# BOOK PUBLISHING

## WHAT IT IS, WHAT IT DOES

# BOOK PUBLISHING

## WHAT IT IS, WHAT IT DOES

### JOHN P. DESSAUER

**R. R. BOWKER COMPANY**
New York & London, 1974
A Xerox Education Company

Published by R. R. Bowker Co. (A Xerox Education Company)
1180 Avenue of the Americas, New York, N.Y. 10036
Copyright © 1974 by Xerox Corporation
All rights reserved
Printed and bound in the United States of America


Library of Congress Cataloging in Publication Data

Dessauer, John P
    Book publishing: what it is, what it does.

    Bibliography: p.
    1. Publishers and publishing.    I. Title.
Z278.D47        070.5'73        74-12162
ISBN 0-8352-0758-7


Figures 3, 4, 5, 6, 7 from *The Printing Industry* by Victor Strauss (Bowker,
1967). Reproduced by permission of Printing Industries of America, Inc.

A.M.D.G.

To the many book people,
living and dead,
who have taught me
by their wisdom and example

WITHDRAWN

# Contents

# Preface

Some years ago, while I was assisting in the direction of a university press, I requested that our parent institution conduct an audit of our operation. They sent me a brilliant young graduate student who was obviously going to go far, was nearly finished with his academic work and already preparing for his C.P.A. examinations. Sitting in my office before the audit he exuded the confidence of youth and of high intelligence. "We'll have you fully audited in less than a week," he assured me, waving his hand depreciatingly at the little publishing house surrounding him.

A week later he was back, definitely the worse for wear, sinking exhausted into a chair. "This must be the most complicated business on God's earth," he exclaimed. "Why, every book is a new and separate product, separately conceived, designed and produced, governed by a unique agreement with its author. My associate and I have worked like beavers and we haven't even completed one fourth the job." He looked at me accusingly, "You should have warned me," he said.

No doubt I should have, but how? I had no comprehensive means of informing him about the ins and outs of book publishing; certainly no simple, basic book that would have provided him with the necessarily broad perspective that would have helped to orient him in his task.

We had a similar problem with our own staff. It was obvious that some of our editors did not know as much about production and about marketing and finance as they should have to perform in their jobs to best advantage. Nor did most of our production, financial, and marketing people know enough about editing or the other operations of the press. At that time not even Gene Hawes' *To Advance Knowledge*, a handbook specifically oriented to university press publishing, was available so we finally solved the problem by conducting a series of lectures for the entire staff in which the various department heads explained the work in which they were engaged. It would have helped enormously had we had a concise, introductory book that would have conveyed the general information we felt everyone working in publishing should have.

I felt the need for such a book again keenly a few years later when I directed another university press and was approached for counsel by a graduate student in literature who was anxious to enter book publishing. Not only was she unaware of the various functions that constitute the publishing process, but her notions about the industry itself were very vague. How, then, was she to decide whether to be an editor or a promotion person (both aspects interested her), or to try to enter the textbook or the general book fields?

On and off during the more than thirty years that it has been my privilege to be associated with the book industry, I have wished for such a book or have run into people both within and without the profession who shared my desire. I therefore present this volume to my readers in the hope that it will appropriately fill a need that has existed for a very long time.

A broad, comprehensive introduction, by its very nature, has virtues as well as limitations. Because it is brief and approaches its highly complex subject in selective and summarylike fashion, it enables the reader to gain a broad comprehension of the field without the necessity of wading through a vast amount of detail. By implication, however, it cannot treat any one facet of its subject in great depth. At best it can only lead the reader into the subject; once there, should the reader feel the need for more exhaustive information, he will have to seek it from other sources. (A good way to begin the pursuit for further knowledge is to refer to the excellent book, *What Happens in Book Publishing*, edited by Chandler B. Grannis, in which practitioners in various publishing areas discuss their crafts, and which contains a valuable bibliography of other specialized works in the field. The reader should also consult the Bibliographic Note at the end of this book).

Book publishing, like all businesses and professions, has its highly technical and complicated aspects and its own unique terminology. While I have attempted to make my discussions of these technical areas—notably of production and finance—as basic and as nontechnical as possible, I will not be able to spare the reader the effort necessary to comprehend intrinsically complex material. Yet I believe that with a minimum of patience and determination on the reader's part these discussions will yield their fundamentally rational and useful content. Since familiarity with specialized terms is essential even to a broad understanding of a specialized activity, I have made it a practice throughout this book to use a term in context without further definition if it has once been explained. To assist the reader's memory, a full glossary of such terms is provided, following the Epilogue.

This book would not have been written had it not been for the help of three colleagues at *Publishers Weekly*. Roger H. Smith first encouraged me to undertake it. Arnold W. Ehrlich took up the encouragement and supported the project with dedication and vigor through difficult periods. John F. Baker saved it in its hour of need. I am deeply indebted to them all, but in particular to John Baker who went far beyond calls of duty and friendship to pour over the manuscript for long hours and to ensure that it would reach its final, satisfactory form.

During the preparation of the manuscript a number of individuals contributed mightily to my education: Leo N. Albert, Ian Ballantine, Fred Belliveau, John N. Berry, James K. Bowman, Marvin S. Brown, John Chipman, Woodworth Chittick, William S. Diefenbach, Paul D. Doebler, Arthur Engel, Paul Forringer, James C. Giblin, George A. Hall, Michael Harris, Saul Herbst, Dennis M. Hudson, Kenneth T. Hurst, Marc Jaffe, Judith M. Kennedy, Charles W. Kraus, Irving Levey, Werner Mark Linz, Charles W. Pepper, Stewart Richardson, G. Roysce Smith, William Smith, and M. S. Wyeth. With the courtesy and generosity characteristic of book people, they committed time, wisdom, and experience to my instruction.

Steven Frimmer, an old and valued friend, not only contributed counsel and insight but waded through the entire manuscript with comments and suggestions. My wife, Elaine, provided constructive criticism as well as priceless encouragement, born of the miraculous love that has graced our late afternoon. My publisher, Richard P. Zeldin took, as always, a personal interest in my doings. Jean Norrington, research librarian at *Publishers Weekly*, was a cheerful and valuable resource. Bowker Librarian Jean Peters was ever gracious and singularly obliging. Editing Supervisor, Roberta Moore, proved that dedication and good cheer are the hallmarks of editorial effectiveness.

To acknowledge the lessons learned and kindnesses received from members of the industry during a generation of active work would fill a whole volume. I trust that my dedication of this book to all who have been of help to me will at least remind them how much I still consider myself to be in their debt.

—*J.P.D.*

# Introduction

We speak of book publishing as an industry and as a profession. Both designations are certainly appropriate. Book publishing is a business conducted, for the most part, for profit. But its practitioners—at least those who do it honor—have motivations that transcend their profit interest. They know that books are no mere commodity, no mere items for consumption that leave their readers much as they find them. Books, like other vehicles of information and sources of entertainment can change, influence, elevate, demean, exalt, or depress those who expose themselves to them. What books are and can be depends heavily on the judgment, integrity, taste, and acumen of those who select and produce them— their publishers.

Thus the publisher plays a vital role, not only in the marketplace but within the culture and civilization of which he is a part, and what makes book publishing a profession as well as a business is the conscious pursuit by the publisher of his responsibilities. He wields his influence with pride, caution, and conscience. He makes his decisions with awareness that he is injecting live matter into the cultural bloodstream. Perhaps too often he fails—tastes can be mediocre, avarice can overcome pride and conscience, even sound judgment can bow to the agitation of noisy fads. Publishing does not become a less significant calling, however, because there are sinners among the elect.

Perhaps one reason why American book publishers will at times succumb to temptation is that essentially they are fighting an uphill fight. Books are not really a very popular commodity in our society. I estimate that American consumers—individual as well as institutional—purchased more than $3 billion worth of books during 1972. This represents less than one half of one percent of the $640 billion in estimated total consumer spending for that year. Even so, nearly $1.4 billion, or 44 percent, of this total was spent on books used in formal education, in elementary, high school, college, and university classrooms and libraries, and therefore does not really represent discretionary spending. Several studies comparing the reading and book-buying habits of Americans with those in European countries have placed our consumption level at the bottom of the list. Improvements in recent years have still far from closed the gap.

Publishers and others interested in the fate of books had often hoped that the achievement of universal literacy would lead to significant increases in book buying. Although we have now closely approached universal literacy, such hopes have gone largely unfulfilled. Perhaps we have failed to distinguish between literacy and literateness, between the ability to read and the habit and enjoyment of so doing. We may also have failed to consider how many books are read though not bought and how many are bought though not read.

Whatever the reasons, the fact is that in our society the interest in and the capacity to enjoy books is confined to a minority. True, in recent decades this minority has grown. There has been a general maturation of American culture in which the rise in educational level and increased affluence have played their roles. And there is reason to believe that the trends thus set in motion will continue and that books, along with other cultural commodities, will enjoy increased acceptance by American consumers.

Some observers had predicted that books and other printed means of information and entertainment would suffer a decline. Led by Marshall McLuhan these prophets had foreseen a general conversion to audiovisual media. The very reverse has occurred. While the audiovisual scene, notably television, has of course grown impressively, books and periodicals have also seen gains. The reason, which apparently escaped McLuhan and others seeing the matter in too simple terms, is that as the thirst and capacity for knowledge and the enjoyment of the arts increase, so does the use of the many and varied means of satisfying them. Not only do tastes and personalities differ, but the same individual, responding to different needs and moods, may find it opportune to read during one hour, see a live play the next, attend a concert tomorrow, and watch some television in between.

Reading itself, of course, is a habit that will differ greatly in nature and character from one individual to the next.

Students read and buy books because they must, although, hopefully, some will enjoy the experience and acquire the lifelong habit of doing so. Professionals —physicians, attorneys, accountants, engineers, scientists—who wish to keep up with developments in their field read and buy books in substantial numbers, as do people seeking job improvement or advancement and those engaged in continuing education.

There is the hobbyist who enjoys reading about his avocation, the traveler who does some of his journeying in his armchair, the playgoer who relives his experience in reading a script, the art lover who visits the great galleries in books of reproductions, the music devotee who deepens his appreciation as he reads the lives of the composers. There is the collector who acquires books for their beauty or rarity, or even the show-off who displays them out of vanity to support the appearance of sophistication. Did we say that book readers and buyers constitute a minority? Not *a* minority—a whole host of minorities of special tastes, interests, vocations, and avocations.

In the course of this book we shall examine the ways in which the book publishing industry attempts to satisfy these varied interests. We shall briefly review its history and examine the environment in which it functions, the qualifications required of its practitioners, the products it creates, the processes employed in their manufacture, their markets and how they are reached. We shall inquire into patterns of ownership and styles of management and into the economics and finance of the process. From this examination we hope will emerge not only an understanding and appreciation of the massive complexity that is characteristic of this field, and of its successes and failures, but also of the important role that book publishing plays in the life of our society.

# Chapter I.

## The
## Past Is Prologue

**Books in History**

Books in one form or another are as old as civilization. We encounter them in ancient Mesopotamia as clay tablets and in ancient Egypt as papyrus rolls. Rolls were also the form they took in Greece and Rome, where bookselling already flourished and the "scriptoria" or copying establishments plied a vigorous trade. Cities like Pergamum and Alexandria boasted of great libraries; the latter is said to have housed at one time as many as 700,000 rolls.

The format of books as we know them dates from the first century A.D. when the codex, a volume of parchment pages bound on one side, was introduced. A massive and often beautiful object, the codex remained the characteristic book of the Middle Ages. The religious and secular works then produced, mostly in monasteries, were often duplicated assembly-line style with copyists, proofreaders, and illustrators each fulfilling separate, coordinated functions.

As early as the twelfth century the stationers make their appearance as commercial duplicators and purveyors of books. Many were attached to the universities then being founded and which were taking over the publishing function from the monasteries. Later the stationers organized themselves into corporations and guilds and, like other craftsmen of the period, assumed monopolistic control over their own profession.

The fifteenth century witnessed two vital developments: the introduction of paper and the invention of movable type. Some bibliographers doubt that Johannes Gutenberg should be credited with the invention of type; they claim that Johann Fust and Peter Schöffer actually printed the Bible which bears Gutenberg's name, and that in any case the Constance Missal antedates that Bible as the first printed book. Be that as it may, the practice of printing books by the new method spread with great rapidity throughout Europe and a wealth of "incunabula," as fifteenth-century books are known, survives. By 1500 books were paginated and title pages listed publishers' imprints and dates of publication much as they do today. In 1501 Aldo Manuzio designed the first small book which thereafter replaced the large and awkward codex.

The Reformation and Counter-Reformation proved to be potent stimuli to reading and the publication of books. Not only were the Scriptures made available in the vernacular and widely distributed, but religious controversy found in the newly established printing presses ready means for spreading argument and counterargument far and wide. If the distribution of a great many books was thus encouraged, so was a good deal of suppression, confiscation, and burning. Censorship became a way of life. Even John Milton, who in 1644 wrote the *Areopagitica,* a ringing defense of freedom to publish, later turned censor for the Commonwealth. But literacy gained ground embracing by one estimate 60 percent of the population of sixteenth-century England.

In 1638 the Puritans set up a press in Cambridge, Massachussets, on which in 1640 the *Bay Psalm Book* was printed. It was among the first of nearly 90,000 titles which were produced in the American Colonies, mostly in English but also in German, Dutch, French, and in Indian languages. Colonial production was of course heavily supplemented by books brought to the new continent from all parts of Europe by immigrants, travelers, and merchants.

## Modern Publishing Begins

During the eighteenth century the common people in the Western world shared a growing belief that they could acquire learning through reading. Women had attended the common schools and helped enlarge the audience for books. The farmer or artisan who was a man of letters was no longer a rarity. This was the era of the founding of the great encyclopedias, such as the *Britannica* in England, and the establishment of circulating libraries in many countries. The cause of authors, who had been restricted by monopolistic printers, was aided by such legislation as the British Copyright Act of 1710 which enabled them to negotiate for favorable compensation and terms.

But if book production was substantial in the eighteenth century, with two million titles issued worldwide, the nineteenth century was a period of even more significant development. Some eight million titles were published. By 1900 a best-selling novel would sell 600,000 copies in the English-speaking world. Urbanization, industrialization, and the impetus given to universal education by the growth of democratic influences were among the principal factors in this growth.

Many publishing houses still active today were founded during this period. Among imprints surviving in the United States who can trace their ancestry to the late eighteenth and the nineteenth century are Lea & Febiger (1785), Abingdon Press (1789), J.B. Lippincott (1792), John Wiley & Sons (1807), Harper & Row (1817), G. & C. Merriam (1831), Houghton, Mifflin (1832), Little, Brown (1837), G.P. Putnam's Sons (1838), Charles E. Merrill (1842), E.P. Dutton (1852), Rand McNally (1856), Ginn & Co. (1867), Allyn & Bacon (1868), Johns Hopkins University Press (1878), and Doubleday (1897). It is noteworthy that many of these publishers specialized from the beginning in educational, professional, and religious books while others addressed themselves to the general public.

During the nineteenth century also paperbound books made their appearance, notably in Germany and France where they became firmly and permanently established. In the United States they managed to flourish briefly during the 1830s, but an adverse postal ruling ended the experiment abruptly in 1843. They were resurrected by 1870 and had quite a vogue, particularly in the celebrated dime novel form. But so large a portion of these books was pirated from foreign editions that the copyright act of 1891 once again effectively put an end to that brief paperback era.

## The Early Twentieth Century

Most of the houses active in the United States today, including some of the largest and most influential, were founded in this century. Some like McGraw-Hill (1909), Prentice-Hall (1913), Simon & Schuster (1924), and Random House (1925) during early decades, others like Atheneum (1959) more recently. The advent of the modern paperback was responsible for the creation of some, such as Pocket Books (1939), Bantam Books (1946), New American Library (1948), and Fawcett World Library (1950); the development of book publishing for direct mail distribution, particularly by magazine publishers, was responsible for the founding of others such as Time-Life Books (1961) and American Heritage Press (1968). New York became the center where most houses operated, but Boston, Philadelphia, and Chicago were also points of concentration. Only recently has the Western region also begun to play a role as a locale for book publishing.

The contemporary era for the book industry dates from the post-World War II period. Not that some of the trends, phenomena, and practices shaping the present scene had not been initiated before. But the educational boom and the general prosperity in the postwar period were among the principal factors contributing to the shape and character of today's publishing world.

It would be fair to say that prior to World War II the industry had, in economic terms, been a minor one in the United States. Its healthiest segments, the educational, professional, and reference book areas, were able on the whole to attract sufficient capital to meet their obligations and opportunities but were not generally regarded as prime prospects for investment. Publishers serving the general consumer were often struggling to keep alive; it is no secret that in some diversified houses the educational department's income would keep the trade department in existence and only the fascination of owners and managers with general consumer books allowed those divisions to function at all.

Salaries in the field during this period, particularly in the trade area, were low. Few authors could support themselves by their writing. A book could rise to the national best-seller list, particularly in nonfiction, by selling less than 50,000 copies. College enrollments, confined to a cultural-economic elite, were modest as were the textbook sales catering to them. The great depression intensified what was then, even more than now, a minority interest in books.

Book distribution reflected these conditions. Booksellers were struggling to survive, caught in an economic squeeze that on the one hand required them to operate in expensive locations in order to maintain traffic and attract customers, while on the other hand did not allow them to sell their wares expensively enough and in sufficient volume to earn an adequate margin. Many communities were consequently not adequately served or not served at all by book outlets. Some of the great bookstores of the nation could not have kept their doors open had it not been for their used book departments, where markups were more adequate, or their rare book sections that catered to wealthy collectors.

As today, booksellers looked with concern on the activities of book clubs. The Book-of-the-Month Club had been founded in 1926, the Literary Guild in 1927. Undoubtedly book clubs stole some sales away from retailers, but they also reached readers who had no access to or no opportunity to visit bookstores and they succeeded by their membership arrangements in making book buying a habit for some consumers who might otherwise have been very sporadic in their purchasing. By their promotion they created wider interest in titles they selected and in fact created new readers who subsequently proved a boon to booksellers and publishers alike. The same could be said of paperbacks when they made their appearance under the Pocket Books imprint in 1939. Though seen initially by many booksellers as a threat, they have on the whole benefited the industry beyond measure.

But these and other marketing innovations, while helpful and important in laying foundations for the future, did not then succeed in bringing prosperity to the industry. Book people, like teachers, scholars, artists, and musicians, in those days before affluence was widespread, were resigned to an existence of genteel poverty. They found other compensations. To be near books, to share if only indirectly in the literary process, to be midwife to an author's blessed event, these were exciting and rewarding. A deep commitment and dedication grew from the love of books that sustained many a publisher and bookseller despite the lack of significant financial reward.

At the same time, however, the industry—in particular its trade publishing segment—suffered from a paucity of business acumen. While there were publishers who, like Alfred Knopf, combined editorial genius with sound business sense they were unfortunately the exception rather than the rule. When an endeavor, by its very nature, attracts people who find their rewards in its nonmaterial aspects, it is not normally going to find the best talent in American business management flocking to its doors. Nor is it likely that the people whom it does attract will arrive with the persuasion that sound management ability is one of the prime requisites expected of them.

Thus many publishing houses became victims of a vicious circle: because they were not successful businesses they did not enlist the interest of good business people—with the result that they remained largely unsound from a business standpoint. Only recently has this trend begun to be reversed.

## War and Postwar

World War II itself played a role in changing conditions in the industry. In a patriotic and enlightened move publishers made available thousands of "Armed Forces Editions" of their books to the military in the field. Books thus became companions and solace, entertainment, and relaxation to countless individuals many of whom might otherwise never have acquired the habit of reading. As these volumes were paperbound they also helped pave the way for the incipient paperback revolution.

The War, furthermore, resulted in the beginnings of the college explosion: the era in which higher education was to become the perceived birthright of the masses rather than of a mere elite. The veterans who flocked into college classrooms under the G.I. Bill established a precedent which, partly successful and partly a failure, has nevertheless become an article of national faith and commitment. The veterans purchased a great many books with government funds, thus giving college publishing its first big postwar shot in the arm.

Shortly after the war's end the new era in paperbound books was born. The titles which Bantam Books, New American Library, Pocket Books, and others who soon joined them were disseminating were not only different in format, size, and price—they used new channels of distribution which books had never before found open to them. By making use of the facilities of national magazine and independent local distributors, books were displayed on newsstands and cigar counters, in drugstores, railroad terminals, etc. The market they created was in large measure new and previously untapped.

Quite a different paperbound development occurred soon after during the early 1950s in the traditional book field when so-called "quality" paperbacks made their appearance. These titles of serious nonfiction and literary classics, while enjoying a certain vogue with the general consumer, found their prime markets in education. Most were used in college courses. During the late fifties, when secondary school programs were upgraded, high schools also contributed to their consumption. In fact, as time went on, both quality and "mass market" paperbacks enjoyed increased educational uses.

Simultaneously with these developments several educational book publishers, noting a trend toward the use of audiovisual materials in the classroom, began to diversify their production by introducing such materials separately or in multimedia combinations. McGraw-Hill had entered the field as a lone pioneer in 1946; other textbook houses did not follow suit until several years later. While the extensive displacement of books predicted by enthusiasts for audiovisual education never materialized, multimedia publishing became a significant factor in the decades that followed.

In fact the growth and upgrading of education on all levels that followed the 1957 shock of Sputnik had profound effects on the entire book industry. Publishers benefited from the massive infusion of federal funds that characterized the late fifties and the sixties. School classrooms, library resource centers, and college and public libraries became the beneficiaries of programs that enabled them to enlarge their holdings of books and of audiovisual and related materials which had rarely before been supported by such funding and certainly never on such a scale.

These events coincided with a consistently growing wave of affluence and also with substantial increases in enrollments on elementary, high school, and college levels (the postwar baby boom was having its effect).

**The Merger Period**

By the early 1960s journalists, economic forecasters, Wall Street analysts, and other custodians of the national crystal ball began to make ecstatic predictions for the future of education, for the use of leisure time, and, by implication, for book publishing. Unfortunately their analyses were often superficial and they badly overstated their case. Nevertheless many of the factors to which they pointed were real and, for a while at least, their forecasts appeared plausible.

They succeeded in whetting the appetite of investors and corporations searching for ways to diversify their holdings. Wall Street was at that time not particularly renowned for its restraint and detached judgment; even so all the earmarks pointed to book publishing as a sound investment with future growth. Thus publishing stocks, particularly those of educational companies, became glamour holdings. And conglomerates began to woo every independent publisher whose future promised to throw off even a modest share of the forecast earnings.

The publishers being wooed were often very happy at the prospect of a merger. Few had the resources to make the growth the new markets promised a profitable reality. Some privately held companies solved the problem by offering shares to the public, though such moves often proved mere stopovers on their way to being absorbed by larger companies. Some, determined to preserve their independence, succeeded in maintaining their status quo. But a major segment of the industry found itself involved in merging, acquiring, or, more frequently, being acquired.

Thus Random House was purchased by RCA after previously absorbing Alfred Knopf and Pantheon Books. Holt, Rinehart & Winston, itself the product of two mergers, became a subsidiary of CBS, as did W.B. Saunders. The Times Mirror Company of Los Angeles made subsidiaries of New American Library, World Publishing Co., Popular Science, Harry N. Abrams, Matthew Bender, C.V. Mosby, and Year Book Medical Publishers, among others. Litton Industries acquired Van Nostrand, Reinhold, American Book Company, and McCormick-Mathers. Xerox took over Ginn & Co. and R.R. Bowker. Meredith Corporation bought Appleton-Century-Crofts and Lyons & Carnahan. Time, Inc. acquired Little, Brown and New York Graphic Society. ITT purchased Bobbs-Merrill and Howard Sams. Harcourt Brace Jovanovich absorbed Academic Press and Grune & Stratton. Encyclopaedia Britannica purchased G. & C. Merriam and Praeger. Raytheon captured D.C. Heath, and so on and so forth.

These mergers and acquisitions have had a profound effect upon the book field. They made resources available without which the industry could probably not have capitalized on its opportunities and fulfilled its obligations to educational and consumer audiences alike. They brought new management and business acumen to the field which had been seriously lacking and which, in many instances resulted for the first time in orderly budgeting, forecasting, planning, and fiscal arrangements. But in many cases they also placed the power of ultimate decision and policy making in the hands of people unfamiliar with books, their peculiarities, and their markets.

**Boom and Aftermath**

What liabilities were being engendered by these changes were not readily apparent during the prosperous sixties. From 1963 to 1969 publishing industry sales, including those of book clubs, increased by 59 percent, from $1.7 billion to $2.7 billion. These were times when books seemed to sell despite the inadequacies of their publishers, when even inferior materials were readily absorbed by a well-funded, gluttonous market. So many factors worked together to benefit the various segments of the industry that almost everyone enjoyed a slice of the pie. Research projects supported by government and foundation grants encouraged acquisition of professional books; generous federal and state budgets, bringing unaccustomed affluence to colleges, universities, and their faculties, augmented sales of scholarly materials; newly founded colleges were stocking libraries; parents eager to strengthen their children's educational resources avidly bought encyclopedias for the home; general and specialized book clubs were flourishing.

There was, in addition, the factor of growing export and foreign sales. The postwar scholarly and scientific community had embraced English as the international language and American publishers were reaping some large benefits. Translations and the leasing of publishing rights to foreign

publishers were also growing phenomena. Soon American publishers of professional and reference materials saw the advantages of founding their own subsidiary companies abroad, thus enjoying the best of both worlds.
It could not last. The 1970s ushered in some substantial reverses. General economic conditions initially declined, then recovered only sporadically. Enrollments in elementary schools, reflecting the population patterns of the preceding years, went on a downward trend. Taxpayers' revolts in many areas curtailed school budgets. College enrollments, too, began to decline even as state legislatures cut appropriations for higher education. Federal support for schools, libraries, and research were threatened and embroiled in political controversy. Home sales of encyclopedias were falling off substantially.

The pace of book industry growth was expectably slowed. From 1969 to 1972 sales increased by only 11 percent, from $2.7 billion to slightly over $3.0 billion, hardly more in some segments than could be accounted for by inflationary factors. Understandably textbook and other educationally related sales suffered above-average reverses.

But if the boom era had apparently come to an end, the industry had matured and advanced significantly during this period and many of the gains appeared to be permanent. Large numbers of new readers had come into the fold. Lower education had been upgraded and higher education expanded to a larger segment of the population with related advances in book consumption. Even if readers and book buyers still represented only a minority, or more accurately a group of cultural minorities, these minorities had grown substantially.

New financial and management resources had come into the industry during the merger period. Many of the new owners and stockholders, sold initially on excessive expectations, had of course suffered disappointments. Many had become affiliated with the industry without an adequate understanding of books, their cultural role, or their commercial possibilities. But as excessive optimism gave way to a more realistic view, the genuine opportunities confronting book publishers in the last quarter of this century were becoming more apparent. Such realism supported by adequate fiscal means and genuine management capability is in a position to capitalize on these opportunities and to overcome the serious obstacles standing in their path such as antiquated, inadequate methods of distribution.

Already signs of continued growth for the book industry are apparent. In the United States, since the beginning of the seventies, more new bookstores have been opened than in any comparable period in history. Several new book clubs, catering to specialized consumer tastes, have come into being. In 1972 mass market paperback sales increased by 10.5 percent over the prior year.

It is against this background, a generally reassuring history despite its share of reverses, that we must take the measure of the industry in its present state.

# Chapter III.

# A
# Broad Perspective

## A Cultural Industry

Book publishing, as we have noted, is both a cultural activity and a business. Books are vehicles of ideas, instruments of education, and vessels of literature. But the task of bringing them into existence and of purveying them to their readers is a commercial one requiring all the resources and skill of the manager and entrepreneur.

It is appropriate, therefore, to describe book publishing as a cultural industry. The theater, film, and record businesses which share these characteristics can be similarly defined. It is important to recognize the dual character and demands of book publishing and of similar enterprises because their success depends on it. Both the environment in which they function and the qualifications of their practitioners reflect this duality; in both instances we must consider cultural *and* business requirements if our enterprise is to flourish.

## A Mass Industry?

What environmental factors have an impact on book publishing? Well—certainly it is influenced by the general cultural climate to which we have already referred. Book buying though a growing phenomenon in America is not a habit with a majority of the population. Sales figures of individual books are most revealing. When a national best seller after going through hard-cover and paperbound editions sells two million copies the industry rejoices and points to it with pride. Yet such a sale represents a purchase by less than 1 percent of the population. An ordinary, mediocre television show on a national network will have exposure to many times that number. The same is true of the major magazines.

The average hard-cover trade book published may sell up to 10,000 copies, the average "mass market" paperback perhaps 100,000. The designation "mass market" for that paperback may be justified when comparing it with the hard-cover volume—but in relation to the total potential market it is something of a fiction. In America books do not really reach the masses—at any rate not yet.

Unfortunately many editorial and marketing concepts the industry has formulated in recent years are based on the assumption that books are a mass commodity. Thus the best seller, which supposedly will reach a mass audience, receives major emphasis; the more specialized book, appealing to a more limited market, is given less attention. Yet all the evidence suggests that in aggregate the industry receives the bulk of its income and support from book buyers who indulge specialized interests and tastes. To the extent that the emphasis on imagined "mass" interests neglects these buyers, the industry is cutting its nose to spite its face.

It would be fair to say, in fact, that the single greatest challenge facing American book publishing today—the goal that would most enable it to reach its potential—is simply to reach effectively the people willing and anxious to buy books. This would entail emphasizing editorial choices aimed at satisfying the real interests of consumers as well as the development of adequate means of placing books into their hands. In both ways American book publishing in the seventies leaves much to be desired. Editorial emphasis is far too much on potential "mass" titles—most of which do not perform as expected. As for obtaining specialized books, such titles are rarely available in retail outlets, are difficult to obtain even by mail, and take interminable time to arrive when ordered. Uncounted book sales are lost in this country every day because willing buyers cannot find what they want on display nor can they order books with reasonable ease.

**Publishing and Education**

Closely related to the general cultural climate as an environmental factor for book publishing is the state of education. Many stresses currently trouble this field: broad public disillusionment with what are perceived to be its failures; demands for greater accountability by educators; rising costs coupled with public reluctance to meet them. Educators themselves are anxious to introduce methods that will improve performance, centering mostly around greater individuation in approach to students.

Recently two trends in the choice of educational materials have been challenging the traditional textbook: the use of general books, particularly paperbacks, and the employment of audiovisual and other nonprint media. Many educational publishers have diversified their products and are in a position to respond effectively to these trends. But industry sales figures suggest that although textbooks have lost some ground, the attrition is far smaller than the lively rhetoric would lead one to believe. If a significant trend is emerging it seems to be that in the majority of schools and colleges the textbook will remain the principal tool of instruction. Other books and other media will play their roles, of course, but they seem destined to remain secondary ones.

This is not to suggest that the textbook is not going to change as conditions change. Certainly new emphases in instruction—including, one must own, new fads—will influence the content and appearance of text materials. We may see more softbound texts, more consumables (materials on which the students work directly and which they, therefore, use up), more modular packages (kits consisting of small units). What is of the essence, however, is that from all appearances printed materials especially designed for the classroom—or for individualized instruction within formal educational settings—remain the favored choice of educators and students alike.

Another factor, touching upon education in a broader sense, deserves the attention of book publishers. The knowledge explosion, TV, and heightened career demands, among other factors, have greatly increased the thirst for continuing education which has always motivated a sizable segment of the book-buying public. (Even thirty years ago I discovered to my amazement that the best-selling books in a somewhat seedy store in New York's Times Square area were not sex manuals but College Outlines. And they were selling not to college students but to truck drivers, subway guards, accountants, and office girls.) This interest does not appear at the present time to be effectively served through normal book outlets, yet holds great potential for publishers who will have the imagination to exploit it.

## Copying and Copyright

Two other rather specific phenomena affecting the environment for book publishing need to be considered here because of their timeliness and significance: unauthorized copying and censorship.

Unauthorized copying of copyrighted materials is a problem that has become widespread since the invention of the Xerox and other copying machines which have made it easy and relatively inexpensive to duplicate not only pages but whole chapters and sections of books. As today no self-respecting public or academic library is without a copying machine and as schools and colleges make them available to their teaching staffs, the opportunities for disregarding the legally protected rights of authors and publishers in this regard are numberless.

The present U.S. copyright law dates back essentially to 1909, long before the invention of the automatic copier. Because of this and other modern developments, notably in such areas as films, television, and recordings, a proposed new law intending to deal effectively with present conditions has been before Congress for several years. Unfortunately considerable controversy has embroiled several areas of the bill, including that of copying permissible for research and educational purposes. On this issue traditional allies in education, the library world, authors, and publishers have become sharply divided.

Authors and publishers have stood on the principle that the right to literary property is a natural right recognized in common law, forbidding, for instance, the unauthorized copying or publication of unpublished writings and correspondence. When a work is published it must enjoy statutory protection from unauthorized duplication for a specific period (the present law provides for 28 years with the possibility of renewal for a like period; the new law proposes 50 years following the author's death without renewal). Without such protection the economic interests of authors and publishers will be seriously threatened and the incentive lost to invest time or money in the production of literary property. On the other hand, the time limitation exists so that after the investors in such property have had an opportunity to gain justifiable earnings, the public—including other authors and publishers—may have free use of the material.

Although the present statute does not specifically provide for it, the courts have ruled on many occasions that limited use of copyrighted matter—such as the quotation of a passage or paragraph in another published work—is permissible and does not infringe on the rights of the original owner. Authors and publishers have indicated that such "fair use," as the courts have termed it, is acceptable as is, on the same principle, the limited copying of books such as a single page for research purposes. But they have insisted that extensive copying—of whole chapters or parts of books—is not acceptable without authorization, and that libraries and educational institutions that make copying machines available to educators or the public have a responsibility to control their use.

Libraries have protested that the responsibility is the patron's, not theirs; libraries are service institutions and should not be used to enforce the law. Educators think that publishers are too restrictive; some can see no wrong in duplicating a chapter or two from a book even for the use of (and sale to) several hundred students. Researchers express alarm over the complexities of a process that requires them to write to a publisher and pay a fee each time they want to copy a dozen pages from a book or journal.

Efforts have been made to resolve these questions and to devise convenient permissions methods for users while safeguarding the interests of copyright owners. A system would have to be created—perhaps for licensing or collecting copying fees—that would be effective yet simple and inexpensive to administer. Certainly if such a system cannot be successfully developed the interests particularly of educational and scientific publishers will continue to be seriously jeopardized. Since investments in their publications are customarily large—and growing in cost—these publishers are highly vulnerable and understandably anxious for an effective solution.

**Publisher vs. Censor**

If the issue of unauthorized copying is volatile and controversial, that of censorship is infinitely more so. It is also far more complex.

Most authors and publishers have traditionally opposed attempts to curtail freedom of expression. Basing their position on the First Amendment, which they contend makes any restraint on publication illegal, they have fought—often courageously and at great personal sacrifice—against efforts at supression and censorship inspired by political, philosophical, religious, and moral persuasions. Had it not been for the battles and unceasing vigilance of many authors and publishers some great works of philosophy, religion, political theory, and literature would not now be available in libraries and bookstores.

What was in the minds of the fathers who passed the First Amendment may be more difficult to establish but judicial interpretation has never regarded it as an absolute guarantee of unfettered expression. Libel and obscenity are among the forms of speech and writing which the courts have consistently held are not protected by the First Amendment. Nor, to recall the ever popular statement of Justice Holmes, does freedom of speech entitle one to shout "Fire!" in a crowded theater.

Some commentators point out, furthermore, that a publisher has a responsibility beyond the law when he makes his decision to publish. He may not have the right to injure another human being without reason whether or not the libel law is sufficiently vague or vaguely interpreted to permit his publication of a work filled with destructive innuendo. The public may have a right to know what is in the public interest but its hunger for sensation may perhaps not be justifiably satiated if in the process a man's right to a fair trial is hopelessly jeopardized.

*Publishers Weekly,* in a July 2, 1973 editorial, critical of the Supreme Court Decision which effectively places the power to determine what is obscene in the hands of local communities, states:

> . . . it may not be amiss to point out that some publishers, by their own actions in recent years, have helped to create a climate in which such a ruling can be regarded as an acceptable one by large numbers of the American people. . . .This is not to say that the publishing industry deserves the new and more stringent approach the Supreme Court has taken; merely that it becomes much harder to say where a stand should be taken when segments of the industry have already gravely undercut normal publishing standards.

Novelist Anthony Burgess, in an article in the *New York Times Magazine* of July 1, 1973 entitled "For Permissiveness, with Misgivings," speaks to the literary issue when he says:

> When novels about sodomy, bestiality, multiple coition and murderous-rape-with-willing-victim cram the bookstalls, what hope has the serious and well-written novel that takes sex as merely one aspect of life? Can the present-day cinema audience watch without restiveness a film in which a couple fall deeply in love without taking off their clothes? Appetites are growing coarser and ears deafer. And there are more pseudo writers about than there should be, capitalizing merely on the freedom to be brutal or erotic or both.

The industry's well-founded case against censorship might be more persuasive therefore, and likely to gain greater public acceptance, if publishers were to exercise more consistently the responsibility that is the inevitable concomitant of freedom.

### What Makes a Publisher?

If the environmental conditions to which we have referred have an influence on the publishing process, the determining factor remains the publisher's decision. It is he who by his judgment, taste, vision, integrity, and business acumen shapes in the end not only the industry but to a significant degree the literary and general culture which harbors him.

What qualifications must he bring to this important role? Granting that dispositions and aptitudes vary greatly from individual to individual, there appear to be certain general traits of personality and mind that are observable not only in the giants who have left their indelible mark upon the profession, but also in those more numerous women and men who in each age have contributed solidly to its progress.

The true publisher moves with equal comfort in the world of mind and art and in the world of commerce. This may not be a common personality combination; in fact it is probably rather rare. But it appears to be an indispensable prerequisite for achievement in book publishing. A publisher who consistently disrespects the demands for quality and worth in the manuscripts he publishes will, despite temporary successes, find his enterprise dying of spiritual starvation in the end; just as a publisher who consistently ignores the commercial needs of his establishment will find before long that his cultural opportunities are negated by bankruptcy.

Curiously in this age of often extreme ideological moralities these compatible, indeed complementary, traits have been thought to be irreconcilable. Some purists express shock at any attentiveness to solvency. The moneymen, at the other extreme, often have no patience with any concern for literary or scientific excellence. "Will it sell?" is their only question. "Will it help build and maintain the imprint so that ten years from now our books will still be received with interest and confidence, and books we published ten years ago will still be selling because of their lasting significance?" may be the question both sides should be asking.

Obviously no publisher of vision can afford to be indifferent to the total atmosphere for writers, particularly for new writers. It is a wise and honorable tradition in publishing that one should give opportunities to new talent so that such talent may eventually produce salable manuscripts. Many an author's first book is published at a loss in anticipation of substantial gains on his second or third book. At times publishers will even knowingly publish an author whose work they suspect will never be successful commercially simply because they assess it to be of such quality and stature that its value to civilization far outbalances any financial loss it may incur. Such publishers display enlightened self-interest for they persuade readers and writers that publishers honestly love books.

But such commitment to the future of writing must be made with sound judgment and with a shrewd eye upon the general fiscal health of the publishing venture. The truly distinguished manuscript deserving the publisher's unselfish support is rare indeed; totally aside from the fact that not-for-profit publishers (like university presses) exist precisely for the purpose of allowing material to be published that may not succeed in the commercial market. That market itself is for most literary and informative writing a simple and true test of merit: if a book cannot be published viably perhaps it is simply not good enough and should not be published at all. Vox populi—vox Dei.

This leads to a second major qualification for the publisher: the ability to empathize with public tastes. Obviously, given the lively cultural pluralism of his audience, a publisher cannot personally share its every enthusiasm, every persuasion, every perspective. But his should be a sufficiently sympathetic imagination to enable him to make judgments on behalf of the tastes and interests he hopes to serve. Whether it be the world of students and teachers or the complex universe of consumers, he should, in evaluating a manuscript, be able to bring their needs, attitudes, and predilections to his decision and act, as it were, as their advocate in making his choice.

A publisher is a specialist in his own profession—but when it comes to learning and literature the publisher must be a generalist. In fact publishing and its sister cultural industries may be the last bastions of generalism in a world in which the vastness of information and the variety of available diversions are pushing most of us into narrower and narrower areas of competence.

Finally a publisher needs courage. It takes courage to place one's faith in an untried author and use one's resources on his behalf, to adhere to quality and standards in a world often addicted to mediocrity, to shoot ahead of the cultural target, and to open new paths in the hope that they may become highways for literature and knowledge.

### Divisions of the Industry

The products publishers develop, the markets to which they are addressed, and the methods used to reach those markets are the principal criteria by which the industry has divided itself into certain categories. Such divisions as trade, text, professional, or mass market paperback publishing have come about naturally because houses engaging in these activities share common editorial objectives and economic concerns.

I say houses but should clarify that this may often mean a department or internal division of a house, particularly since the days of diversification and merger when many formerly independent enterprises became parts of empires.

In defining and describing the industry's divisions and, later, the various publishing functions, it becomes necessary to adopt a standard terminology. Words such as "trade books," "editorial," or "production" are generally in use throughout the industry but they do not always have the same meaning in every establishment that employs them. Local conditions have in fact introduced considerable variation into the industry's vocabulary. Since this makes communication between publishers difficult and precise comparisons of their activities impossible, standard terms and definitions have had to be developed and are employed in the statistical surveys conducted for the Association of American Publishers (AAP). I have generally utilized these terms and definitions throughout this book.

In keeping with this approach I have also adhered to the AAP definition of books themselves. This definition includes all nonperiodical hard-cover volumes regardless of length; all juveniles, hardbound or softbound regardless of length, except coloring books; and all nonperiodical softbound volumes of more than 48 pages. Normally a softbound nonperiodical publication of between 5 and 48 pages is considered a pamphlet although it may be classified as a book if generally accepted as such (as for example a short text-related workbook or a volume published as part of his regular program by a mass market paperback publisher).

The following are the industry's major divisions:

*Trade books* are designed for the general consumer and are sold, for the most part, through bookstores and to libraries. They may be hardbound or paperbound and include works for both adults and children.

Typical trade books are hard-cover fiction, current nonfiction, biography, literary classics, cookbooks, hobby books, popular science books, travel books, and art books. Also books for self-education, such as those in foreign languages, books on sports, music, poetry, and drama. The main distinction between trade books and textbooks is that the latter are designed for classroom use rather than for general consumption and contain pedagogical apparatus such as summaries and test questions. It does not follow, however, that trade books are not used in classrooms or for educational purposes. In fact, in recent years, increasing numbers of trade titles have been bought for use in colleges and schools. This is particularly true of trade paperbacks—often referred to as "quality" paperbacks— which are widely used in college courses.

It should be noted that juvenile trade books range anywhere from picture books for the prereading age to works for "young adults" in their latter teens.

*Religious books* include Bibles, testaments, hymnals, and prayer books (but traditionally exclude Sunday school materials). This category also embraces other works of specifically religious content, such as theology and popular devotional literature.

In recent years religious publishers have increasingly engaged in the production of titles which, though of interest to a religious readership, are nevertheless not specifically religious in character, as for example material on social work, racial problems, and world peace. Such books are classified as trade books or as textbooks, depending on their content and intended market, rather than as religious materials.

*Professional books* are, as the designation implies, books directed to professional people and specifically related to their work. AAP surveys distinguish among three major areas of professional publishing: *Technical and Scientific Books* which treat of subjects in the physical, biological, earth, and social sciences as well as technology, engineering, and the trades and are addressed to practicing and research scientists, engineers, architects, technicians, mechanics, and teachers in these and allied fields; *Medical Books* designed for physicians, nurses, dentists, hospital administrators, veterinarians, pharmacists, *et al.*; and *Business and Other Professional Books* addressed to businessmen, managers, accountants, lawyers, librarians, or other professional individuals not covered under the technical, scientific, and medical categories.

As with trade books, the use of professional books in educational programs is widespread. However, if the editorial character of a volume and its predominant intended audience is professional and its educational use represents a secondary market, the book is classified in the professional category. When professional publishers publish textbooks—for example, medical publishers' nursing texts—the textbook classification applies.

*Book clubs* could be regarded as a retail market channel rather than as publishers, particularly as for the most part they do not originate the materials they distribute to their members but acquire the rights from other publishers. However, traditionally book clubs have been considered to be part of the publishing industry, and as a few clubs do originate books and as all clubs prepare separate editions for their specific distribution, the classification has some rationale.

AAP surveys provide for distinctions between *consumer* and *professional* book clubs. Consumer clubs in turn involve those who cater to *general interests,* such as the Book-of-the-Month Club and the Literary Guild who offer a great variety of titles without attempt at subject specialization, and *special interest* clubs whose members have particular subject enthusiasms, such as cooking, the outdoors, or the military, or who represent a special population group such as do students served by clubs which distribute paperbacks in the schools. Professional book clubs partake of the characteristics of professional book publishers so far as their offerings and audience are concerned.

*Mail order publications* are books created for the general consumer and are marketed to him by direct mail. The principal differences between book club and mail order publications programs are that the latter are originated by the publisher who does the marketing and the publications are distributed without the specific commitments by the purchaser which characterize book club memberships. Although mail order publishers often market series or multivolume sets on a so-called continuity basis (i.e., after placing his order the purchaser receives volumes automatically unless he instructs the publisher to stop), the buyer incurs no obligation nor enters into a membership arrangement of any kind.

Mail order publications, too, have secondary markets consisting of trade sales through bookstores and to libraries, as well as of educational sales similar to those enjoyed by trade books.

*Mass market paperbacks* are softbound books on all subjects whose predominant distribution is through "mass" channels: newsstands, chain stores, drugstores, supermarkets, and the like. Many are reprints of hard-cover trade books; others are originally published in this format.

It is often very difficult to discover the differences between trade and mass market paperbacks. (Sometimes the originating publisher's imprint provides the only clue.) Generally mass market paperbacks use less costly paper and employ covers more likely to attract the "mass" audience than do their "quality" counterparts. Yet they, too, enjoy large secondary markets in trade outlets (book and department stores) and in educational settings.

*University press* books provide an instance where the content of titles and the methods used in their distribution are disregarded in their classification and the sole criterion employed is the originating source. University presses which are, for the most part, not-for-profit departments of universities, colleges, museums, or research institutions, publish mostly scholarly materials or titles of regional interest. However, occasionally they produce trade books and textbooks as well which are then categorized here rather than in the area which content and market would dictate.

University presses publish hard-cover and soft-cover books. Their principal customers are scholars and libraries but many titles, particularly paperbacks, are used in classrooms. Bookstores absorb some sales, notably of trade-oriented materials.

*Elementary and secondary textbooks* are hard-cover and soft-cover textbooks, workbooks, textbook-related tests, manuals, maps, and similar items all intended for classroom use and equipped with specific pedagogical features which distinguish them from consumer-oriented materials such as trade juveniles. The industry refers to producers of these materials as "elhi" publishers.

Many publishers in this field also produce audiovisual and manipulative items such as films, filmstrips, slides, recordings, transparencies, duplicating masters, games, magnetic boards, etc. Sometimes these are combined with books or at least with printed components (cards, pamphlets, etc.) in so-called multimedia packages or kits.

Schools are the primary market. (AAP surveys consider kindergarten to the eighth grade the elementary grades and grades 9 through 12 high school.) Lately some junior colleges have begun using elhi materials. Government and libraries (other than school libraries) also constitute secondary markets.

*College textbooks* include hard-cover and soft-cover textbooks, pamphlets, reprints, course-related tests, and other materials, and certain audiovisual items such as films, slides, and cassettes. "College" here embraces all higher education (grades 13 and up), from junior college to postgraduate level. The upgrading of secondary school programs has created an interesting additional market in high schools for college publishers. Government, industry, and libraries also account for some of their sales.

It is probably more difficult to distinguish between college textbooks and trade books than it is between their counterparts on the elhi level. Some publishers have even produced trade and textbook "editions" of the same title with differences so slight (such as that the trade edition is equipped with a dust cover while the text edition is not), as to make the task of classification almost impossible.

(AAP survey practice utilizes the criterion of predominance in making some distinctions: if a book finds its principal market in the textbook area, it should be classified there, if in the trade-book area then in that category. Where distribution is evenly divided and two quite separate editions are actually marketed, each edition is considered to be a distinct title and classifiable in its own area.)

*Standardized tests* are a small industry segment closely related to textbook publishing. Standardized tests, as distinguished from "objective" tests which accompany specific textbooks and materials, measure intelligence, ability, aptitude, achievement, and other personality traits. Schools and colleges employ such tests and the evaluation services provided by their publishers, but significant markets exist also in industry and other areas outside formal education.

*Subscription reference* books are principally sets of encyclopedias marketed by their publishers to consumers on a door-to-door or direct mail basis. Since this marketing pattern often involves package arrangements, other reference or self-educational materials such as dictionaries, atlases, sets of the classics and similar publications originated by these publishers also fall under this heading. Sizable secondary markets include public and educational libraries and schools.

It is noteworthy that nearly every division of the industry enjoys substantial markets outside its primary sales focus. This growing phenomenon is of relatively recent origin. Prior to World War II, product and market distinctions were nearly synonymous: trade books sold almost exclusively through bookstores and to libraries, elhi textbooks to schools, college textbooks to students in higher education. The advent of the mass market and the growing practice, in education, of supplementing texts with other books have served to blur what were once fairly precise market lines.

The industry has sometimes found it difficult to adjust its organizational structure to these changes. Most publishing houses have retained the product-oriented divisional and departmental arrangements of the prewar era while attempting to meet new marketing opportunities by making interdivisional sales arrangements or creating sales departments independent of their editorial counterparts. On an industry-wide basis the divisions we have enumerated continue to prevail mainly because they still provide opportunities to publishers in similar economic circumstances to compare experiences and address common problems.

The complexity of the field is such that no reliable figures are available citing the number of publishers active in each division. The R.R. Bowker Co. maintains a list of more than 6,000 book publishers in the United States of which approximately 1,000 produced five or more titles during 1972.

*Literary Market Place,* an annual Bowker publication, lists the latter individually, enumerating some of their specialties and areas of interest. The Association of American Publishers does, however, provide annual estimated sales figures for these divisions. The figures for 1972 are shown in Table 1.

Table 1

ESTIMATED 1972 BOOK PUBLISHING INDUSTRY SALES
BY AAP SURVEY CATEGORIES

| Category | Millions of dollars |
|---|---|
| Trade (total) | $442.0 |
| Adult hardbound | 251.5 |
| Adult paperbound | 79.6 |
| Juvenile | 110.9 |
| Religious (total) | 117.5 |
| Bibles, testaments, hymnals, and prayer books | 61.6 |
| Other religious | 55.9 |
| Professional (total) | 381.0 |
| Technical and scientific | 131.8 |
| Business and other professional | 192.2 |
| Medical | 57.0 |
| Mass market paperback | 252.8 |
| Book clubs | 240.5 |
| Mail order publications | 198.9 |
| University presses | 41.4 |
| Elementary and secondary text | 497.6 |
| College text | 375.3 |
| Standardized tests | 26.5 |
| Subscription reference | 278.9 |
| Other | 154.8 |
| | $3,007.2 |

The figures in Table 1 include domestic as well as export sales (not, however, sales of subsidiary companies of American publishers operating in foreign countries). The last category, "Other," embraces nonbook sales such as sales of audiovisual products, as well as sales of book overstock at sacrifice prices ("remainders") and sales of unbound pages ("sheets") to foreign publishers.

Publishers generated these sales from nearly half a million titles in print. Of these, according to *Publishers Weekly*'s "Weekly Record" to which most publishers report, nearly 27,000 were new titles and over 11,000 were new editions published during 1972.

Publisher's receipts are not identical to consumer expenditures. Many books are sold by publishers at a discount to bookstores or to wholesalers—who in turn market to bookstores and other retail outlets—and bookstores and wholesalers must have their markup on the merchandise before it is sold to the consumer. Only in cases where the publisher sells directly to individuals or to libraries and institutions (which then makes the library or institution the consumer), is the publisher's sales income identical to the consumer expenditure.

Eliminating nonbook sales, and confining the estimate to the domestic market (excluding, therefore, all export and foreign sales), consumer expenditures on books in 1972 are shown in Table 2.

Table 2

1972 ESTIMATED DOMESTIC CONSUMER
EXPENDITURES ON BOOKS

| Category | Millions of dollars | Percent of total |
|---|---|---|
| Trade | 624 | 20 |
| Religious | 185 | 6 |
| Professional | 339 | 11 |
| Mass market paperback | 371 | 12 |
| Book club | 233 | 7 |
| Mail order publications | 191 | 6 |
| University press | 44 | 2 |
| School (Elhi) text | 477 | 15 |
| College text | 375 | 12 |
| Subscription reference | 279 | 9 |
| | 3,118 | 100 |

**Industry Markets**

As we have seen, publishers' customers include individual consumers and institutions to whom they market directly as well as through intermediaries such as retailers, wholesalers, and jobbers. More specifically the major domestic market areas may be described as follows:

*Retail outlets* include bookstores; book departments in department stores; shops selling religious, stationery, and gift items; museum stores; chain stores, supermarkets, and drugstores; and newsstands, among others. Professional books are often sold in medical and engineering supply stores, hobby books in hobby stores, art books in art supply stores, etc.

Of the above, book, department, and other stores which have traditionally handled books for the general consumer are thought of as trade outlets. Chain stores, drugstores, supermarkets, and newsstands comprise the so-called "mass market."

*College stores* are often classified separately since they provide the principal channel for books utilized in higher education. However, they also account for substantial noneducational sales to the students and faculty whom they serve.

Publishers may deal with the above retail outlets directly or through *wholesalers.*

*Libraries* include public, college, and university, and special (i.e., industrial, research, or special interest) libraries. School library sales are usually classified with sales to schools and institutions. Some library sales are consummated by publishers directly; however, most are supplied through the facilities of *library jobbers,* i.e., specialists in supplying the library trade.

*Schools and institutions* comprise school systems, districts, depositories, classrooms, resource centers, libraries, and school stores, as well as other educational institutions public or private from kindergarten level through grade 12.

*Direct to consumer* transactions are those in which the publisher or book club markets directly to the individual by mail or door-to-door.

*Other* markets for publishers include industry, government, premium users, foundations, research establishments, etc.

Table 3 shows estimated 1972 consumer expenditures for the market categories just described.

Table 3

1972 CHANNELS OF DOMESTIC BOOK DISTRIBUTION

|  | Estimated consumer expenditures | |
| --- | --- | --- |
| *Channel* | *Millions of dollars* | *Percent of total* |
| General retailers | $698 | 22 |
| College stores | 525 | 17 |
| Libraries | 348 | 11 |
| Schools and institutions | 712 | 23 |
| Direct to consumer | 783 | 25 |
| Other | 52 | 2 |
|  | 3,118 | 100 |

In addition to these domestic markets publishers enjoy *export sales* to foreign bookstores, libraries, and individuals. Sometimes they make arrangements with foreign publishers for the sale of an entire edition of bound books or of unbound sheets which the foreign publisher then markets under his own imprint. A number of American publishers operate subsidiary companies abroad to which they export books and sheets but which also manufacture indigenous editions and originate titles in their own territories.

Finally, publishers gain important income from the marketing of domestic and foreign *rights*. Book clubs and paperback publishers will purchase the right to reprint books, as may magazines for certain portions of a book or for serialization of the whole. Foreign publishers will buy translation or reprint rights. Motion picture and TV rights, though often controlled exclusively by the author, are also occasionally a source of revenue for the publisher. "Subsidiary" rights as the industry terms them are of particular importance in the economics of trade-book publishers.

## The Publishing Process

The basic functions of the publisher involve the selection of manuscripts or the planning of projects; the preparation of manuscripts for the typesetter; the supervision of the book manufacturing process; marketing and publicizing; the processing of orders; the warehousing and shipping of inventory; and the necessary financing, accounting, and housekeeping tasks attendant upon the preceding obligations.

From these fundamental responsibilities evolve the functional areas of publishing: editorial, production, marketing, fulfillment, and administration.

*Editorial.* The editing task is basically twofold: the selection of manuscripts and their preparation for publication. In its first phase the editor chooses or recommends a manuscript after satisfying himself that it has the merit and salability that warrants placing it on his list. Or he may conceive of a project and find an author to undertake it. In the second phase he will work with the author to ensure the best possible presentation of his subject and material. Because the process is varied and complex it encourages a certain amount of specialization, and there are editorial readers (who do nothing but give first readings to manuscripts), procurement editors (who visit authors to solicit their work), creative editors (who dream up projects and subsequently find writers to undertake them), and copy editors who are experts on grammar, punctuation, and language usage as well as demons on accuracy. Most editors combine two or more of these functions in their daily tasks. All editors are, or should be, master diplomats for they must constantly work and negotiate with that most temperamental species, *homo scrivens.*

*Production.* The AAP definition of production involves the supervision of the manufacturing process. This includes the planning and designing of the physical book, choice of materials for it, and the selection of and relations with suppliers throughout its typesetting, printing, and binding.

*Marketing.* This function includes personal contact selling, advertising, promotion, and publicity.

*Fulfillment.* This area covers order processing, invoicing, handling of accounts receivable, payments and collections, credit control, shipping and warehousing, and the maintenance of sales and inventory records.

*Administration.* Fiscal, personnel, and general business management, including the accounting function, fall under this heading, as do corporate organization, policy, and planning.

We shall be discussing these publishing functions in detail, as they are exercised in various divisional settings, in the succeeding chapters of this book.

## Industry Activities and Associations

The record of the book field in dealing with its common problems is a strangely mixed one. On the one hand some publishers groups have maintained good information services and statistics for many years, and textbook publishers in particular have established effective joint relations with national and local governments. Trade-book publishers have often united in battling censorship. But only recently have general and textbook publishers joined in one industry association, and the organizations representing publishers, retailers, and wholesalers have barely begun to attack their most serious common difficulties, such as inadequate distribution.

Book people are often known and admired for their rugged individualism which stands them in good stead when they must make difficult editorial decisions. Unfortunately the same staunchness of spirit often makes them less than wholly receptive to the needs and possibilities of cooperation. Here as in other ways the influx of new management and ownership has been an advantage; as the record of recent years proves, the industry has now overcome the inertia that characterized much of it for generations and is solidly on the way to forging an effective industrial community.

In the forefront of this development is the Association of American Publishers created in 1970 by the merger of the American Book Publishers Council and the American Educational Publishers Institute. Organized into divisions corresponding generally to the historic groupings described earlier, the new body has displayed unprecedented vigor in dealing with the political and commercial problems of the industry. In carrying out its tasks AAP has cooperated with other publishers groups such as the Educational

Media Producers Council of the National Audio-Visual Association, the Information Industry Association, the Association of American University Presses, and the Children's Book Council. AAP has also joined forces with the American Booksellers Association, the National Association of College Stores, and the American Association of Book Wholesalers in exploring solutions to the industry's critical marketing and distribution problems. And it has continued the long-established relationship of the publishing community with the Book Manufacturers Institute in developing and promulgating specification standards, particularly in the textbook field.

One of the most significant developments of recent years, the introduction into the United States of the International Standard Book Numbering System, also enjoys AAP sponsorship, along with that of the American National Standards Institute and the R.R. Bowker Co., which administers the program. This system, to which most major book-producing nations now subscribe, assigns a unique number to every title which also identifies its country of origin and publisher. Plans exist for expanding the system to assign numbers also to nonprint media, and to institutions and dealers who purchase books and other materials, thereby opening up the possibility that in the near future all ordering, invoicing, and record keeping will lend itself readily to standardized computerization.

Other industry organizations and activities that should be noted here are the American Library Association, the Authors League of America, the American Institute of Graphic Arts (to which book designers belong and which sponsors annual exhibits and awards for excellence in the field), the Council for Periodical Distributors Associations (wholesalers handling mass market paperbacks), and the National Book Committee whose role it is to enhance popular interest in and appreciation for books and which receives some organized as well as individual support from the book community. *Literary Market Place,* the directory for the industry, lists details for the above and related organizations.

One certainly hopes that the impetus toward a common approach to shared problems which the growing activities of these organizations have provided will continue to be felt. As a cultural industry the book field is far too dependent on public attitudes and public policy to afford its members the luxury of autocratic isolation.

# Chapter III.

## How
## Books Are Created

# ADULT HARD-COVER TRADE BOOKS

As long as there is popular interest in a subject writers will write books about it and publishers will publish them. The horizon for trade books is therefore practically unlimited and the topics they cover are legion.

There is fiction. Since the days of Thomas Deloney in the sixteenth century the novel has been an institution in the English language. In recent years there have been reports of its imminent death which have proved, however, to be greatly exaggerated. Perhaps the novel no longer plays as central a role in popular diversion as it did in Dickens's day when it appeared in installments which so gripped their readers that people would crowd the dockside of ships arriving from England and shout to the captain inquiring whether Little Nell was still alive. Perhaps the tragedy is that many novelists today lack Dickens's genius or at least his discipline and vision. But no one can look at the popular consumption of novels in both hard and soft covers and persuade himself that the medium is biting the dust.

On the contrary, the cat has had kittens. No longer are we content with fiction, or even its traditional whelps historical fiction and romance, but we have developed mystery fiction, science fiction, and gothic fiction among other offspring. Occasionally we even sell a collection of short stories, proverbially a tough nut in publishing experience.

There is topical nonfiction: books dealing with the great issues of the day. There are biographies, ranging from Alexander the Great to Alexander Pushkin. There is history—American, Asian, Australian, and Afghanistani-an. There are reference works: encyclopedias, dictionaries, and atlases. There is the whole range of "how-to" books on bridge, gardening, cooking, modern languages, various crafts, hobbies, and sex. There are populariza-tions of science and scholarship. There are books on art, drama, and poetry and on travel and leisure time activities. There are the cartoon, picture, and novelty titles which the trade's snobs nobly refer to as "nonbooks." One marvels at the ingenuity of authors and publishers in satisfying, stimulating, and occasionally even inventing topics of interest.

When the publisher thinks of the market for his titles he recognizes that some will have a short life, others may go on selling for years. Most fiction is likely to fall into the first category, as will probably topical nonfiction, whereas a good biography or work of history, 'a basic reference title, a helpful how-to book, or a sound popularization are likely to become part of what the publisher calls his "backlist": titles that consistently contribute to his income year after year.

Whether a book becomes a best seller or not may have little to do with its life expectancy, however. A successful novel may sell half a million copies in two years (after which it will probably enjoy another life cycle in paperback), but subsequently disappear from the publisher's list. A work of philosophy or science on the other hand may become a best seller at its beginning yet continue its career for decades thereafter. And of course the large majority of backlist titles never come even close to making the national best-seller list.

On most of his titles the hard-cover trade-book publisher hopes to earn income from subsidiary rights. If the book appeals to a wide audience he is likely to sell reprint rights to a mass market paperback publisher. If it could enjoy application in school or college classrooms he will place it in his own or another publisher's quality paperback program. The major book clubs may choose it, or at least make it available to their members, if its prospective audience is broad; if more limited in appeal it may be selected or listed by one of the numerous special interest book clubs that have sprung up in recent years. And for many books there is the opportunity of publication in Britain or translation for release in other languages.

**Agents and Their Role**

Most trade books are placed with publishers through literary agents. Although many of the best and most prestigious houses still read manuscripts submitted directly by authors—"unsolicited" or "over the transom" in trade parlance—the actual record of acceptance of such manuscripts is small, even diminutive, in comparison with the number which reach publication after they have had an agent's attention.

The agent's role has been augmented in recent years for a number of reasons. As book markets have grown, both successes and failures in trade-book publishing have begun to involve much larger commitments, expenditures, and risks. The professionalism which agents represent in scouting for and screening manuscripts, advising authors on their writing, and negotiating on their behalf with publishers has been welcomed by both sides. Agents seek out authors—at writers' conferences, in academic institutions, by scanning literary magazines for promising talent, or even among nonliterary celebrities—encouraging them and guiding them to produce publishable manuscripts. They sift submissions by hopeful writers, discouraging the presumably untalented or unfashionable, while working constructively with those who appear to have potential. By the time an agent submits a manuscript to a publisher it has presumably passed a rigorous test and is in such shape as to warrant that publisher's serious consideration.

Should the publisher be interested, the horse trading begins. Royalties, advances, and guarantees against royalties, author's shares in subsidiary rights all must be worked out to mutual satisfaction. Most authors feel neither qualified nor temperamentally inclined to struggle with the publisher over these matters; yet, as very substantial sums are often involved they are happy to have an agent's services and counsel in settling them. Furthermore, with an agent in the picture, motion picture, TV, and foreign rights are often reserved to the author exclusively and the agent undertakes to make arrangements for and negotiate these contracts as well.

In fact, though publishers often stoutly refuse to admit it, agents have taken over some of the traditional functions of the trade-book publisher: manuscript screening, finding new writers, conceiving book ideas, and recruiting authors to produce them, working with the author in shaping up the manuscript, and negotiating on his behalf for certain subsidiary rights. However, publishers continue to pursue these tasks on their own, thus paralleling, supplementing, and occasionally duplicating agents' efforts.

## The Selection Process

Within the firm, screening, creating projects, and assisting the author are the roles of editors and their supporting staff. In houses where unsolicited manuscripts are welcome they are often given a first reading by a junior staff member who prepares a report which together with the manuscript is reviewed by a staff editor. Such a report addresses itself to the significance of the work, its subject matter, the quality of the writing, and its market potential and recommends either further consideration or rejection. The staff editor on the basis of the report and his own examination of the manuscript will then decide whether the material should be declined or further examination is warranted. In cases where an outline or sample chapters are submitted the procedure is much the same. If the material has come through an agent it will of course reach a staff editor or even a supervising editor immediately.

Except for a manuscript that appears to warrant an immediately favorable decision—such as a spectacularly well done novel submitted by a reliable agent—a promising work is given additional readings within the house or by outside experts. If the manuscript treats an established subject, inquiries are made into existing or previously published books and their performance in the marketplace. Is the new title really needed? Will it contribute enough to command the support of its intended audience? Can sufficient copies be sold to ensure a profit? Or barring this possibility are there vital cultural considerations, such as the discovery of a major new talent, or possibilities of favorable returns on future books to warrant the investment? It is only after inside readers and authorities in the field have answered these basic questions affirmatively that a title is likely to be recommended for publication.

The procedure is modified if the house has taken the initiative in approaching the author or agent or in generating the project. In such cases a proposal may be drafted by the author or the initiating editor which must be approved before a contract can be signed. Such a proposal may be sent to outside experts for comment unless the merits and nature of the project are sufficiently persuasive to make such a step unnecessary. Similar methods are employed in the consideration of a hardcover edition of a title originated by a paperback house, of a foreign manuscript for translation, or a foreign publisher's title for publication in this country.

**Money and Auctions**

When a title with major marketing possibilities is under consideration and its appeal to a mass market paperback publisher is a foregone conclusion, the trade publisher may well explore possible reprint arrangements and the mass market paperback publisher's likely commitment before he makes his own decision. He will do this not only because the subsidiary income will loom large in his own profit projections but because he will be asked to pay a very steep price (as high as a million dollars in rare cases) by the author and his agent for the acquisition of the manuscript. In fact major books are often "auctioned off" among publishers, i.e. literally sold to the highest bidder.

This phenomenon as well as the generally very considerable escalation in author demands in recent years has been a concern to many publishers, accustomed as they had been to modest advances and to an equal share in nearly all subsidiary income earned by the author. Today it is not unusual to pay several hundred thousand dollars in guarantees (nonreturnable advances) against royalties for a top novel. Superior nonfiction, which ten years ago could be obtained for $5,000, may demand as much as $25,000. A celebrity writing his autobiography with the help of a collaborator may command as much as $100,000.

True, the average good novel or nonfiction manuscript may bring no more than $15,000 (a mere 100 percent increase during the last decade), and first novels only $2,500. In fact, as M.S. Wyeth, a prominent trade book editor, points out, the generally higher cost of literary property may occasionally work against the interests of new writers who are left by the wayside while mad auctions for obviously more salable properties are going on. Yet one can hardly regret the fact that some writers at least are receiving sufficient reward for their labors to provide them with a decent livelihood. Nevertheless the inflationary spiral seems to have gotten out of hand.

The problem is, simply, that most of the auctioned books are not earning their advances. In fact, very often such books have turned out to be dismal failures whose value was more perceived than real and who benefited from the ability of a plausible agent to sell the big sizzle on a small, tough steak. The reason the auctioneers have succeeded thus far is that a few publishers—both paperback and hard-cover—are anxious to expand, have ample resources, and have been willing to pay inflated prices thus forcing others in the industry to go along if they are anxious enough to lay their hands on the auctioned properties. Some publishers, realizing the futility of the entire exercise, never went along; others have decided to give up trying. Conceivably the inflationary trend may already have been somewhat dampened.

### Rights and Loyalties

More is involved than advances and guarantees, however. While royalty rates have not been seriously affected—they still begin at 10 percent of the list price in most contracts, graduating upward to 15 percent and in some rare cases to 20 percent as sales increase—shares of subsidiary income have been substantially affected. The traditional 50–50 percent split of paperback and book club income has begun to give way in many cases to a 60–40 percent relationship in favor of the author, particularly where paperback royalties are concerned. Some publishers have preferred to arrange for a graduated scale which begins at 50–50 percent, turns to 60–40 percent at $100,000, culminating in a 70–30 percent ratio near $200,000. A model contract recommended to its members by the Authors League even suggests a scale of 50–50 percent on the first $10,000, 60–40 percent on the next $10,000, and 70–30 percent above $20,000. Of course there are still publishers who believe that the established line should be held. They argue that a trade publisher's stake in subsidiary rights income is so great that he cannot operate without a decent share of it. If he is forced into doing so, he will not have the resources to gamble on new and untried authors or even on marginal books and in the end writers as a whole and of course their agents will suffer.

Such publishers express concern over the basic attitude underlying these developments which they see as excessive greed on the part of authors and agents. They point out that many authors are no longer as loyal as they once were, that they jump from publisher to publisher with every new book just to get the best possible deal. How can the publisher justify his gamble on a first book—which presupposes the likely success of a second or third book—when he has no assurance that the author will not go elsewhere with manuscript two or three?

Multiple contracts, which commit publisher and author for two or more books running, are one solution to the loyalty problem, at least in cases where the risk factors are low. But other points continue to be hotly debated. The Authors League model contract, for example, suggests limiting the original publisher's licensing term to 28 years (as opposed to the customary full span of copyright) and proposes more drastic provisions than publishers now allow under which rights would revert to the author if the book is not available in retail outlets or if its sales fall below a given level after 10 years. (Now rights usually revert to the author only after the book goes out of print in all editions.) Subsidiary rights which the publisher had not licensed or relicensed after 7 years would similarly revert to the author.

No doubt there are shortsighted excesses in the pressures some authors and agents have exerted and no doubt there are long-term losses in the erosion of many author–publisher relationships. But constructive relationships are often a casualty in contemporary society where distrust and hostility are thought to be enlightened attitudes and taking the long view is rare. Authors, by nature often more emotional than most people, may reflect no more than the general trend. And some have suffered serious disappointments in their associations with publishers—because of publishers' inefficiencies or because of their own excessive expectations and lack of understanding of the field. If in many instances an adversary atmosphere now overshadows these relationships, perhaps there is some blame and some innocence on both sides.

## Cost Considerations

If the publisher is thorough and dedicated to intelligent financial planning, he will, prior to making his publishing decision, carefully examine his prospective investment and return on every project. Anticipated sales income and earnings from subsidiary rights must be weighed against advances and royalties payable, manufacturing cost, promotional expense, and overhead. This calls for carefully prepared estimates of sales, manufacturing cost, and price projections (with perhaps several variations of all three since price, size of printing, and projected market are inextricably interrelated). Once optimal printing and price are decided, including provisions for anticipated reprintings, the financial prospects of the title can be forecast.

The prudent publisher will therefore not make a decision until he has consulted various experts on his staff: the sales manager, the subsidiary rights manager, the production manager, the business manager, and the manager of financial planning. Strangely enough the traditional editorial meeting—a revered ritual at many publishing houses at which a good many decisions to publish are still made—often excludes production and financial representation, a sad indication that, from a business standpoint, many trade publishers are still flying by the seat of their pants.

## Why Books Fail

Perhaps the excessively intuitive character of many publishing decisions provides a clue to the very high rate of failure among trade books and to the fact that trade-book publishing is among the least profitable categories in the business. There are additional reasons which deserve examination.

Faulty editorial judgment is certainly one of the principal causes. Sometimes an editor is overly impressed by an author's previous record; or he fails to do his homework by not obtaining sufficient expert opinion on the manuscript or by choosing the wrong reader. His own enthusiasm or that of the agent may get the better of him. Or he may be under management pressure to fill his quota—in many houses editors are judged and rewarded according to the number of manuscripts they bring in—and may be reaching for a borderline property which had better be left alone. As trade-book editor Steven Frimmer suggests, he may also be guilty of a simplistic approach to success, trying to imitate last year's best seller with a book which, by the time it is published, will be badly out of fashion.

The house's marketing efforts may also be ineffectual—although as every publisher knows no amount of advertising will turn an obvious failure into a success. By far the single biggest reason why trade books fail, however— even some excellent titles that deserve a better fate—is sheer numbers. There are simply too many books published, certainly far more than there is room for in bookstores and libraries, far more than can be noticed and reviewed, far more than the hard-pressed editorial, marketing, and fulfillment staffs of publishers can handle efficiently.

Take fiction. The better bookstore or library can probably make room for a few hundred new titles each year. In 1972 publishers whelped no less than 2,000 new titles upon their defenseless outlets, by conservative estimate twice as many as could have been successfully marketed.

This is not a new story. O.H. Cheney, in his lively and revealing *Economic Survey of the Book Industry 1930–1931*, listed the flood of titles as one of the business's main problems. That too many books are published is a subject on which it is possible to elicit universal agreement from publishers, no matter how much they may differ on other matters. Why then does the deluge continue?

There are a number of reasons, some of which were implied earlier: unwarranted editorial enthusiasms, overly persuasive agents, the lazy urge to imitate success and to flood the market with carbon copies of yesterday's money-maker. There is the desire to keep people on the payroll occupied; since we published 200 titles last year we must publish 200 titles this year, even if some are not too good. There is even what passes superficially for corporate planning which may commit a house to a given size program simply to meet its projection, an approach that may work in the hardware business but hardly in a cultural industry.

But by far the most significant factor in overproduction is what may be described as the buckshot approach to publishing, the lightning-will-strike theory, playing the lottery, or the gold-rush syndrome. The idea is, says the trade publisher who subscribes to this suicidal concept, that trade books are unpredictable because the public is unpredictable. Fickle is the word—they take the "sleeper" to their bosom while turning up their noses at the hot prospect everyone swore would make millions. The answer? Place as many entries in the stakes as possible, take a flyer on as much material as seems to hold promise and you can afford—lightning may strike some of it. And indeed lightning seems to have struck enough of it from time to time to have permitted the practice to survive (although a good many publishers who operated this way have disappeared from the scene, bankrupting their imprints).

It is not difficult to rationalize the choices that are made in this chaotic process; even marginal books can be described as a "contribution to learning and literature." Furthermore the habit of thinking in this way, reinforced by predetermined size lists and editors' quotas, becomes a sacred ritual in time: carried on behind handsomely paneled walls on which hang autographed photographs of best-selling authors, it assumes full respectability and even, superficially, the aura of success.

There are signs, however, that the new business consciousness on publishing and retail levels is making the lottery obsolete, to say nothing of authors who realize that when distribution channels are clogged good writers suffer a great deal more than bad. More and more talk is heard about birth control—from retailers who plan to cut back on their new title purchases, from publishers who are convinced that careful selectivity, sound market research, and wise planning can make a few titles far more successful and profitable than buckshot-style whelping ever could. Not until the industry as a whole is convinced, however, or at least until its major producers are persuaded of this wisdom can the average title published receive a fair and equitable chance in an honestly and efficiently managed market. Since all those concerned—publishers, wholesalers, retailers, and libraries—have a great deal at stake here one dares to be somewhat optimistic about new approaches on this vital point.

The American consumer is, unfortunately, obsolescence-prone. Though serious book buyers may be less so than others, they too have often been conditioned by publishers and book clubs to go hungrily searching for the latest rather than the best. The simple fact is, however, that a cultural experience such as reading is only very superficially dependent on novelty—Henry Fielding still reads better than most novels on the best-seller list and Spinoza has it over the conventional wisdom any day. It is difficult to understand why publishers have permitted themselves to become so fervently trapped in emphasizing the new—it's so much less costly to sell backlist items on which type and plates are paid for and which require hardly any promotion and often not even any royalty payments. Furthermore, since the quality of most backlist titles—which have had to establish themselves by survival—is far greater than that of most new items, the satisfaction of readers and their appetites for buying more will be more consistent if they are urged to partake of such proven and established titles among available books. From every standpoint, cultural as well as economic, publishers would be well advised to reduce their new title production.

**Editing the Manuscript**

Once a manuscript has been accepted for publication it becomes the subject of further editorial ministrations. The staff editor who has taken special responsibility for it will now work with the author to help him achieve the best organization, the most appropriate emphasis, the right tone, the optimal length, and the proper slant for his work. He will be assisted in this task by a staff or free-lance copy editor—a specialist on grammar, punctuation, and English usage who will also check facts, quotations, and citations for accuracy.

Editors are sometimes accused of overediting. Yet without their fussing many a manuscript would go into print with contradictions and inconsistencies, tiresome repetition, glaring errors, awkward constructions, and tortured phrases. Many an author has been saved from the wrath and scorn of critics and readers by the alertness and punctiliousness of his publisher's editorial staff. Editors *do* overedit, of course, when they substitute their own taste, their own approach, their own view of a subject for that of the author. Nowhere is the essential midwifery of publishing more apparent than in the editor's task when he must literally inhabit an author's soul and whisper to him as though from within, seeing the world and the subject with the author's eyes and hearing the cadences of language with his ears.

There are celebrated cases of editorial empathy, like that of Maxwell Perkins who became Thomas Wolfe's literary mentor and without whose labors Wolfe's novels would never have become possible. Such instances of intimate collaboration may be rare; yet most good authors have words of praise for their editors and pay tribute to their understanding, skill, and diplomacy.

## ADULT SOFT-COVER TRADE BOOKS

The quantitative effects of the paperback revolution are all around us. Hardly a segment of publishing has failed to be touched by it; from potboiler to modular textbook the economics, convenience, and fashionable popularity of the soft binding have created new markets, new audiences, even new uses for books. One does not have to embrace the extreme position of wild paperback enthusiasts, who would have us believe that their product will soon replace the hardbound book entirely, to acknowledge the astounding potential, in some measure yet untapped, of paperbound books.

If the quantitative impact of paperbacks has been great, so has their qualitative influence. As the cultural maturity of Americans deepens—a maturity manifested in significant degree by the reading population which grows not only larger but ever more discriminating—the softbound book continues to be both a major cause and effect of our advancing civilization. Nowhere has this been more apparent than with the paperbacks published by trade publishers which have justly earned the appellation of "quality."

The numbers of quality paperbacks are smaller, and their prices higher, than of books conceived for the mass market. In 1972 some 366 million units were sold by mass market paperback publishers at an average cover price of $1.03, while trade publishers sold 80 million units at an average list price of $1.82. Their markets differed significantly as well: nearly 60 percent of trade paperbacks flowed into the educational market, while only approximately 30 percent of mass market paperbacks were thus distributed. (This does not include the paperbound volumes directed to school children through student book clubs.) And, although these distinctions like all others are becoming less precise as the entire paperback phenomenon continues to gain momentum, trade paperbacks are generally more handsomely designed and printed on better paper than their mass-oriented counterparts.

They had different "inventors" as well. Robert de Graff, who founded Pocket Books in 1939, is credited with initiating the mass market entity; Jason Epstein who persuaded Doubleday & Co. in 1953 to launch Anchor Books is considered to be the father of the quality version. It was Epstein who realized that growing college enrollments, scarcity of copies on university library shelves—particularly of out-of-print works of scholarly importance—the tendency to widen the range of collateral reading coupled with decreasing reliance on the core textbook (particularly in humanities and social science courses), would all work together to provide a ready market for reprints of significant writing in these fields. The general public, furthermore, was ready to respond to more serious paperbound offerings than those which the mass market publishers had generally been able to provide (even if some titles, like the Mentor Books published by New American Library, had paved the way for several years for a quality dimension to the revolution).

The early development of quality paperbacks was a wonder to behold. Out-of-print titles that had slumbered quietly on the discontinued lists of university presses and scholarly societies and which in their lifetime had sold perhaps 1,500 or 2,000 copies were suddenly resurrected and began to enjoy sales of 3,000 even 5,000 copies in the new format, not to speak of a few which sold in the tens, even the hundreds, of thousands. Soon backlists and out-of-print lists were feverishly combed by publishers hoping to sell rights and by publishers hoping to establish quality imprints. From an academic standpoint the concept was highly successful; in fact it accelerated the move away from unique emphasis on textbooks and toward a broadening of general book use in college courses. Characteristically it also led to overproduction and a serious surfeit of titles so that some publishers who had entered the field suffered damaging economic reverses.

The time has long since passed when an out-of-print title may readily be found for successful incorporation in a paperback program. Titles planned for original trade paperback release, a phenomenon evident even at the beginning of the quality era, are more common now, even though publishers still reprint a good many of their own and other publishers' books in maintaining their paperback lists. Occasionally a title is released simultaneously in soft and hard covers largely to gain critical attention because some review media are still reluctant to notice paperback originals. The availability of a hardbound edition is also an accommodation to libraries.

The selection process is usually placed in the hands of editors who specialize in this field and includes, as it does in the hardback area, screening and creating projects. Royalty rates are traditionally lower than in the hardback field; quality lines pay author or originating publisher (who then shares the income with his author according to contract) 5 to 8 percent of list price. Advances are generally modest reflecting anticipated royalties from a first printing of 4,000 to 10,000 copies. Of course top sellers may be reached for more eagerly and may even be subject to auction by the originating publisher or agent. When rights are licensed by the originating publisher the contract term itself is limited to 7 or even 5 years after which it expires. Some contracts are then renegotiated and renewed. The originating publisher usually insists on a delay of a year or more in the appearance of the paperback in order to protect the hard-cover market during that time.

The number of outlets for paperbacks is growing. According to G. Roysce Smith, Executive Director of the American Booksellers Association, most booksellers devote 35 to 50 percent of their display space to them. Bookstores specializing in paperbacks are also increasing in number. In consequence, trade paperback publishers, who at one time relied almost exclusively on the college market, have begun to produce more material for the general audience, especially the youth audience which, they have discovered, is particularly receptive to their medium. Culture or counterculture, paperbacks are apparently a favorite youth commodity, so much so that the small format appears to matter less than the soft binding. Recent years have witnessed some remarkable successes, such as the *Whole Earth Catalogue,* where oversized, high-priced paperbound volumes have outsold nearly everything else in sight.

At the same time some trade publishers and some mass market producers are creating hybrid titles and series: softbound books that have a place in both traditional trade outlets and in at least some of the better mass market facilities. If a book can by this means enjoy a market of 50,000 to 100,000 it represents a valuable expansion over the normal trade distribution and appears to be particularly suited to certain fiction, timely nonfiction, and craft and self-help titles that receive at least a substantial portion of their support from youth readers.

## LIBRARY REPRINTS

When the boom stimulated by federal funding enriched public and university libraries in the 1960s it became apparent to some publishers that libraries might now have enough money to pay the high prices for reprints of important out-of-print materials that would have to be charged if they were made available in small editions. These publishers proved to be correct. Libraries responded solidly and a small subindustry developed which reprinted some of the scholarly and reference classics that time and the previously forbidding economics of small reprints had made unavailable.

The subsequent decline in library funding as well as the inevitable saturation resulting from filling much of the limited need which exists in this field has since reduced the momentum of this activity. Yet it persists and appears to have found a permanent place within the industry.

Closely related to this activity are the various services, such as that provided by University Microfilms in Ann Arbor, Michigan, which make out-of-print materials available on an on-demand basis, on microfilm, microfiche, or in actual soft- or hardbound book format. Some publishers who deal largely with libraries have even begun to release a film or fiche as an alternative form of publication for a new book or a title still in print. As many libraries are hard pressed for space, these alternatives hold a certain attraction. However, to date the publishers report that they have failed to achieve the glowing results that had been predicted for these forms of publication. Once again the book, whose imminent replacement by new media has so often been prophesied, appears to be holding its own.

## JUVENILE TRADE BOOKS

Children's books have been buffeted by a variety of currents in recent years, some of them contradictory, which in combination have spelled slow growth and even discouragement for a number of publishers. On the positive side has been federal funding for school and public libraries which has made the market heavily institutional so that today some 75 percent of all children's books are sold to schools and libraries. On the negative side the consumer has been reluctant to buy large quantities of most children's books and has resisted price increases, which in tune with general economic trends have affected juveniles.

No doubt there is a great deal more competition for a child's time today than there was in former years when books might have played a more dominant role. Leisure reading, as an activity, competes with the affluent child's sports, hobbies, elaborate toys, or the second or third TV set. Also school work is often a bit tougher today, more time consuming, and involves a good deal more mandatory reading by the youngster.

The result is that some publishers who at one time contributed significantly to the production of children's books have greatly curtailed or even eliminated their programs. Since children's books, like other publishing areas, have always suffered from overproduction this curtailing has had at least the salutary effect of reducing the excess somewhat. In consequence some of the publishers who have remained in the field are doing well in both sales and profits.

While the principal market for children's books is institutional there is a substantial secondary market in bookstores and even in mass market outlets. These retail markets have recently been expanded by the arrival of the paperbound juvenile, an experiment which is enjoying impressive growth on the surface but is turning out to be a rather thorny rose for publishers. Printings must be quite large to satisfy economics, but markets are as yet not sufficiently responsive to justify them.

It is interesting to note that the management and editing of children's book programs has generally been a feminine bastion in a world which, though not as inflexibly masculine as some, has nevertheless been male dominated. (It can be argued, I believe, that book publishing has offered above average opportunity to women for many years; however, since the general average has been quite low women who claim that their opportunities in publishing do not truly equal those of men can muster some persuasive evidence to support their case.) Be that as it may, women have certainly dominated the children's book corner of the industry and the inroads there in recent years have, interestingly enough, been made by men.

Although there is quite a diversity even among the few houses still publishing children's books regularly—some aim their hard-cover products almost exclusively at the institutional market while others cultivate retailers more—in general their method for selecting manuscripts and the terms they extend to authors are much the same.

At most only a third of the books are handled by agents; few are created or planned by their publishers; most arrive over the transom. Since children's manuscripts, particularly those for the lower age groups, are short (many only ten typescript pages), the burden of examining them is not excessive even though the acceptance rate may be as low as one fourth of 1 percent or four acceptances in one thousand submissions.

(Commenting on the mass of manuscripts submitted, children's book editor James C. Giblin wonders why aspiring authors do not acquaint themselves better with what is being published—by examining books in their local library, for example—thus avoiding so many false starts and efforts doomed to disappointment.)

About half the manuscripts arrive with illustrations. Often these cannot be used, however, even if the manuscript is publishable, and the publisher must find experienced and competent illustrators. Among the titles published perhaps a third are designed for the picture book age, i.e., to third grade level; another third for ages 8 to 12; and the remaining third for ages 12 and up, including so-called "young adults." Of course these days adult books are read by "young adults" as much as, or even more than, titles classified as juveniles, just as many young adult titles published by juvenile houses are also listed as adult titles in promotional literature to libraries.

Royalty advances and guarantees in this field are modest. On a picture book the author and illustrator may each receive $1,000 to $2,000 against royalties to each of 5 percent of the list price. Books for the intermediate and upper age groups may bring the author $1,000 to $2,500, while the illustrator, whose contribution probably consists only of some ten line drawings and a jacket design, may receive a flat fee of $750 to $1,500 or even $2,500 if he enjoys a major reputation. Royalties to the author might be as high as 8 percent; should the illustrator receive royalties rather than a fee these might be 2 percent. Better established authors may command a graduated royalty such as 7.5 percent on the first printing, or 7,500 copies, and 10 percent thereafter, in rare cases rising even to 12.5 percent at perhaps 15,000 copies. Conversely once a book is established and enjoys a steady but slow sale, royalties might be renegotiated downward to make it economical to keep the book in print.

First printings on picture books vary with their complexity and cost. (The greater the initial fixed manufacturing cost the greater is the tendency to print in larger quantities in order to distribute that cost over a larger number of units—a tendency which is not always sound from a financial viewpoint.) A two-color volume might enjoy a first printing of 7,500 copies. A four-color book may be printed in the 12,000 to 15,000 range if the primary colors used in printing are preseparated by the artist (i.e., plates can be made directly from his artwork) or even in the 30,000 range if so-called process color is employed in which the colors are separated by camera, an expensive method. Printings in the 8–12 age group normally run 6,000 to 8,500 copies and in the 12-and-up bracket 5,000 to 7,500.

Since the market for juveniles is heavily institutional and since many libraries have particular binding requirements, the publisher may prepare a specially bound library edition or sell sheets to a "prebinder," a firm specializing in binding books to the particular specifications of their library customers.

Needless to say, printings, royalties, and advances go up substantially if one is dealing with a highly popular author whose following embraces consumers in addition to institutions. As for mass market titles, those in hard covers are often classics in the public domain and therefore not subject to royalty, or they represent repackaged titles on which a reduced royalty has been negotiated.

Somewhat the same is true of the new paperbound juveniles most of which are reprints of hard-cover items. As many of them sport color illustrations and carry low list prices, large printings (30,000 to 50,000) are the order of the day. The publishers who have launched them, some of whom are trade while others are mass market houses, are seeking to establish them more firmly so that the market will respond in proportion to the necessary printing commitment, an objective which has thus far eluded realization in many cases.

Where the paperbound format in children's books has been a phenomenal success is in the student book clubs operated for some years by such firms as Scholastic Magazines and Xerox Education Publications. These firms purchase book club rights from publishers and prepare their own editions which are then marketed through the classroom, with teachers acting as agents for the clubs. When such arrangements are concluded they usually provide for 6 percent royalty based on the club price which the publisher then shares on a 50–50 percent basis with the author and/or illustrator. Hard-cover children's book clubs, on the other hand, some of which work through schools and teachers while others reach their members directly, will generally make arrangements paralleling those in the adult field.

## MASS MARKET PAPERBACKS

Compared with other mass media, books with their 100,000 to 200,000 average sales do not usually reach audiences of a size deserving the "mass market" description. Still—no other development in twentieth-century book publishing has contributed as much to their wide dissemination as that which Robert de Graff launched with Pocket Books less than four short decades ago. Occasionally a softbound best seller does roll up very impressive sales figures: eight million, ten million, even twelve million copies. And if such sales reach less than even one tenth of the population, one can be encouraged by the fact that each year best-seller figures appear to grow larger—a happy indication that the paperback is indeed becoming more of a mass commodity all the time.

An interesting characteristic of the mass paperback field is that it embraces a relatively small number of publishers. Fewer than twenty houses produce any significant volume of sales, and, of these, five imprints—Bantam, Dell, Fawcett, New American Library, and Pocket Books—play a dominant role. Among the second-tier houses some like Avon and Ballantine have recently enjoyed impressive growth, however, and the general prosperity which has been typical of this industry segment is likely to continue to stimulate not only increased activity by present producers but additional entries into the field.

Anyone investigating the possibility soon discovers that the potential rewards may be equaled or even exceeded by the hazards, however, which may explain why relatively few publishers have braved the waters. For one thing the sheer investment—in guarantees to authors, in printings, in publicity campaigns—can be staggering. For another, market conditions border on the chaotic and only a solidly established, editorially shrewd and extraordinarily capable sales and fulfillment organization can even begin to cope with them effectively.

**A Problematic Market**

The bulk of mass paperbacks is distributed through nearly 600 independent news wholesalers throughout the United States who serve some 90,000 outlets most of which are newsstands and drugstores, but which also include bookstores, department stores, college stores, and schools. To reach the independent news wholesalers, publishers employ the facilities of a national magazine distributor or their own sales organization, often a combination of both.

The ability and sophistication of independent wholesalers in serving their book customers vary drastically from one to the next. Some have developed excellent techniques for selecting, warehousing, and delivering books which have proved to be efficient and profitable; some even operate retail outlets of their own. Others unfortunately approach the task haphazardly and with varying degrees of confusion. The consequences of these conditions are quite staggering: approximately half of all books shipped to wholesalers remain unsold, and while some are returned to the publisher whole, most are discarded after the covers have been torn off and submitted for credit.

In fairness to wholesalers one must recognize the publishers' share of responsibility for these conditions. In 1972 mass market publishers produced some 2,200 new releases, or an average of nearly 200 titles monthly. Even some of the better outlets served by wholesalers cannot accommodate more than half of such releases; they may have 90 to 100 pockets for display, some of which should be devoted to best sellers and backlist items that will produce more revenues for the retailer than will certain of the new titles. For the relatively few establishments served by wholesalers that can support a larger selection, there are many more whose facilities are even smaller than the average. For the market as a whole to display adequately the mass titles being produced each month is a physical and mathematical impossibility.

Publishers have come to recognize this, and those who are well organized and responsible have made attempts to deal with the problem both individually and by participating in industry dialogues with wholesaler representatives. The most important step, greater selectivity in publishing new releases, is apparently already being implemented: 1972 title production represented a 27 percent drop from the 3,000 which had been published in 1971. Other problems, notably the inability of many wholesalers to select salable titles from the flood and to serve their outlets intelligently and efficaciously, remain largely unsolved.

One solution publishers have favored—though wholesalers are often grieved by it—is to intensify their direct selling efforts to retailers and trade jobbers. Here selectivity in buying is greater and merchandising ability is often superior and the results show it. Returns from bookstores, college stores, department stores, supermarkets, chain stores, and trade jobbers amount to only some 20 percent of shipped goods, not an ideal situation perhaps but certainly a much better one than the wholesaler picture and no worse than the experience of trade publishers in the same market. Furthermore, direct sales are usually more productive in maintaining best sellers exposed and a solid backlist title on the shelves—again because the customer is often a more sophisticated, efficient merchandiser of books.

The mass paperback industry's total marketing pattern is quite revealing in this respect: some 63 percent of all units are shipped to wholesalers but only 53 percent of units actually sold are so channeled. Direct transactions (including export to overseas markets) account for only 31 percent of shipments but for 39 percent of actual sales. The balance—6 percent of shipments and 8 percent of sales—is accounted for by so-called "special sales," such as bulk shipments to industry for premium purposes.

**The Best-seller Emphasis**

One consequence of the difficult wholesaler market has been that some publishers have placed extraordinary, even excessive, emphasis on best sellers. A publisher who produces such a best seller becomes a welcome supplier to the wholesaler; a publisher's list that consistently contains best sellers may be perceived as worth stocking month after month, certainly in preference to a list which cannot boast as many best sellers.

Soon the publisher's anxiety to capture a best seller for his list becomes intense; the stakes are certainly thought to be high enough. If one is a smaller publisher wishing to establish oneself more thoroughly in the market the need to have a best seller may be regarded as essential. In consequence competition for top books becomes more intense and the guarantees offered go up and up—one million dollars is no longer an unbelievable or unheard of figure. Soon the titles of the second rank or titles with outside best-seller potential are caught up in the inflationary spiral and guarantees for them reach six figures. And the title which used to be available for $15,000—and still is hardly worth more in real terms—is beginning to bring $40,000 or even $60,000. Only routine acquisitions are still likely to command the once common $5,000.

Not everyone in the paperback field is happy with these developments. At the 1973 Annual Meeting of the Association of American Publishers, Oscar Dystel, president of the industry's leader, Bantam Books, warned his colleagues against the shortsightedness and steadily diminishing returns of a policy favoring swollen guarantees. Nor does every publisher in the field regard the competition for best sellers as the only path to editorial success. Ian Ballantine, for example, whose gifts for innovation are well reflected in the Ballantine Books list, has developed new concepts and new series and discovered new titles and new authors which have become successful without the burden of drastic overpayments in guarantees.

**The Selection Process**

Most mass market softbounds are still reprints leased from hard-cover publishers for 5 to 7 years (after a waiting period of a year or so). And in sheer numbers titles still predominate that appeal not to the reader of best sellers but to buyers with specialized tastes: science, western, mystery, or gothic fiction addicts, sports fans, astrology buffs, fanciers of witchcraft, war history enthusiasts, people looking for self-help and self-improvement. And since some 30 percent of all sales reach the educational market, there are long lists of classics, reference titles, and serious nonfiction on all levels—to say nothing of the children's books which, as we noted, are a new if somewhat struggling phenomenon. As Marc Jaffe, Bantam's editorial director, never tires of saying, "there are many mass markets."

Original paperbacks have been with us for a good many years, but recent developments have proved to be a stimulus to paperback houses prepared to take the initiative in developing titles. Guarantees can be somewhat smaller if one deals with the author directly rather than through a hard-cover publisher; in fact, why not have the hard-cover publisher pay a guarantee for his privilege of launching the title initially or simultaneously? As there is often a respectable sale in hard covers—to libraries if to no one else—and as review coverage is often nonexistent unless a title appears in the traditional way, there is a strong incentive to proceed in this fashion.

But in certain genre, notably westerns, mysteries, science, and gothic fiction, and so-called "instant" books on current events, there may not even be a sufficiently large sale in hard covers to justify that effort and many today appear in soft covers only. Thus the editorial activities of most mass market paperback houses parallel those of the hard-cover trade firms: they screen, procure, and create titles with the best of them, even while they are in constant touch with the hard-cover houses for reprint rights.

Royalties, like guarantees, have risen in recent years. Approximately 8 percent of the cover price is the base rate, extending usually to about 150,000 copies, then increasing to 10 percent. In rare cases it may graduate to 15 or even 20 percent. Some modifications have been introduced by publishers who have developed more "quality" or hybrid programs where the marketing effort is more selective, the returns lower, waste smaller and the royalty structure more in keeping with that employed by trade paperbound publishers. Of course the printings in such instances are also smaller, amounting perhaps to 50,000 to 75,000 in contrast to the 200,000 characteristic in mass title instances.

The growth of original title production, the ever rising demands of authors and agents, the blurring of mass and quality paperback distinctions, all appear to be working together to introduce new concepts and techniques into this fast developing field. Oscar Dystel has urged that hard-cover and paperback publishers find new ways of working together, perhaps jointly sponsoring and jointly developing new titles and series. Trade editor Stewart Richardson, noting the distinct though overlapping markets reached by hard-cover books and by quality and mass paperbacks, foresees more instances when the career of a title might be in three formats beginning, say, with a hard-cover edition, going next into mass market for a limited time to satisfy the broad consumer interest, and finally arriving in trade paperback format for a long-term career as an educational and select consumer item. Houses such as Dell, Ballantine, and Harper & Row, on the other hand, are pressing on in their development of hybrid books which enjoy a simultaneous following in every camp.

## RELIGIOUS BOOKS

For reasons only vaguely related to those which brought prosperity in the sixties and an erratic recession in the seventies to certain other industry segments, the religious book field underwent a significant cycle of its own. In large measure it paralleled the fortunes of organized religion itself during recent decades.

There was the postwar religious boom, when peace of mind and soul were offered in national best sellers and when optimistic churchmen could speak of a religious revival in American society. A nation seeking normalcy and security, shaking off the aftermath of depression and world conflict, living under the shadow of nuclear annihilation and nobly articulating its public and international responsibilities was a scene in which religious practice and religious publishing could flourish. Not only the traditional denominational presses and religious publishing houses but the large general publishers, several of whom founded or expanded existing religious departments, were busy catering to the growing interest. Traditional editions of Bibles, hymnals, devotional volumes, and prayer books sold in substantial numbers. Inspirational works in hard covers and in paperback reached thousands. Church-sponsored educational programs consumed carloads of books.

Was it affluence, the civil rights struggle, Vietnam, the Vatican Council, the youth rebellion of the sixties, the sexual revolution that changed it all? Or was it a combination of these and other factors? God alone knows. The fact is, however, that as liberal denominations conceived of their religious responsibility increasingly in terms of social issues, the specifically religious character of their concerns was no longer apparent. Many "religious" books became indistinguishable from other works on peace, race, poverty, and civic involvement, just as church membership lost some of its distinguishing character and could be subsumed in political and social action.

The mood of the nation generally had certainly changed enough to outdate the once successful inspirational volumes with their emphasis on personal salvation. Action, involvement, ecology, public morality—these were now the fashionable subjects for religious reading. These changes coincided, furthermore, with organizational and liturgical reform in several faiths. The easing of traditional rigidities within Catholicism brought about by Vatican II, for example, and the far-reaching changes in ritual which it decreed, had a profoundly depressing effect on the sale of missals, prayer books, and other perennial standbys. Ecumenism, accepted by most denominations, caused a lessening of emphasis on any, including liturgical, practices that advanced strictly denominational interests, therefore also causing a drop in the demand for denominational hymn and prayer books. And of course both laity and clergy were defecting from Catholic and some Protestant churches at a rate that would have been unbelievable just a decade before.

Interestingly enough this fate was not shared by the fundamentalist Protestant denominations or those with a generally evangelical cast. Their attendance continued solidly, their Bibles, prayer books, and inspirational literature continued to find a ready audience. Eventually the more liberal scene also began to shake down and stabilize itself. Werner Mark Linz, president of Seabury Press, the publishing imprint of the Episcopal Church, who headed the Roman Catholic publishing imprint Herder and Herder before it was merged into Seabury and who is therefore in a unique position to assess all fronts, believes that the decline of nonevangelical religious publishing has now "bottomed out."

Actually when taken in its totality, thanks to the stability of the evangelical book market, the religious field did not suffer major attrition. What had suffered badly for a time had been the Catholic segment, the liberal denominational imprints, and those general houses which had benefited from the popularity of certain religious books in happier days. And just as there are indications that while some of the denominations have suffered, religion as such has not, owing to a revived interest in the subject in colleges, a popular curiosity about Eastern faiths, and such widespread phenomena as the Jesus movement among youth, so it would now appear that the subject of religion is as live a topic for book treatment as ever and only its denominational involvement has lessened.

Publishers who stuck to their guns during the recession have survived and are doing well. Their lists have been pruned, their plans refined, the quality and aim of their offerings have been sharpened. While there are now fewer general houses active in the field, the denominational imprints continue committed and the independent religious publishers, notably those with an evangelical orientation, are as active as ever.

The market for religious books is still sizable. The R.R. Bowker Co. lists more than 4,000 stores handling religious titles, more than 3,000 of them stocking Protestant, 2,000 Catholic, and more than 1,000 Jewish books. This in itself is an indication that ecumenism has advanced and that there is a good deal of publishing and selling across denominational lines. The Christian Booksellers Association, a group enrolling mostly evangelically oriented Protestant stores, numbers 1,500 members. General and college bookstores handle some of the most popular titles, and direct mail is a common method of distribution employed by both publishers and certain booksellers. A number of book clubs serve both the professional and lay segments of the field.

Religious publishers' lists fall generally into one or more of four categories: Bibles and devotional manuals; inspirational books for laymen; materials directed to professional clergymen and theologians; and textbooks for use in religious education programs. Needless to say, particularly during the present era of blurring distinctions, serious theological works may sell to laymen (although perhaps not as readily as they did a decade ago), and some titles, such as those on Eastern religions, will circulate far beyond a strictly religious audience. As has always been true, the publishing of theological works and of religious scholarship may require a financial subsidy which is one reason why denominational houses that are not organized for profit can devote themselves to it. Such support may come from Bible sales or similar income which then may also be used to market certain devotional or inspirational books at or near cost in order to give them the widest possible dissemination.

Very few religious authors come to publishers through agents. Their manuscripts either arrive over the transom or are obtained by procurement editors at conferences and meetings; or the authors may come to the attention of the house through their writing, through their teaching or their preaching. Royalties conform to conservative textbook standards; advances are modest if paid at all. First printings are often considerably smaller than those common in the trade field; it is characteristic for a religious book to get off to a slow start but, once established, to enjoy a long and solid existence. Of course if a title has trade-book character, because the author is a celebrity for example, the terms it commands may well be similar to those of a strong trade book as will be its printing and sales pattern. By implication somewhat the same is true of religious textbooks, particularly those which find wide use in adult and youth parish education programs.

Bibles and devotional manuals are, of course, in a class by themselves. Most editions are well established and have predictable sales year after year. The commissioning of a new translation or edition, often shared these days by several denominations, is a major undertaking consuming a number of years and sizable endowments by the sponsoring group. The sales of a successful Bible are, then, often quite spectacular with some editions soon running into millions.

## PROFESSIONAL BOOKS

Professional book publishing ranks with the most profitable categories in the industry, a record which even the winds of change, blowing as lustily here as elsewhere, have been unable to shake. Recent growth in certain areas, such as medicine and business, has shown particularly encouraging patterns.

Professional books are fundamentally tools of work. The best titles are indispensable to their purchasers; certain reference volumes promulgating standards or data universally utilized in a profession have almost totally predictable markets strictly related to the number of individuals practicing or teaching or the number of companies active in a field. A publisher who is fortunate enough to have such a work on his list—and some run to several volumes and command substantial list prices—and who can count on a continuously active response as he publishes updated and revised editions, is indeed fortunate. Of course the investment and the expertise necessary to create and publish such books are also substantial.

The recession which has buffeted some of the professions has of course been felt by publishers. Curtailment of federal research grants, cutbacks in the space program, the ecology crisis and related disenchantment with technology particularly among the young, and the financial crunch in higher education—these have contributed to the flat performance of, for example, materials in science and technology. Thus there has been a noticeable decline in demand for books in engineering particularly of works which are theoretical in nature. Disciplinary shifts have also troubled publishers. "Physics has gone out of fashion" observes scientific publisher,

Michael Harris, explaining that professionals like other people "move with the money" and that the former physicist might now be found working on a biophysical project which is both academically and practically more popular. The creation of new disciplines or subdisciplines requires extraordinary alertness on the publisher's part as he must publish for tomorrow, not yesterday. It also makes his marketing effort more difficult as people who could be reached with relative ease a few years ago through membership rosters of professional societies and subscription lists of disciplinary journals are becoming more elusive.

A related phenomenon, that of increasingly narrowing specialization brought about by the refinement of research and the knowledge explosion, has been aptly termed "twigging" by Curtis Benjamin, former McGraw-Hill president and chairman. As the various scientific branches grow more numerous twigs, and the twigs in turn do some twigging of their own, the number of subjects for books grows proportionately but the audience for them tends to shrink. Michael Harris believes that twigging has on the whole been beneficial because of the opportunities it has provided for significant books to come into being, but everyone agrees with Mr. Benjamin's contention that contracting markets are creating economic problems of serious proportions. When one adds to this the difficulties publishers are experiencing because of unauthorized photocopying, which tends to diminish their marketing opportunities even further, one recognizes that some books whose appeal is extremely narrow can no longer be published profitably despite their obvious merits. Publishers of professional books, like those in other fields, feel an obligation to their constituents to publish some titles of superior quality despite the certain knowledge that they will create losses. However, given the hard economic realities, they must forego publishing some less extraordinary though worthwhile items in the hope that scholarly societies or university presses will take up the slack.

Paradoxically professional publishing suffers from overproduction just as other industry segments do. Of course the concentration is on the "popular" subjects rather than on the very narrowly specialized, and the pressures that create a title surplus—attempts to duplicate yesterday's successes, ill-considered editorial decisions, the feeling on the part of small houses that they must grow to gain sufficient recognition in the field—are very similar to those pertaining elsewhere. There are the added hazards resulting from the need to anticipate developments in the professions themselves.

One of the most critical problems plaguing the professional book publisher is the inadequacy of existing distribution facilities. Bowker lists nearly 1,700 stores claiming to carry professional books of which, in the estimation of most informed judges, some 500 might qualify to the extent of carrying even a marginally adequate selection, and less than half of those might be described as satisfactory outlets. Many dealers lack well-trained staff; they are uninformed about new publications, do not know their own inventory or keep adequate controls over what they sell. Often a book is sold within a week of its arrival at a store but then not reordered until six months later when the publisher's sales representative pays his next visit. One cannot help but contrast this state of affairs with the impressive expertise and efficiency of European professional booksellers who bring to their enterprise knowledge, sophistication, and initiative—in other words a professionalism of their own—that makes them notable instruments in the progress and dissemination of knowledge.

Because retail outlets are so often unsatisfactory, direct selling has been one of the principal marketing tools of publishers. Medical and law houses usually maintain sales forces calling on private practitioners, law firms, and hospitals. Scientific and business publishers cannot usually justify such arrangements economically and therefore engage extensively in direct mail promotion. The effectiveness of direct mail has recently been blunted somewhat, however, by the consequences of disciplinary shifts and twigging. Furthermore, most professional customers would prefer to examine a book before buying it and opportunities for so doing are simply nonexistent in the vast majority of cases. It is impossible to estimate the sales losses to publishers resulting from these detrimental conditions.

On the bright side has been the success of American professional books abroad. Since English has become the international language of science and scholarship, and American technology and management techniques have in the past been regarded as advanced over those of most other countries, American books in these fields have found ready acceptance overseas. More than 20 percent of professional publishers' income currently results from export sales. Unfortunately continued success of such magnitude is unlikely as American preeminence in many areas is being successfully challenged by Japan and some of the highly industrialized European nations.

Most professional manuscripts result from the publisher's editorial initiative. Many title ideas originate with house editors who often themselves are competent in a discipline and become aware of the need for treating a certain subject from their contacts with the field. In many cases—since specialization makes it impossible for a house editor to deal with equal effectiveness with every subcategory of every discipline—the house retains a competent scholar or practitioner to act as editor for a series in his specialty. Such editors, chosen for their ability to deal with other professional writers, to originate ideas, and to keep abreast of their special fields, are usually responsible for most of the book ideas in their series.

House editors carefully scan technical, scientific, and medical journals as well as periodicals in the management, accounting, data processing, and computer fields for ideas and potential authors. They attend professional and scholarly meetings where they often make contacts directly with authors or gather useful suggestions for book topics and for writers who might develop them. Occasionally they find it advisable to involve two authors in a volume: an outstanding authority in a field who may be, however, not too effective a writer and an individual of perhaps less celebrated standing but able to communicate clearly and effectively the great man's ideas and knowledge. Some publishers even have a staff of house writers available to collaborate with authors.

In other cases editors may encourage the preparation of a multiauthored book. This is usually germane where a massive reference tool requires the competence of many hands; it is also pertinent when a relatively new and fast-moving subject needs to be rapidly treated and no single author would be able to find the time or be able to work rapidly enough to do it justice. It isn't easy for a busy professional to sacrifice many hours and his normal income to write an entire book; he is often able, however, to prepare an essay or a chapter. In any case, be it complete book or contributed essay, many professional authors would not even be writing but for the encouragement of publishers' editors. As medical publisher Fred Belliveau points out, persuading authors to write is one of the professional publisher's principal functions.

In all some 80 percent of professional books are generated through in-house initiative, and only 20 percent arrive over the transom. Agents are only infrequently involved. Advances are paid occasionally but are rarely sizable. Royalties may be 10 percent of the list price or 15 percent of the publisher's receipts (which are less than the list price since discounts are extended to retailers and institutions and even occasionally to individuals such as teaching faculty), except on direct sales where they may be as little as 5 percent (the rationale given being the supposedly greater cost of direct marketing, a not altogether persuasive argument). Contributors to multiauthored volumes are often paid a flat fee of $5.00 to $7.00 per page instead of a share of royalties. Where one of the small but important professional book clubs selects a title, publisher and author will share equally in the royalty which usually represents 10 percent of the club price.

Most authors of professional books, like most authors in other areas, are not likely to amass fortunes as the result of their writing. They are not usually motivated by the prospects of gain in any case but by professional pride, considerations of prestige, the urge to communicate significant findings to their peers and to serve their disciplines. However authors of major handbooks, reference works, or leading work tools in their field have at times seen their royalties exceed their regular income, and a few have become quite affluent thanks to their publishing successes.

In recent years a number of professional publishers have added products in other media to their programs: microfilm, microfiche, data banks, slides, films, and audiocassettes are among the items one now finds on many medical, law, technical, and business lists. Such products have significantly rounded publishers' offerings and augmented their income without displacing or even diminishing their book production. It is noteworthy that the demand for such nonprint products seems to be a parallel to rather than a substitute for books; in fact, in many cases where publishers have offered microfilm or fiche as an alternative form of acquiring a book in print, libraries and individuals have continued to select the book, passing up the alternative.

## SCHOLARLY BOOKS

Scholarly books are published for the most part by not-for-profit, subsidized enterprises: research institutions, university presses, museums, and learned societies. The reason is basically simple: audiences for scholarly books are small. Consumers of such books are reluctant to pay the very high prices which would result from normal profit markups on high unit costs dictated by small printings; therefore commercial publishers do not usually find it possible to undertake the production of scholarly materials.

University presses, which account for the bulk of scholarly title output, have had an interesting history. Still numbering probably less than one hundred in the United States—an exact count is difficult to establish since small publications programs exist on many campuses which may or may not be classifiable as university presses—they have, however, nearly tripled their numbers since World War II. Several causes have contributed to this proliferation: the growth of higher education itself, the greater affluence of universities during the fifties and sixties, and the unique role which publication plays in the academic process. Recent budget cuts have snuffed out the life of some of these enterprises and threatened a few more and nearly all have been forced to curtail their programs. Nevertheless the majority seem to be weathering the storm.

Most presses owe their existence to a genuine need for making scholarly works available and their lists bear eloquent testimony to the importance, both qualitative and quantitative, of their contribution. Others, however, appear to have been called into being less from real need than from such academic pressures as an exaggerated emphasis on institutional prestige and a faculty promotion system that gives undue weight to a man's list of publications irrespective of their value. To operate a press has become a status symbol at some institutions of lesser rank, as well as a hope for ready access to print for certain second-rate academic authors whose chances for salary increases and advancement are dependent on their ability to present a publications list to a promotions committee.

Given these pressures and the unfortunate wastefulness of some universities particularly since their boom years, academic publishing presents a somewhat checkered picture even today. Ill-disguised dissertations, hastily compiled symposia, and excessively esoteric monographs still find their way into print even under some very prestigious labels. Current economies are serving to reduce this tendency as are contemporary alternatives to book publication—microfilm and fiche and photocopying—through which materials can be made available that have limited value but not sufficient merit to warrant book publication.

A potent force for setting and advancing standards in the field has been the Association of American University Presses (AAUP) which by its admission policy and various programs has kept the goals of excellence consistently before its sixty-odd members. Reflecting unquestionably the commitments of the majority, it has preached rigorous selectivity, meticulous copy editing, attractive design, and high quality in production. As a result several university presses have become industry pioneers and some significant innovations, notably in design and production, were first introduced on academic campuses.

University presses to some extent partake of the characteristics of trade, professional, and textbook publishers. While most of their titles are addressed to specialists, particularly faculty in higher education, some are aimed at a wider audience, usually a regional one, of general consumers. As many presses are attached to state universities, they have naturally assumed the obligation to publish books about their state and region for a local readership. Some have also published textbooks, usually of an experimental type or designed for highly specialized graduate level courses where enrollments are small and commercial publishers find the risks unduly great. Many presses have quality paperback programs with titles that are often found on college and graduate course reading lists. Very occasionally a university press book even becomes a best seller, a major book club selection, or a widely adopted text. These instances are rare however because presses are not normally equipped, editorially or through their marketing machinery, to select, develop, or distribute materials for large commercial markets.

Most manuscripts reaching scholarly publishers are unsolicited. The campus on which a press is located is probably its prime source for submissions, although many presses prefer to limit the number of books by campus authors, just as some scholars prefer to be published by off-campus presses. The reasons given by both, that seeking off-campus associations lessens the danger of a faculty becoming "captive" to its press and the press to its faculty, is not however persuasive to all practitioners in the field. Agents are hardly ever involved. A few presses employ procurement editors traveling to other campuses, often competing with a press located there or with other presses similarly engaged in procurement. Some press directors have noted, however, that they believe such a practice to be in conflict with stated objectives of service to scholarship and the nonprofit status of university presses.

A key problem in scholarly publishing is the evaluation of manuscripts which in most cases can only be undertaken by other scholars in the field. Great care must be taken to select readers whose judgment will be both competent and impartial; academic rivalries and disciplinary disputes must not be allowed to influence objective scholarly assessments. Most presses will obtain three favorable reports before they decide to recommend a work for publication. Such recommendation is then usually made to a faculty committee, representing the parent university, with whom rests the ultimate power of decision to publish.

Arrangements with authors vary. A royalty of 10 percent of the list price is common although in some cases such a royalty is deferred until certain costs are met or a minimum number of copies, possibly 1,000, are sold. Some contracts provide for a royalty of 15 percent of the press's income from the book which, with the usual discounts, may amount to less than 10 percent of the list price. Occasionally a particularly costly volume may be published without a royalty or the author may be paid a flat sum. And in certain cases, when development expense of a title is expected to be very large and its market particularly narrow, a subvention may be required before the press can consider publication. Such a subsidy may be furnished by a grant or a fund but most presses will not accept subventions furnished personally by the author as such a practice smacks too much of vanity publishing. (Vanity publishing is the industry's term for an arrangement wherein an author pays the entire publication costs to a publisher who specializes in such work.) Presses with paperback programs usually provide for lower royalties (5 to 7 percent) on softbound editions.

The largest market for scholarly books is libraries: academic, special, and public. College bookstores absorb a significant portion as do general retail outlets. Domestically some 10 percent are sold by mail directly to scholars, reflecting the effectiveness of direct mail promotion which also accounts for much of the university library sale since these libraries usually respond to requests from faculty who have been circularized. AAUP, through its service subsidiary American University Press Services (AUPS), maintains extensive academic mailing lists which many presses utilize in their promotional efforts. Other promotion includes advertisements in scholarly journals and, less commonly, in general review media as well as exhibits at scholarly meetings. (AUPS also manages a cooperative exhibit program which is supplemented by individual press displays and the use of commercial exhibit services.) The trends that have benefited the foreign sales of commercial publishers have also augmented the overseas activities of university presses to the point where some now operate foreign distribution offices. In 1972 some 14 percent of all university press sales were export.

The greatest problem facing scholarly publishers today is money. The parent institutions, which traditionally have supported their publishing enterprises with cash subsidies and free services, are themselves struggling with shrinking budgets and are seeking acceptable ways to prune their expenditures. The press is often a vulnerable entity because it is not readily perceived to be related to the university's teaching or research role.

Nothing could be more shortsighted, however. Often the only way in which some of the most significant teaching and research taking place on a campus can be disseminated to the scholarly community at large is by means of adequate, competent book publication. Because the scholarly community is small—most university press editions do not exceed 2,000 copies—commercial publishers cannot assume the burden should universities decide to disclaim it. On the contrary, current pressures in the commercial field are if anything intensifying the need for well-managed, able and alert not-for-profit publishing enterprises. If the better presses now on the scene are not adequately supported, everyone—but most of all the academic community itself—will be severely impoverished.

Some institutions and some press managers are tempted in these difficult times not to confront this issue but instead to imagine that it can be solved by presses engaging in activities that might show a profit such as the publication of textbooks and trade books. Totally aside from the possible conflict this might create with commercial publishers who would rightly wonder why they should be subjected to competition from tax-exempt institutions, this appears to be a self-defeating strategy also from a practical point of view. Even commercial publishers are hard put to keep up with changing conditions in consumer and educational markets; even with large-scale procurement efforts, sizable capital resources, and ambitious marketing programs—which university presses could never hope to match—commercial houses often find it difficult to gain representation in the overcrowded and intensely competitive areas of textbook and trade-book publishing. If university presses attempted intensively to enter these fields one suspects that they would quickly and fatally increase their losses.

No—the answer is what it has always been: a firm, reliable commitment by the parent university to its press because it recognizes that along with its other teaching and research programs its publishing effort represents a unique and irreplaceable contribution to knowledge and culture.

## SUBSCRIPTION REFERENCE BOOKS

Few achievements in the publishing world are as impressive as the compilation and production of a multivolume, major, general encyclopedia.

When such a work is developed on a level of high quality and competence it represents both a rich fruit and a significant tool of civilization. In a world of exploding knowledge it also constitutes a publishing challenge of unrivaled proportions.

The challenge is of course a perpetual one. The well-established reference sets, which have justly earned their reputation, are subject to continuous revision. Reprinted annually they attempt to incorporate as much updated and new information as possible. Their publishers also issue annual supplements or yearbooks so that sets purchased in previous years may continue to be useful to their owners.

In the eighteenth century, when they were first created, encyclopedias served the entire literate population. As differentials in educational levels became more significant and as encyclopedias were recognized to be valuable tools in the education of children, publishers began to issue sets for various levels of age and sophistication. Today, among the dozen or so leading sets published by American houses are the works aimed at elementary-school-level children and at those attending high school or readers with a secondary-level education, and the scholarly sets that are intended to serve college and university students or graduates.

The development of a new set, or the major overhauling of an established one, represents a multimillion dollar investment. Scores of house editors and researchers, hundreds of contributors, and many consultants in specialized fields must collaborate on the text, to say nothing of the illustrations and maps commissioned or located for the purpose. In every case selectivity of material and authors, level of detail, and the nature of the presentation figure importantly in a managing editor's plans and decisions; in the case of children's encyclopedias, reading level and vocabulary limitations are additional considerations.

The same complexities, albeit on a more limited scale, figure in the task of perpetual revision. Constant decisions must be made regarding the incorporation and the extent of treatment of new facts and developments, the need for change in previous articles and entries, and the illustrations and maps that support the text. Special editorial problems arise from the limitations of existing format and length into which revisions and additions must be incorporated. All this must be done under the pressure of inflexible deadlines; it is proverbial in the field to speak of next year's revisions even as the pages for the current edition are going to press.

Domestically encyclopedia publishers market the major portion of their product directly to homes and businesses; more than 70 percent of their sales in the United States are consummated through large staffs of field salesmen. Such sales usually include an arrangement for the automatic supply of yearbooks and may involve package deals which include other reference materials, series of classics, globes, slides, viewers, etc. Other domestic marketing efforts comprise sales to libraries and schools, covered also by sales travelers, as well as intensive direct mail programs which in recent years have sometimes branched off into book club and mail order operations marketing other publishers' titles to the consumer.

The last development has been inspired in part by the fact that of late domestic encyclopedia sales have fallen off drastically—by approximately a third between 1969 and 1972—and publishers have looked for ways to take up the slack. The reasons for the sales decline are probably several, among them the economic recession, the "saturation" selling in which publishers engaged during the prosperous sixties, consumer criticism of and resistance to high-pressure or deceptive sales techniques, editorial weaknesses in the products themselves, declining birth rates, and readier access to reference works provided to children in newly established school libraries and resource centers.

But if domestic sales have been declining, foreign sales have been growing at an impressive rate—about a third between 1969 and 1972. These foreign sales represent some export but mostly the indigenous revenues of subsidiary companies overseas where English-language as well as adapted translations of American sets (in addition to locally originated products) are marketed. So important has this foreign production become that today some 47 percent of encyclopedia revenues of American publishers are generated abroad, making this segment of the industry the most international of any in character.

## ELEMENTARY AND HIGH SCHOOL TEXTBOOKS

Schoolbook publishers constitute the largest industry segment on the basis of revenues; they are also among the divisions which have traditionally operated in the most businesslike fashion. By its very nature, elhi publishing has always demanded long-range planning, sizable investments, carefully designed marketing strategy, and fiercely competitive selling. These circumstances have discouraged the excessively intuitive decision-making that has characterized some of the other areas of the book publishing world. Paradoxically, however, recent developments have loosened the very rigidities of the adoption process which have hitherto conditioned the nature of this field.

At one time nearly every state in the union exercised strong central control over the textbooks used in its classrooms. Usually only one title or series per subject and grade level won the approval of the state selection board; such an award was a rich plum indeed and publishers would work feverishly—sometimes even unscrupulously—to gain and retain it.

Changing educational and political forces have eroded this monolithic structure. Only 23 states now retain some control over the selection of textbooks and even the most authoritarian will approve four or five titles per subject and grade level, permitting districts to select from the list at their own discretion. In the remaining states, districts, individual schools, or even individual teachers are at liberty to choose with almost total freedom from whatever may be available for their needs.

The impetus for this development—which is ongoing and gaining momentum—has come from both the teaching profession and the public. Teachers, serving communities with differing needs and character, have exerted pressure for greater discretion in the choice of materials that would suit their circumstances, be they urban, suburban, rural, advantaged, or disadvantaged. The public, often highly critical of educational performance (why can't Johnny read? why can't he add?) has supported these efforts, seeing in the trend toward individuation some hope that children would derive greater benefits from the national investment in the educational process.

Much has been made of the fact that in introducing diversity into the materials selection process, the educational community has toppled the traditional textbook from its preeminent position. Not only are many more textbook titles now in use than in earlier days, thus fragmenting their impact, but nontextbooks, notably paperbacks, and nonbook items such as card kits and periodicals, have replaced the old textbooks in many instances. Audiovisual materials, manipulatives, and other nonprint products, furthermore, abound and are said to be on the verge of replacing books altogether.

The shift may be more apparent than real, however, and journalistic enthusiasm coupled with the fadism which for a while gripped the educational scene drunk on its own prosperity, may have served to create an exaggerated impression. No doubt the iron hold which a few books once had on the materials market has disappeared, probably forever. No doubt more general books, paperbacks, periodicals, kits, audiovisuals, and other materials will continue to take important shares of that market. But there is a noticeable trend which schools and publishers are reporting and which industry sales confirm, indicating a strong adherence and in some places even a return to textbooks as basic teaching tools—not the textbooks of yesterday, but new textbooks—many of them paperbound, many modulized, many designed for individualized instruction, and most of them reflecting the contemporary conviction that the innate fascination of knowledge and learning, rather than a rote emphasis, should be conveyed to their young users.

To some extent this trend emerges out of disillusionment, because of the promises which the substitute materials failed to keep. According to many reports, students simply do not take audiovisual experiences as seriously as they would have to were they to become the mainstay of the learning process. Audiovisual materials are often too frail, furthermore, to withstand the harsh wear of daily use; from one end of the country to the other many a broken language laboratory, piece of jammed hardware or torn software, and half-demolished kit is gathering dust in a schoolroom. While many such materials continue to be highly useful and respected, there appears to be a growing consensus that such usefulness is limited, is mostly supplementary in nature, and must be judiciously employed to be effective.

This new discrimination and perceptiveness is reinforced by another, very significant new development in education: the pressure for accountability. Maybe learning should be fun say the advocates of accountability—it should certainly be basically absorbing and respond to that innate curiosity which is a fundamental human trait—but it should also stick. After a youngster is exposed to it for the required number of years, assuming a minimal willingness to learn which he must bring to the process and without which any school is totally powerless to teach him, he should have something to show for the investment made in his education. If despite a reasonably good disposition on his part he is found to be incapable of functioning and surviving in the contemporary world, the schools have failed him. These days school boards and parent groups are often demanding a demonstration of the school's effectiveness, of teachers' competence, and of the value of the materials acquired at public expense. Momentary fads, no matter how fervently advocated or embraced, are not usually able to sustain the scrutiny which an accountability-oriented public is now often ready to exercise.

## How Elhi Titles Are Developed

Ideas for the overwhelming majority of elementary and secondary textbooks originate with their publishers. Salesmen, consultants (i.e., teachers who are employed to demonstrate products to other teachers), editors, and managers all travel, attend national and regional meetings, and are constantly alert to new trends and developments in the field. Authors already on the list are also valuable sources for suggestions which are then explored and investigated.

Such exploration assessing the market, evaluating existing and competitive materials, curriculum trends, and other factors likely to affect the success of a new book or series, is vital. The lead time from idea to finished product may be two or more years, the investment may run from one to several million dollars. The risks, particularly in today's volatile markets, are therefore very high. Only a carefully analyzed income and cost projection strongly indicative of a profitable return on a project will encourage management to undertake such risks on behalf of its stockholders.

Once a project has been decided upon, authors are sought who can undertake it. A school publisher often develops his authors by stages and over a period of time. Usually they are teachers who have established a reputation for effective teaching and writing, who ably communicate with today's youngsters and have demonstrated their ability to motivate them to learn. Many are innovators or pioneers in curriculum development. Their thinking is likely to be representative of a sizable segment of their profession, and they are usually good speakers for they must serve as the principal advocates of the new product before their peers.

Authors come to the publisher's attention through salesmen and consultants—his eyes and ears in the field—through editorial contacts and on the recommendation of other authors or teachers. They may have written articles for journals or delivered papers at meetings. The publisher may initially assign an author a small task such as writing a supplementary bulletin for an existing text; later he may ask him to prepare a workbook or to conduct tests on a new product. In this manner he determines whether the author can write effectively, to age level. Often more than one author will finally be selected for a textbook; in some series where several grade levels need to be served as many as fifteen authors may be engaged in the development of a project.

Authors' royalties average 6 percent of publisher's income for elementary materials, 8 percent for secondary titles. Workbooks and supplemental items may carry a 6 percent royalty or may be paid for under a flat fee arrangement (perhaps $1,000 for a 150-page workbook). Advances if paid at all are small and designed to help the author meet expenses such as typing of the manuscript. However, even though unit prices of schoolbooks are usually not very high (in 1972 they averaged under $2.00 for elementary and under $3.00 for secondary hardbound and paperbound texts and workbooks combined), the sheer sales volume of some titles can result in handsome incomes for their authors, considerably larger very often than their regular salaries as teachers.

### Validation and Testing

Testing materials in the field, thereby discovering their weaknesses, if any, and making needed changes before publication, is a growing practice with school publishers. Some testing has always been done, notably by authors with their own students; recently, however, some state adoption requirements, economic considerations, and the general trend toward accountability have intensified publishers' efforts in this direction.

Testing, if well designed and implemented, will establish the workability of a program in a variety of geographic and cultural settings. It will enable the publisher to present a more convincing case to adoption authorities, whether they require such testing or not. It will also provide protection for the publisher against failure of a project in which he has invested substantial time, energy, and money.

Testing can take many forms and can be conducted on various levels of sophistication. One can, for example, measure reading ability before and after the application of a program that purports to teach children to read. The test criteria and methods of measurement then become important considerations. More frequently however testing may simply involve having the author and selected teachers use page proofs of the book in actual classroom situations. "Bugs" discovered in the program can then be identified and removed and gaps in its effectiveness can be noted and filled.

Reading levels and the progressive introduction of word complexity into a series spanning several grades are key considerations in many projects. Computer programs have been developed that are able to check this feature and even to assist in the writing of such volumes. Computers generally, of course, are used on a wide scale in various testing procedures.

## The Government as Author

A number of important publishing projects have been developed under the sponsorship of the U.S. Office of Education. When such ventures are compiled, at USOE Regional Laboratories, for example, the developers usually play the publisher's role up to the copy-editing stage or even the camera-ready or master stage, so that the publisher who finally releases the materials needs to do no more than produce or duplicate and distribute them.

Some very valuable projects have thus come into being, particularly in areas where basic research was needed, such as speech therapy and biology. A questionable aspect, however, is the practice which duplicates the publisher's know-how and facilities at public expense, or even develops projects in areas such as basal reading which are already overcrowded with products. Schoolbook publisher Charles W. Pepper points out that the laboratories have been most helpful when they have explored new areas utilizing resources publishers cannot normally command—such as the $100 million which the government invested in the speech therapy program—or when they have allowed publishers to collaborate with them in early stages of a project thus avoiding needless duplication of expertise.

Interested publishers are invited to bid on such government projects, with emphasis placed on their capacity for giving the materials distribution, meeting quality editorial and production standards, and paying adequate royalties. Since elhi publishers, given their intensely competitive stance and sizable investments in existing projects, might not display much enthusiasm for a venture that competes with a book or series already on their list, USOE has consistently refrained from awarding contracts to publishers with competing properties.

## The Uncertainties of Public Funding

Since the major portion of elementary and secondary education in this country is supported by public money (private schools on this level are rapidly decreasing in number and significance), elhi publishers are understandably concerned about recent tendencies on all levels of government to curtail educational budgets. With many communities voting down school bond issues, with major cities running out of funds before the end of the school year, and with the federal government indicating some reluctance to support public schools as heretofore, their concerns are real. Furthermore, increasing portions of school budgets are being consumed by teachers' salaries and building and maintenance costs, all of which have risen at rates much higher than the rate of price increases of books and related products, thus threatening disproportionately high cuts in the acquisition of educational materials.

To some extent, one imagines, the harsh economies advocated by budget-pruning legislators are a reflection of public disenchantment with educational failures during a period when schools have received more money and educators higher salaries than ever before in history. Coupled with the new "show-me" attitude manifested by accountability, it may well indicate a determination to have education perform or reform. But one doubts that it is a sign of American disenchantment with education itself; if anything, the fervent disillusionment is the reverse side of a coin of excessive expectations. Perhaps the educators who have contributed to both exaggerated hopes and overwrought disappointments by promising more for education than it can possibly deliver would be well advised to introduce a new realism into their discussions with the public.

In any case, I am inclined to agree with market research analyst Paul Forringer that the commitment of the public to educational growth and excellence is likely to continue over the long term. States will probably assume a greater share of the burden now carried by local communities—if only to respond to demands for greater equality in such expenditures—and the federal government will continue to play a major role. While publishers may, along with other suppliers of the educational market, find themselves at temporary low points (after all elementary enrollments, reflecting the birthrates of recent years, are currently dropping) long-range prospects for solid public response to educational needs are good. School publishing is therefore likely to remain the sturdy, reliable performer it has always been.

## COLLEGE TEXTBOOKS

If it is true that increasing complexity and diversity are the hallmarks of cultural maturity and advancing civilization, what is happening to higher education is on the whole profoundly encouraging. For despite diminishing enrollments, hard financial times, and the confusion that accompanies any major transition, diversity is becoming increasingly manifest in the teaching programs of colleges and universities. And the college textbook, like its elhi counterpart, is becoming a less monolithic and more individualized entity.

Consequently, like their elhi brethren, college publishers are working harder these days. The "big" textbook, with a sale of 200,000 each year is, with rare exceptions, a thing of the past. It may now have a sale of 100,000, or in certain disciplines may be disappearing altogether. As a result publishers must develop a greater selection of titles both of the basic text variety and of the "supplemental" type which is where a great deal of the action now is. In the humanities and some of the social sciences, particularly, the typical course requirement today is a number of titles rather than a single, massive volume. There may still be a fundamental survey-type book, especially in freshman or sophomore program, which provides the backbone and outline of the course and which, in fact, contains references to and points in the direction of some of the supplemental titles. The survey text, like the supplemental materials, may be paperbound; and many of the books used are not texts at all but quality or mass market paperbacks (resembling the pattern established earlier for recommended, as opposed to required, materials which for some years have included a wealth of titles published by nontext houses).

This is less true of science courses, both physical and biological, where the traditional, hardbound textbook still predominates. Nevertheless even here variety is the new watchword and the huge adoption has given way to a variety of smaller ones. And in certain median fields, such as economics, one is likely to witness manifestations of both patterns depending on the orientation of the school and the instructor.

Institutions, faculty, and students together are shaping these developments, and their attitudes determine the nature and type of book used. In elite colleges one is likely to encounter the greatest variety, the least reliance on texts, the most extensive choice of general and scholarly materials. Upper level and graduate courses are more freewheeling than introductory programs. Four-year colleges and two-year schools that enroll mostly students who will transfer to four-year institutions, are likely to be more flexible than schools that cater for the most part to career or vocationally oriented students enrolled in two-year terminal programs. In the latter case, where students are often unable to afford several books and are less inclined to pursue knowledge for its own sake, the old-line textbook pattern is still the norm. More and more institutions and departments are permitting individual instructors to make their own choices, however, and more instructors are influenced in their decisions by student response.

Despite these profound changes, and despite the significant influx into the field of materials published by general houses, the majority of books currently being used in college programs continues to be produced by textbook publishers. It is likely to remain so. The reasons are that although course materials can no longer be as rigid as before, must be more stimulating of intellectual curiosity, more responsive to contemporary interests, and more pluralistic in content, they will nevertheless succeed best in the majority of cases if they are designed and tailored specifically for the educational process. We are witnessing, in other words, not the death, but the metamorphosis of the college textbook.

### New Publishing Initiatives

This metamorphosis does indeed require the textbook publisher to work harder. For one thing he must keep in closer touch with the many fields of study, observe rapidly changing trends, anticipate developments, and make available what is likely to be in demand tomorrow, not what reflects the abandoned concepts of yesterday. This forces him to rely more intensively on his own judgment and to do more homework. In the past college publishers would characteristically approach a distinguished teacher or scholar, inquire into his writing activity, hopefully persuading him that he should place his book with the house and rely almost totally on his familiarity with the field to produce a viable and successful work. While some publishers did engage in market research, few looked sufficiently into such questions as existing competition, satisfaction and dissatisfaction with books being used, and expressed needs and preferences by those likely to adopt the materials. In some cases even such factors as total enrollment and potential market share were only imperfectly guessed at. In consequence, like other industry divisions, college publishing during the fifties and sixties suffered from serious overproduction.

Today, with success or failure dependent on a multiplicity of small decisions involving perhaps hundreds of supplementary titles that might sell only 10,000 to 20,000 in paperback annually, along with some basic texts selling only half of what they once did, the correct answers to these market questions are vital. Nor can any publisher afford to disregard the impact on sales of the significant used book trade carried on by college stores and among individual students or be oblivious to the bothersome phenome-non—no doubt economic in origin and aggravated by the growing number of books being assigned—whereby students fail to buy recommended or even required materials, getting by with sharing or even ignoring some of them.

So the college publisher must plan. What is needed in both basic and supplemental texts? What features should the material offer? Who is best equipped to write it? The publisher may still rely on his sales travelers to maintain contact with the faculty, to bring back ideas, to report trends and developments. But it is the editor who today must conceive the project and work more intensively than heretofore with the author in shaping it into an effective teaching tool. The market researcher for his part must provide reliable data on its competition and market potential.

The role of the faculty author or advisor is accordingly changed, perhaps in some ways diminished. What may matter less than a man's distinguished reputation is the competence and intelligibility with which the material is presented so that students will regard it as acceptable. A significant sign of the times, according to James Bowman, McGraw-Hill Book Co. vice president, occurred when in preparation for a recent edition of Samuelson's *Economics*—the *most* successful college textbook of all time—McGraw-Hill obtained comments from students in all parts of the country which the Nobel-Prize winning author found most helpful in improving and clarifying some points in his classic work. Publishers, notes editorial and business executive Woodworth Chittick, are more willing today to employ less established yet imaginative and able writers. Should they encounter a great man whose ability to communicate fails to equal his disciplinary competence, they are more anxious than ever to find a collaborator for him—perhaps even a staff writer—so that prestige and wisdom may be matched by intelligibility and efficacy.

College textbook authors' royalties are in the 10 to 16 percent of list price range. (Sometimes comparable arrangements are made based on publishers' income.) Occasionally on a book of considerable potential an escalating royalty formula may be employed. Advances are made to help an author meet out-of-pocket expenses, such as permissions fees on a book of readings, but such advances are rare and normally modest.

A number of college publishers have entered the audiovisual field to produce films, slides, transparencies, records, and cassettes. As in other publishing areas, notably elhi, such products have made their way and have become significant sources of income for their originators. Generally however they have supplemented and complemented rather than competed with the book programs of their publishers.

# Chapter IV.

# How Books
# Are Manufactured

The soul of a book—its ideas and contents—must be housed in a suitable body. Thus from their beginnings books have enjoyed the attention of master designers, illuminators, and craftsmen. The great codices of the Middle Ages are precious museum treasures. Since the Renaissance outstanding typographers have designed the typefaces in use to this day. Some of the world's greatest artists have illustrated and designed books: Daumier, Matisse, and Picasso come readily to mind. The custom of collecting books for their beauty has been established for centuries.

It is not likely, or even desirable, that every book published should be a great work of art. But every book should offer to the reader a functional attractiveness that makes the content fully accessible and that conveys by its arrangement and appearance the purposes of the author. Text should be as easy to read as possible. Illustrations should be well reproduced and appropriately integrated with the text. Binding should be as durable as required by the character of the book and the reader's needs.

Good functional design helps to sell books. The reader browsing in a bookshop may not have the slightest inkling of what constitutes good book design, but if he finds the package he holds in his hand visually inviting he is more likely to buy it. How clearly the pages are laid out, how readable the type is, how striking the illustrations are, and how well they are coordinated with written matter may well have a bearing on his decision. This is particularly true of professional, educational, hobby, craft, and how-to titles. Sheer beauty of design is bound furthermore to have an influence on people with discriminating literary tastes who are likely to be more sensitive than average to aesthetic factors.

Within a publishing house the responsibility for creating the book as a physical entity lies with the production department. Very few publishers own their own printing facilities so this responsibility normally involves dealing with commercial typesetters, printers, and binders. A production manager and his staff are therefore involved in the following basic steps while the physical book is brought into being: planning, cost estimating, scheduling, design, selection of suppliers, purchase of paper and cover materials, and the supervision of typesetting, printing, and binding.

What the production staff does is a great deal more comprehensible when one has a basic acquaintanceship with the technical areas with which that staff must deal: typesetting, printing (including book papers), and binding.

## Type and Its Characteristics

Anyone who has ever played with a rubber type kit, or used a typewriter for that matter, is acquainted with the rudiments of typography. There are, to begin with, certain basic differences between type faces. The most common variety of letters employed in printing (including the type in which this book is set) is some version of the letters used by the ancient Romans:

# ABCDEFGHIJK

These letters are characterized among other features by the cross strokes at line endings which are known as "serifs." There are other styles of type faces which lack these serifs and which are therefore known as "sans serif":

# ABCDEFGHIJK

Roman faces are generally considered to be more readable than sans serif and are therefore more commonly used for setting text. Sans serif faces are occasionally employed for body type but are more often used in setting headings, captions, and tabular material.

Within the families of roman and sans serif there are many type faces of which some of the most popular are shown in Figure 1. Each face is available in the capital letters of the alphabet (caps or upper case), usually in two sizes (large caps and small caps), as well as in the small letters (lower case), in addition to numerals, punctuation, and certain symbols (such as the asterisk). There are also items such as superior numbers ([1]) used in references to footnotes. Most faces are available in a slanted version known as "italic" which is used for emphasis, notes, or captions. Type faces usually are available in a variety of weights: light, demibold, and bold. Most text composition employs light weight exclusively, with the bolder weights reserved for headings. (Figure 2 shows variations of regular and italic faces in different weights.) A complete set of letters, numerals, punctuation marks, and symbols in a given slant or weight is known as a "font."

An important factor in type selection is size. In typography a special system of measurement is employed based on "points." A point is a shade less than $1/72$ inch; 12 points make a "pica" which is therefore a little less than $1/6$ inch. A foot is equivalent to approximately $72 1/2$ picas. The size of a letter is predicated on its height; when it is measured, however, it is not the letter itself but the "body" on which it is mounted that determines its size (see Figure 3). As a result, because of design variations, there may be noticeable differences in, say, the 12-point size of different type faces.

There are also considerable differences in the width of fonts. Some are set narrow and close together (condensed), others are more rounded and spread (extended). Some faces are even available in condensed and extended versions. These features not only have an effect on legibility but they can seriously affect the "measure" (width) of a line containing the same number of "characters" (letters). Consequently they will affect also the length of the entire book.

Baskerville

ABCDEFGHIJKLMNOPQRSTUVWXYZ
ABCDEFGHIJKLMNOPQRSTUVWXYZ
abcdefghijklmnopqrstuvwxyz
1234567890$

Bodoni

ABCDEFGHIJKLMNOPQRSTUVWXYZ
ABCDEFGHIJKLMNOPQRSTUVWXYZ
abcdefghijklmnopqrstuvwxyz
1234567890$

Century Expanded

ABCDEFGHIJKLMNOPQRSTUVWXYZ
ABCDEFGHIJKLMNOPQRSTUVWXYZ
abcdefghijklmnopqrstuvwxyz
1234567890$

Times Roman

ABCDEFGHIJKLMNOPQRSTUVWXYZ
ABCDEFGHIJKLMNOPQRSTUVWXYZ
abcdefghijklmnopqrstuvwxyz
1234567890$

Folio Light

ABCDEFGHIJKLMNOPQRSTUVWXYZ
abcdefghijklmnopqrstuvwxyz
1234567890$

Helvetica Regular

ABCDEFGHIJKLMNOPQRSTUVWXYZ
abcdefghijklmnopqrstuvwxyz
1234567890$

Univers #45

ABCDEFGHIJKLMNOPQRSTUVWXYZ
abcdefghijklmnopqrstuvwxyz
1234567890$

**Figure 1.** Commonly used type faces. The first four, Baskerville, Bodoni, Century, and Times Roman, are roman faces; the last three, Folio, Helvetica, and Univers are sans serif. Shown for each face are large caps, lower case letters, and numbers. Small caps are shown in the roman faces, but are not available in sans serif.

Univers #46 Italic

*ABCDEFGHIJKLMNOPQRSTUVWXYZ*
*abcdefghijklmnopqrstuvwxyz*
*1234567890$*

Bodoni Italic

*ABCDEFGHIJKLMNOPQRSTUVWXYZ*
*abcdefghijklmnopqrstuvwxyz*
*1234567890$*

Bodoni Bold Italic

*ABCDEFGHIJKLMNOPQRSTUVWXYZ*
*abcdefghijklmnopqrstuvwxyz*
*1234567890$*

Century Bold Italic

*ABCDEFGHIJKLMNOPQRSTUVWXYZ*
*abcdefghijklmnopqrstuvwxyz*
*1234567890$*

Times Roman Italic

*ABCDEFGHIJKLMNOPQRSTUVWXYZ*
*abcdefghijklmnopqrstuvwxyz*
*1234567890$*

Folio Light Italic

*ABCDEFGHIJKLMNOPQRSTUVWXYZ*
*abcdefghijklmnopqrstuvwxyz*
*1234567890$*

Helvetica Semi-Bold Italic

*ABCDEFGHIJKLMNOPQRSTUVWXYZ*
*abcdefghijklmnopqrstuvwxyz*
*1234567890$*

**Figure 2.** Some type face variations. Note the slant of the italic face when compared to its regular equivalent in Figure 1. Also note the differences in weight, such as between Bodoni and Bodoni Bold in the second and third examples.

Legibility is the major consideration in the choice of type. Generally a line should not exceed in measure one and one half alphabets (or 39 characters) since the eye has difficulty maintaining focus on a larger number of letters. Smaller than 8-point type is difficult to read in most fonts; notes might be set in 6-point but one should avoid so small a size for the body of the text. Usually the upper limit for adult books is 12-point type; of course volumes for younger readers will often be set in much larger sizes.

White space on a page is also important. Adequate margins rest the eye and prevent that crowded appearance that often makes reading a strain. Even more significant is the spacing between lines known as "leading." A critical factor in eye fatigue is the jump from the end of a line to the beginning of the next; the eye has difficulty locating the succeeding line if the spacing is insufficient so most composition allows for a point or two of leading.

A typesetter who encountered the following instructions on a manuscript:

Set body in 10/12 Garamond × 24 picas

would know that the text should be set in 10-point Garamond, with a distance of 12 points from the bottom of one line to the bottom of the next, thus providing for two points of leading. The measure, or width, of the line would be 24 picas.

In addition to faces suitable for body copy there are others known as display type which are particularly appropriate for headings or title pages. These may be quite elaborate and are available in sizes larger than those in which text faces are customarily furnished.

**How Type Is Set**

There are five basic methods by which type is set today: by hand, on monotype machines, on linotype machines, through computers, and by so-called "cold" type. As sophistication in both computer and cold-type composition grows, it becomes increasingly difficult to make distinctions between these last categories.

Type is still set by hand, as it was in Gutenberg's day, for some title pages and jackets, or where display type is involved. Some publishers of gift editions, like the Peter Pauper Press, set entire books this way. Needless to say, the practice is rare in this mechanized age.

In hand-setting each letter—which presents an appearance such as that shown in Figure 3—is placed in line individually, and spacing between words and lines is inserted by means of metal slugs or strips. (Line-spacing metal contains a good deal of lead, hence the term "leading.") The spacing between words is subject to skillful adjustment so that lines may end evenly ("justified") at right-hand margins.

It is in the art of spacing words and letters that the typographer's craft comes to the fore. When spacing becomes uneven and awkward, when lines, paragraphs, and pages are poorly balanced or riddled with unsightly blank streaks ("rivers") it is a sign of poor craftsmanship.

Far more speedy, and therefore more common and economical than hand-setting, is the use of linotype machines. Utilizing a keyboard not dissimilar to that of a typewriter, the compositor sets one line at a time. As he presses the keys, matrices (molds) of letters and spaces are assembled which he occasionally adjusts by hand to achieve the proper balance and justification of lines. Each line is then cast individually in hot metal.

In monotype composition, which is generally more costly than linotype, a keyboard is also used but letters and spaces are cast individually rather than in complete lines. Because this provides for greater flexibility both for copy and spacing within the text, monotype is employed for complicated technical composition involving, for example, mathematical symbols and

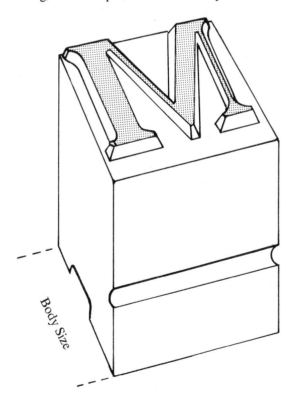

**Figure 3.** A letterpress type character, showing the mounting of the letter on the body.

equations. Dictionaries and reference works are also often set in monotype because they require complicated variations of fonts and linotype is less versatile than monotype in the employment of several fonts simultaneously.

In all methods of metal type composition, lines of type are assembled in long trays known as "galleys" from which proofs, appropriately designated as galley proofs, can be pulled. Editors and authors use them to indicate text corrections. In hand-setting and monotype, the compositor makes corrections by removing the faulty individual letters or words and making the needed substitutions. In linotype the entire line in which an error has occurred must be reset. This creates the possibility that a new error may be made in another part of the line even as the first mistake is corrected and necessitates a new reading of the entire line to ascertain that it really corresponds to the specified copy. Extensive corrections going beyond typographical errors and involving changes of words, phrases, or even sentences, usually require the resetting of entire paragraphs since every line must be rejustified.

Once galley proofs are corrected, the compositor breaks the galleys into pages in accordance with instructions from the publisher indicating the desired number of lines per page. At that time he also inserts page numbers ("folios"), placing odd numbers on right-hand pages ("recto") and even numbered folios on left-hand pages ("verso"). At the same time chapter headings are inserted as well as "running heads" (the lines at the top of pages that identify chapter or section and often repeat the title of the book itself).

Certain pages may not carry folios or running heads, for example blank pages facing chapter openings, the title page, or so-called "half-titles," i.e., pages such as the recto preceding the title page, or the parts of a book, on which title or names of parts are shown in sizable, sometimes decorative type. Often a different folio sequence, of roman numerals, is provided for so-called "front matter": preface or foreword, acknowledgments, and table of contents. From the made-up pages are pulled the "page proofs" which serve publisher and author for a final check of the entire setting.

### Recent Typesetting Methods

An innovation in typography that stands between metal and computer methods is filmsetting. In this process, utilizing either linotype or monotype systems and keyboarding, the matrices are photonegatives which are used to produce a film from which proofs are exposed. Depending on the complexity and sophistication of the equipment, either galleys are furnished or they are bypassed and pages are supplied immediately.

The various computerized typesetting systems—though they may employ a variety of electronic methods, such as encoding on tape or disc, machine printout, or projections of entire pages by cathode ray tube—have one thing in common: they attempt to automate a significant portion of the work that would otherwise have to be performed by human minds and hands. Word-breaks are an example. A good typographer is sufficiently familiar with the language to make the proper word separation at the end of a line. Programs have been written—not always with total success—which attempt to undertake this chore. Another example is justification. Often adjustments are needed because a line runs slightly over or under when standard interword spacing is employed, which the skilled typographer effects either on the keyboard or by hand. Complex programs have been written to automate this task as well.

Fundamentally, there are three program levels in computer composition: the basic systems program which involves general factors like word-breaks and justification; an intermediate level program which contains general instructions for the particular setting—font, spacing, leading, indentations, style features; and, finally, the specific keyboard instructions which are part of the encoding. It is possible, therefore, to effect changes of intermediate level features such as size of font without having to make changes in the encoding itself. It is also possible to have type set by a person with relatively little training: for example a good typist in a publisher's office may be able to encode the manuscript on tape which is then forwarded to the compositor.

Characteristically, instructions for paging the book are part of the intermediate level program; consequently, proofs are furnished immediately in page form and the galley stage is bypassed. This presents special challenges and problems to editors, authors, and production people accustomed to dealing with galleys. For example, it is considered desirable when reading galley proof to eliminate so-called "widows" (i.e., dangling single words or a very short line at the end of a paragraph). When this is done in a typical linotype setting, no problem arises: the compositor simply resets the last line of the paragraph as shortened by the editor and the widow is eliminated.

In a computer setting, proofreading is followed by a correction pass against the original encoding (including any instructions for eliminating widows), and the entire book is then reset from the corrected encoding. As a result, paragraphs and pages may shift in the resetting and new widows may be created. It is wise, therefore, to wait for the last proof before undertaking such cosmetic changes; even then one must look ahead carefully at the full effect of each and every change. In fact, production expert Dennis Hudson believes that some changes in final computer proofs are more wisely made with scissors and paste (that is, by pasting a reset, reproducible line of type directly on the proof), rather than by yet another correction pass on the computer.

Cold type—a term designed to distinguish certain methods of composition from those employing hot metal—can utilize equipment ranging from a simple typewriter to automated installations of considerable sophistication.

In its most primitive form—on an ordinary typewriter with a carbon (one-time) ribbon—the text will be set without proportional spacing and with unjustified right-hand margins. Common typewriters do not space letters proportionately because each key is the same width and the machine is constructed to move ahead by the same distance as each letter is used. But of course the letter "m" is wider than the letter "i," and in metal typesetting the body on which each letter is mounted varies proportionately in width with the letter itself. Certain typewriters, the IBM Executive for example, are available with proportional spacing, and some are even able to justify lines if the copy is run through twice.

Automated cold-type systems, such as the IBM-MTST, the VariTyper, and the Compugraphic, provide proportional spacing and justification;

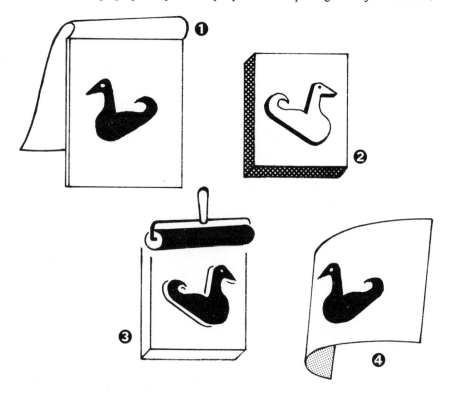

**Figure 4.** Diagrams showing four stages of printing production. The first picture symbolizes original images, the subject matter of printing. The second shows how original images appear on a printing-image carrier for relief printing, letterpress for example. The third picture shows the ink image on the image carrier, and on the fourth picture you see the final printed image on a sheet of paper.

however, quality and appearance are less satisfactory than in hot metal or in the full-fledged computerized systems, such as Videocomp. But these cold-type processes are very economical and they are becoming more successful as the technology improves and a greater selection of type faces becomes available.

**Printing and Its Methods**

There are three methods of printing in wide use today: letterpress, offset (or lithography), and gravure.

Letterpress is the traditional process, basically a continuation of the way books were printed in the fifteenth century. In this method ink is applied to raised surfaces which impress their image on paper (see Figure 4).

We have, however, come some way since Gutenberg's time. Today's presses can print on large sheets, 128 book pages at one time, with so-called

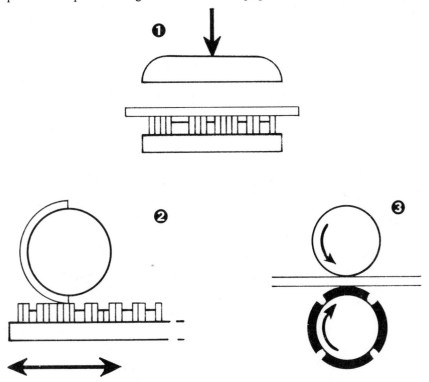

Figure 5. In platen presses (1) the platen and the bed are flat; in flatbed-cylinder presses (2) the bed is still flat but the platen is replaced by an impression cylinder; in rotary presses (3) the plate cylinder takes the place of the flatbed, and both members of the printing unit are cylindrical.

"perfector" presses making impressions on both sides of the sheet simultaneously. While some printing is done directly from type, particularly on short runs for scholarly and professional publishers, the use of plates molded from type is far more common. For some years these plates were made of metal, but in recent decades plastic plates have become more common. Mass market paperbacks on the other hand are printed mostly from rubber plates.

There are two types of letterpresses: flatbed presses, which hold the type or plates on a plane and print on sheets of paper, and rotary presses, which bend the plates over cylinders and print on sheets or rolls (webs) (see Figure 5). Rotaries work at far greater speeds than flatbeds and are therefore more economical for larger runs, such as for mass market paperbacks which employ them almost exclusively.

A recent and important invention is the Cameron Belt Press in which the plates are carried on a continuous belt, and impressions are made in sequence on a continuous roll of paper. This system permits considerable economies on short runs but its uniqueness requires that a book be planned especially for the process.

Since World War II offset printing has made heavy inroads on the letterpress process and, except for mass market paperbacks, most books today are printed by this method. Offset is basically photographic (it is even sometimes called "photo-offset"). Type and illustrations are photographed, and from the negatives thin metal plates are made which are bent over cylinders. The to-be-printed images have been etched slightly into the surface of the plate and the ink adheres to the etched areas. Adjoining the drum on which the plate rotates is another cylinder covered with a rubber blanket onto which the plate offsets (hence the name of the process) these images. The rubber-covered cylinder in turn rolls against and prints on the paper (sheets on a flatbed, or a web on a rotary press).

There are a number of reasons why publishers prefer the offset process to letterpress, most of which have to do with speed and economy. Generally offset presses used in book work are faster than their letterpress counterparts. They also provide better quality on inexpensive papers. While most paper for offset printing must be "sized" (i.e., covered with a special coating), the cost of this coating is relatively low, while the difference in price between paper that will provide satisfactory results in letterpress printing and that which will be acceptable in offset printing is substantially greater. On web offset presses, furthermore, folding is combined with printing in a continuous operation, thus offering substantial savings of time and money.

Platemaking and the storage of plates is another consideration. Most offset plates are used only once as it is relatively inexpensive to burn a new set of plates from existing negatives should a reprint be required. (Deep-etched offset plates, which can be used repeatedly, are less commonly employed.) It is rather easy to store negatives; certainly it is less cumbersome and space consuming than the storage of metal or plastic plates. Since many books published are eventually reprinted—and the publisher almost always hopes that they will be—the existence of negatives from the start, from which new plates can be quickly and economically made, is a favorable consideration. Should the reprint never materialize, the investment in negatives and one-time offset plates will have been less than that which would have produced letterpress plates.

One of the major advantages offered by offset is the greater facility it provides in preparing illustrations. In fact, it would be fair to say that the offset process has made possible the use of illustrations in books which could not possibly have included them when only letterpress was available, and it has substantially simplified and reduced the production cost of illustrated books in general.

There are basically two types of black-and-white illustrations: those involving line only (without shading of any sort) and halftones where shadings or tones occur. An example of a line illustration would be a geometric diagram or a pen-and-ink drawing; photographs are examples of halftones.

Regardless of the printing process used, all illustrations, be they line or halftone, must first be photographed. In letterpress so-called engravings are then prepared that present the images to be printed in raised form. This is achieved by projecting the image onto a sensitized metal surface and subsequently etching out and hand-tooling away all areas not to be printed. In the case of line illustrations this process is time consuming but relatively simple. When it comes to halftones, however, it becomes far more complicated. Halftones are reproduced by means of small dots, often indistinguishable to the naked eye and only clearly visible under a magnifying glass. These dots are larger and appear closer together where a dark area is desired; they are smaller and seem farther apart where a picture is lighter. The dots are created by photographing the original through a screen of crisscrossed lines: where the picture is darker, larger dots result, where lighter their density is less. By projecting the image through the screen onto a sensitized metal plate and then etching and hand-tooling out the not-to-be-printed areas a good halftone engraving can be made. Needless to say, however, the effort is costly and demanding.

The greater the density of the screen (i.e., the greater the number of individual dots per given area) the better the quality of an illustration will be. In letterpress the maximum density of screen that can be used with good results is 110 lines to the inch; even then to achieve success with such a screen requires not only a very carefully tooled engraving but also a high-grade coated paper which is itself quite costly.

In contrast offset illustrations are much more easily prepared. Provided the negative is good, the plate which is burned from it is likely to be satisfactory; no hand-tooling and repeated acid baths, such as are standard procedure for letterpress engravings, are necessary. For halftones finer screens can be used: 130 to 150 lines per inch are common. In consequence the fidelity, contrast, and tonal quality of offset illustrations are superior. Some scientific and medical halftone illustrations are still prepared by letterpress as a certain sharpness and precision in tooling the plate is characteristic of the best in letterpress engravings. But as the quality of offset has improved enormously in recent years, these instances have grown consistently rarer.

The same may be said of color printing. Color illustrations are prepared in one of two ways: either the colors are preseparated by the artist, or they are separated photographically in what is known as "process" color. Preseparation is certainly logical where only two colors are involved: the artist simply prepares two separate versions of his picture, each showing the area in which one of the colors is to be used. Each color is then applied in a separate impression on the press, although two or several simultaneous impressions can be run on certain large color presses.

When it comes to full (multi) color, the printing process takes advantage of the fact that not only can the eye not distinguish small dots individually, but also that it tends to mix primary colors (yellow, red, and blue) into the full range of the spectrum provided the printed dots are effectively arranged.

A good artist, conversant with the graphic process, can so preseparate colors and so instruct the plate maker as to achieve astounding variations, combinations, and richness in his color illustrations. Where photographs or paintings are to be reproduced, however, process color is usually employed. Cameras utilizing red, blue, and green filters, photograph the original, extracting the primary colors from it (see Figure 6). From these photos plates are made, with a fourth plate, for printing black, added to strengthen outlines, shadings, and contrasts. The dot arrangements employed are highly elaborate and ingenious and require great care on the part of camera men, plate makers, and printers to ensure correctness of position, right registry (precise coordination of various impressions), and the right balance of inks.

As in black-and-white halftones, these steps are greatly facilitated by offset printing and good quality at lower cost is easier to achieve than by letterpress. The flexible rubber blanket on the offset press makes it possible to develop a clarity yet softness of reproduction which is more faithful to the original and more pleasing to the eye.

The whole process of paging and of integrating text with illustrations is easier and faster, and therefore more economical to achieve, in offset than in letterpress. In the latter process heavy type and engravings must be placed (locked up) together in pages to be printed from directly or to serve in molding plates. Just handling the sheer weight of type and blocks is a chore compared with the simple offset-based method of making reproduction proofs of the text, shooting negatives of the type proofs as well as the illustrations, and finally stripping the negatives together in accordance with the page design. Plates are then quickly burned from the negatives.

Photogravure printing is a rather expensive process usually reserved for art books and other heavily illustrated volumes. Also known as "intaglio" printing it is celebrated for its soft halftones and pleasing color work. Sunday supplements of newspapers are often printed by this process. Unlike letterpress, where the printing surface is raised, and offset where it is practically flat, in gravure it is indented. Plates are made by etching the indentations into metal, a process that traces its origins to the engraving art of the Middle Ages and the Renaissance.

Gravure presses may be sheet-fed or web-fed. Papers used must have a

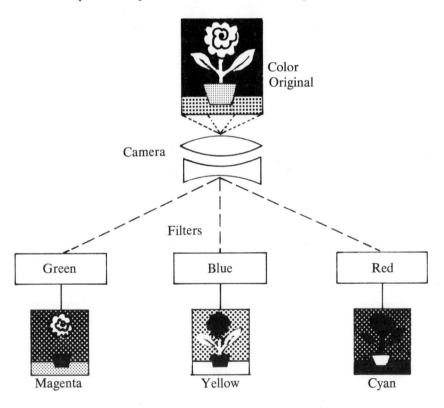

**Figure 6.** Schematic diagram of color separation photography.

high absorbency level as the stock must literally blot the ink out of the indentations. Before offset printing developed to its present state and provided such satisfactory halftone and color work, gravure was the only process that offered a mellowness of tone not achieved by letterpress. Like letterpress it has had to give way to the steadily advancing offset supremacy.

## Paper

Book papers come in many weights, sizes, and colors. The intended use of a stock will determine its desirable features and the grade that will be selected.

In regard to quality, there are two classes of commonly used book papers: so-called "free" sheet and groundwood stocks. The former is used for better books and is intended to last without turning color; the pulp employed is of higher caliber ("free" of groundwood) and has been bleached and chemically treated to ensure permanency. Groundwood papers, used for mass market paperbacks for example, tend to be somewhat grayish in color and to turn brown after some months. Recently some manufacturers have developed groundwood stocks that are coated and therefore present a better initial appearance. Some papers milled have rag content; they are used in better Bibles but only rarely for other books because of their high cost.

Within the above classes available papers vary in substance weight, bulk, finish, color, and opacity. Weight is determined by basis ream weight; a 50-pound paper is one of which a standard ream (500 sheets, 25 × 38 inches in size) weighs 50 pounds. (There are occasional variations in standard measurements which are noted in manufacturers' specifications.) Bulk is shown by indicating the number of pages to the inch after the paper has been "smashed," i.e., air trapped between the pages has been squeezed out.

The combination of weight and bulk is a major consideration in the choice of stock as it will affect the overall appearance of a book. Many weights are available in standard and high bulk, the latter resulting from whipping more air into the pulp as the paper is milled. Of course some papers are characteristically low or high bulk to begin with, depending on their fiber content and the manner in which they were milled. Most adult books are printed on papers ranging in substance weight from 45 to 60 pounds. Children's books are often printed on 70- or 80-pound stock.

Opacity is an important factor. A paper with poor opacity will allow the text or illustrations from the reverse page to show through which makes for very unsatisfactory reading. The chemical titanium, when added to book paper, increases its opacity. Finish is similarly significant. Antique finish, which is velvety in character, is usually employed for trade books. Coated papers are used for certain art books and scientific and medical texts, although advances in offset printing have reduced the demand for coated papers which at one time were essential for printing letterpress illustrations. Some papers are "calendered," i.e., they are run between metal rollers at the mill in order to provide them with a smoother finish. Machine-finish and English-finish papers, often used in text and reference books, are of this variety.

Paper colors range from blue-white to various shades of cream. A great deal of experimentation with nonglare papers has been done and even some coated stocks are available today with low-glare characteristics. Grain is also a factor. As paper runs off the milling machine the fibers flow along the length of the paper. It is desirable to have the grain run parallel to the binding edge (vertical) of a book when printing because subsequent folding and trimming will then occur with, rather than against, the grain and make production easier while resulting in a more attractive product.

**Binding**

The binding process involves folding the large press sheets down to book size, gathering the folded pages in sequence, sewing them together if necessary, and attaching end papers and a cover to them. If desired a dust cover or jacket can be placed over the binding.

Press sheets hold a multiple of pages, the number—usually divisible by four—depending on the sheet size, the book-page size, and the size of the press. As many as 128 pages are common today, but 64, 32, and 16 pages per sheet are not unusual. Since most papers will not fold well if the sheet contains more than 32 pages, and as the handling of very large sheets is cumbersome, the sheets are usually cut to 32-page maximum size as they come off the press.

At the bindery—which may be located either in the same manufacturing plant or at some distance from the printer—the sheets of 32 pages (or less) are folded to individual page size. Depending on the type of folding machine employed, the binder will have instructed the printer to arrange ("impose") the pages in a certain order so that they will come out in correct sequence after folding. What results are uncut booklets known as "signatures."

The signatures are arranged in proper sequence in a process called "gathering." Once gathered they can be bound together in a variety of ways. The traditional method is "smyth-sewing," by which a special sewing machine threads the pages of each signature together and all the signatures to each other. This process is still employed in the case of large art or reference books, with titles that are expected to receive very hard use, and where superior quality of product is desired.

The more common process today, however, is adhesive or "perfect" binding. In this method the back folds of the gathered signatures are ground off and a very strong, highly elastic adhesive substance is applied to them. Thanks to the development of excellent glues, perfect binding is proving to be as lasting and satisfactory as sewing.

Some books are "side-sewn," i.e., the stitches instead of penetrating the backs of signatures are taken through the side, making for a very tight and secure binding able to withstand extraordinary punishment. Booklets of 64 pages or less are often saddle-wire stitched, i.e., held at the backs by metal staples. One can also employ side-staples, thereby providing a sturdier hold and one that can accommodate a larger number of pages.

At this point the cover is ready to go on. If it is a paper cover, it is simply held by the adhesive of the perfect binding or adhesive is applied to the backs of the sewn signatures and affixes the cover to them. (Note that paperbacks are square-backed.) As a final step in paperback binding, pages and cover are trimmed together to specified size.

If the book is to have a hard cover ("case binding") the cases must first be made. They consist of "boards" over which the cover materials—made of cloth, plastic, or treated papers—are folded and glued. Sometimes the

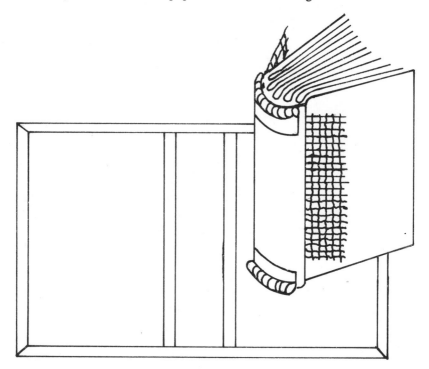

**Figure 7.** Diagram of the rounded and backed book and a binder's case prior to casing-in, or combining the book and its cover.

cover design has been printed on the material in advance; more commonly the cases are stamped with ink or foils.

Endpapers are then attached to the sheets. (They are the heavy pages at beginning and end, sometimes decorated or of colored stock, glued on one side to the case.) The entire set is then trimmed to size. Most books are cut evenly on all three sides; however one may leave the front and bottom untrimmed for a "rough front and foot" (also know as "quad open") which is quite stylish and attractive. If the top is to be colored ("stained") this is also done now. Mounted on the back, which is forcibly rounded as a rule, is a broad strip of reinforced gauze ("crash") to which the so-called "head-and footbands" (usually made of brightly colored threads) adhere at top and bottom. Finally the case is attached by gluing the overlapping crash and endpapers to the inside of the boards (see Figure 7).

The traditional practice is to stack the freshly bound book horizontally between heavy, metal-rimmed boards for some 24 hours so that glues can dry properly and the case can assume its trim shape with a deep, sharp crease at the edge of board and "spine" (back). Binderies with more modern equipment achieve this with so-called "building-in" machines that season the cases in a few seconds. Dust covers, be they craft wrappers or colorful jackets, go on last.

A significant departure from the usual printing and binding process is the Cameron Belt Press which not only prints but folds, collates, and perfect-binds, all in one operation. It is for this reason that its use requires special planning; it is certainly difficult to convert a project to the Cameron process after planning to produce it by another method or to change to an alternative approach once a book has been designed for production by the Cameron system.

**Planning and Design**

Like every aspect of book publishing, production does not and cannot work in isolation. At one end it touches upon the editorial process, at the other upon the marketing program, and throughout it must be conscious of costs and the dictates of sound capital investment. When a production manager and his staff plan and produce books they must coordinate their efforts with their editorial, marketing, and financial colleagues.

Hopefully the production staff will have become involved in a project from its very beginning, even before the manuscript was accepted for publication. It will then have had an opportunity to provide early cost estimates, to note any special manufacturing problems, and to communicate effectively with editors and the sales department as overall plans for publication of the book were formulated. As soon as possible after the acceptance of the manuscript the production department likes to design the volume, make plans for its manufacture, and formulate a schedule for the various stages of the process. Often this is done from a duplicate manuscript even before it is copy edited (although it is advisable in that case to have the editorial department indicate in some detail the nature and extent of the editing anticipated).

A preliminary step in designing the book requires that the length of the text be established by means of a "character-count," a quite precise determination that enables the designer to anticipate the number of lines of body type that will have to be set. The designer then lays out the volume. Title page and other front matter may be drawn specifically; chapter openings and headings and the overall scheme for paragraphs and pages may require only a general layout and/or specifications. Included will be trim size (i.e., page size, exclusive of binding), typographical instructions for body type, notes and headings, running heads and folios, instructions for margins and spacing, depth (number of lines) of page, and placement of the various elements on the page.

Illustrations must be sized (i.e., their dimensions must be specified), they must be marked for reduction or cropping if necessary, and their placement on pages must be indicated. A heavily illustrated volume may require more extensive and detailed layout.

In planning his layout the designer realizes that the book must come out ("cast off") to "even forms," i.e., the total number of pages must fit exactly on the large sheets utilized in printing; if they do not, several blank pages may be left over and look awkward at the back of the volume. To achieve an even castoff the designer must carefully estimate space that will be consumed by text and illustrations, taking into account partially blank pages (at the ends of chapters, for example), blanks, and half titles. As he has a good deal of flexibility—in choice of type, depth of page, sizing of illustrations, and allowing for blank pages—he can usually achieve this objective without too much difficulty. Of course the more complex a volume, the more difficult the task. In certain cases final determination of some elements is not possible until pages are made up, with the designer himself dummying up the more demanding projects.

Paper must be specified next. The designer, knowing what paper the publisher stocks at various printers, or what the printer is able to furnish or even purchase on special order, will make his selection with the character of the book and its particular printing needs in mind. He must also be conscious of special standards or requirements which, in the case of elhi books for example, are quite rigidly defined for both paper and binding.

If the volume is to have a hard binding, the designer will also provide instructions for endpapers, top stain, head- and footbands (if any), boards, and cloth or other binding materials. He will, furthermore, design the printing or stamping to be applied to the case. He may or may not design the jacket, or the paper cover in case of softbound volumes, as this task is sometimes left to special cover artists. Generally speaking, if the designer is on the publisher's staff, he is likely to prepare simple typographical covers but leave more complex artwork, requiring original paintings or photography, to outside specialists. Free-lance book designers are usually retained with the understanding that they will furnish jacket or cover art as part of their service.

Not every book needs to be fully designed. Many publishers employ standard designs for series and for certain types of books, which then require minimal attention on the designer's part—perhaps in laying out front matter and sizing illustrations only. This approach is sound from both an economic and an aesthetic standpoint: there is a desirable logic in having books in series or by the same author bear an identifying resemblance.

In addition some general consistency of format and paper use is also highly desirable. At the moment there appears to be an unnecessarily wide diversity of trim sizes on the lists of individual publishers and even more so for the industry as a whole. The economic consequences of this diversity are staggering: vast sums and innumerable hours are wasted daily on press setup time and paper changes which are totally unproductive and of no value to publishers whatever. Enormous savings could be achieved each year if more standardization of trim sizes could be introduced. Manufacturers have been urging publishers to do this for years, but publishers and their designers have been slow in complying. Manufacturers have pointed out that many more press runs could be "ganged up" (i.e., run in sequence without costly makeready and paper changes) if more titles were manufactured in identical sizes. Preparation time could be greatly reduced, press running time substantially increased, plant efficiency of manufacturers vastly improved, and therefore their charges to publishers impressively lowered. Some publishers reply that the individuality of their products, and by implication their marketability, would be adversely affected by standardization. It is difficult to see how. Even if books were all printed in one of, say, ten standard trim sizes and on one of twenty different makes of paper, designers could still express enormous individuality through typographical treatment, style, and layout. In fact, as better designers will be the first to admit, limitations are usually a challenge rather than an impediment to the truly creative artist.

Studies have revealed that existing variations in size are often so small from one title to the next that by very minor adjustments some one dozen sizes could be developed for the entire field which could be used satisfactorily in 90 percent of all cases. Those exceptional books which, because of their special nature and unique problems could simply not be accommodated by the standard sizes, could still be designed for an odd or special size. The point would be, however, that for the vast majority of books substantial savings could be achieved by both publisher and manufacturer which would increase profits, result in lower prices for the consumer, and, conceivably, even higher royalties for authors.

Another very serious consideration that militates in favor of trim-size and paper standardization is the current paper shortage. Paper mills, unable to supply the industry's total demand, have already decided to curtail the range of their offerings and are eliminating certain special and rarely used grades from their lines. Standardization would enable them to gain greater plant efficiency thereby increasing their capacity and ability to meet publishers' needs.

Unfortunately designers are often the stoutest opponents of standardization. Their resistance is a symptom of an even more serious and fundamental shortcoming that is an occupational hazard in book design: overemphasis on the aesthetic and corresponding failure to meet the functional demands of their task. Obviously good design is essential in the production of books, but good design means first and foremost good *publishing:* clarity, readability, ready communication, inviting appearance, service of the reader and of the author's purposes. The designer who sacrifices readability to "arty" typographical devices, who lays out pages that may look superbly balanced but set the text too small or in confusing arrangements, who lets illustrations bleed off the page (i.e., run to the very edge) but permits important details to be cropped off in the process, is not truly fulfilling his function. Self-expression may be a legitimate aim in any artistic endeavor, but in functional design it must become subservient to and accept the limitations of the objectives which the designed product seeks to serve.

Production managers often complain that designers develop ideas that are difficult and costly to implement, consume unnecessary time, and yet add little to the usefulness and value of a book. Designers when confronted with such criticism then often murmur about the "crass commercialism" of publishers and their failure to appreciate real talent. Interestingly enough the truly great designers, who have left their impact on the development of the book as an objet d'art, have been those who have served with equal effectiveness the aesthetic as well as the functional requirements of their profession.

### Selection of Suppliers

Choice of suppliers begins with decisions about process. Shall we set the type in hot metal or through a computer? Shall we print by letterpress or offset? Use sheet-fed or web-fed presses? Case-bind or paper-bind? Perfect-bind or smyth-sew? Character of the book, consumer expectations, level of quality in production, size of printing and anticipated reprint needs, scheduling, and related economic considerations will figure prominently in such decisions.

A good production man knows his suppliers. He knows their equipment capability, the speed with which they work, the efficiency and quality of their workmanship. Is cost a major consideration? He may find typesetters and printers with low rates but busy schedules and plan a longer production cycle in order to save money. Is speed a major factor? He may be willing to pay a somewhat higher price for prompt service. Is quality the predominant consideration? He may be willing to sacrifice both time and money to achieve it.

Some production plans can become very complicated. Sometimes type is set abroad—particularly where complex scientific and technical composition is involved—with reproduction proofs (special pulls of the setting which are perfect enough to be photographed for platemaking) flown stateside where offset negatives are made from them. Because a particular printer offers economical and efficient offset facilities, the printing may be done by him, and he in turn will ship flat sheets to a bindery whose prices and capability for case binding are similarly favorable. In other instances an integrated book manufacturer, offering complete typesetting, printing, and binding facilities, may be awarded the entire job.

For certain projects the number of alternative facilities capable of doing good, prompt, and economical work may be limited. This is the case, for example, with mass market paperbacks. For certain specialties only foreign sources may be satisfactory; for example on large, economical, high-quality process color runs, overseas printing may be preferable to domestic manufacture. Because of dollar devaluation and cost inflation abroad the economic advantages of foreign printing have been greatly diminished, and as American technology and skill in color printing are steadily improving, domestic manufacturers find themselves increasingly in competitive positions.

Speed in producing a book or the ability to deliver a fast reprint is often a vital consideration, particularly where a book may be a potential best seller. Similarly the economics of ganging up books in series or of like format—original printings together with reprints—will argue for placing jobs with certain manufacturers. Paper must then be in supply at such plants, and one of the most demanding logistical problems confronting a production department is the need to have the right paper in the right place in the right quantity at all times. Cost conscious and efficient publishers have learned increasingly to help solve this problem through standardization—in the variety of papers they will use and the number of trim sizes they will normally employ.

## Estimating Costs

To determine costs of manufacture in advance is vital, not only as a control over the process and as a guide in making decisions regarding methods and suppliers, but also because these costs are significant factors in the setting of retail prices. In fact many publishers use unit manufacturing costs of first printings as bases for price decisions; a popular traditional formula in trade-book publishing, for example, places price at from five to six times that cost.

Such formulas may have some utility, although far more sophisticated and effective methods, which measure total publishing cost in relation to total income based on projected price and subsidiary revenues, can and are being employed. But in any case, manufacturing expense remains a major factor in the pricing structure.

Choice of process and supplier and cost estimates are obviously interrelated and interdependent, and production people must often weigh several alternatives before making the optimal decision. Of course with many, perhaps most, titles pricing and process decisions will be routine; such titles may be part of a series or conform to established patterns which can be safely and advantageously followed.

The basic cost unit in typesetting is the "em"; i.e., charges are predicated on the space consumed by the lower case "m" in a given font and the equivalency of "ems" represented by a particular setting. Since there is more to typesetting than straight body type, however, and since even text composition is sometimes highly complicated, involving mathematical symbols and scientific formulas, estimates are usually based on costs per page which take into consideration the nature and complexity of the entire setting.

Costs per page in turn are contingent on such factors as size, capacity of the page (i.e., the number of characters or words that can be accommodated—see Table 4), the complexity of setting body type, notes, and headings, and the method of typesetting employed. Generally monotype is the most costly process, with linotype next in line, followed by the various computer methods, and finally by the several cold-type methods. Normally straight text composition in trade-book formats will run at $5.00 to $7.00 per page; a scientific monograph or a reference volume may run $25.00 a page or even more in certain cases. This includes an allowance for author's alterations (AA's) for which there is a charge. Printers' errors (PE's) are corrected at no charge.

If the publisher has assumed the responsibility for furnishing illustrations—more commonly the author's concern—the cost of producing these in-house or on the outside must be calculated. Sometimes even if the author has provided illustrations they require touching up or further work which, unless it can be charged to the author, will have to become part of the estimated expense. The publisher normally commissions cover art which likewise is added to the projected total.

Printing cost estimates usually involve negatives and/or plates. Here the process used and the number and type of illustrations included will significantly affect totals. Letterpress halftones are very expensive, offset

TABLE 4

Average Words Per Printed Page for Certain
Book Trim Sizes[a]
(10/12 type size)

| Trim size (inches)[b] | Type area (picas) | Approximate number of words |
|---|---|---|
| 5 3/8 × 8 3/8 | 24 × 40 1/2 | 450 |
| 6 × 9 | 27 × 44 1/2 | 550 |
| 6 1/2 × 9 | 29 × 44 1/2 | 600 |
| 6 7/8 × 10 | 32 1/2 × 52 1/2 (double col.) | 650 |
| 7 1/2 × 9 1/4 | 37 × 48 (double col.) | 800 |
| 7 1/2 × 9 1/4 | 36 × 48 (single col.) | 575–595 |
| 8 1/2 × 11 | 37 1/2 × 53 1/2 (double col.) | 830 |

[a] The estimates shown in this table were compiled by Dennis Hudson and reflect design practices in use in 1973 in the College Department of John Wiley & Sons.
[b] To allow for illustrations and tables, assume that in the first three trim sizes one half page would be used per unit; in the next three sizes, one third page per unit, in the last size one fourth page per unit illustration or table.

halftones less so. Color plates, particularly process plates, are far more costly than black-and-white. Presswork costs, on the other hand, will depend on the length and complexity of the book (halftones add also to presswork expense as does, for example, so-called "open matter," i.e. extensive occurrence of short lines such as in poetry, drama, or narrative dialogue), and the number of impressions in the run. Of course negatives and plates will cost the same regardless of the number of copies printed; presswork however will vary with the size of the printing, including any ganging up with other books that may be possible.

A strange logic appears in many cases to determine the size of first printings. Some publishers argue that since fixed initial manufacturing costs (typesetting, art, negatives, and plates) will involve a lower investment per unit if the number of units manufactured is larger, therefore as many copies should be run at the beginning as possible. This kind of reasoning seems to stem from the practice of basing list price on a predetermined multiple of manufacturing cost and literally concluding that a lower price can be justified or a higher total of fixed cost tolerated simply because more copies are being printed.

What matters is not the unit cost of a first printing in relation to price but the total lifetime earnings of a book in relation to its total lifetime costs. As production executive John Chipman points out so wisely, to concentrate one's income planning on the first printing and ignore both the cost and earnings from likely reprints is unrealistic. On the other hand to run a sizable first printing in order to lower unit costs and in the process acquire excess inventory is altogether foolhardy. Cash is unnecessarily tied up, warehouse space is needlessly occupied, administrative costs in controlling the surplus inventory are needlessly incurred without having any real advantage to show for the effort. In most cases a printing, be it original or reprint, should represent a supply for no longer than a season (six months) or at most a year. Should the economics of the case not warrant a printing small enough not to last beyond this period, then the book should probably not be published or reprinted at all unless strong secondary motives exist for doing so or the sponsor is a not-for-profit publisher performing a service for scholarship or culture.

What usually makes sense then is a modest first printing, permitting the publisher to watch a title's performance before making a larger commitment, with well-laid plans for running a fast reprint when and if it becomes needed. If, as so often happens, a book sells well below expectations, such a first printing may then be just sufficient or at least it will not be a major disaster which would only aggravate the losses already incurred on the fixed publishing expenses of the project.

Part of the loss that can be thus prevented would involve paper, and in view of the paper shortage that would be a blessing in any case. In estimating paper consumption, the number of forms (aggregate of pages printed on one side of a press sheet) must be calculated, divided by two (as there are forms printed on each side of the sheet), and then multiplied by the number of planned impressions. As some of the stock will be wasted in printing and binding, an allowance for spoilage must be added in accordance with specified industry standards. Tables furnished by paper houses show ream weight of papers in various grades and sizes and as paper is sold by weight its costs can be calculated accordingly. Free sheets are more costly than groundwood, coated papers more expensive than antique- or machine-finish stock, paper with rag content the most expensive of all.

Most book papers run in the 25 to 30 cents per pound range. Savings are realized in buying paper by the carload, with some mills offering preferential rates at 10,000 pounds. If the printer is asked to furnish the paper he will add a markup of 15 to 20 percent to his cost of the stock. Smaller publishers who cannot command sufficient purchasing power to work advantageously with the paper houses directly may find it worthwhile to deal with paper merchants who represent several mills.

When it comes to binding cost, the biggest portion lies in folding, gathering, sewing, or perfect-binding, not in casing-in, i.e., attaching covers.

For this reason—and since printing costs remain the same irrespective of the type of binding employed—the variable manufacturing costs (paper, printing, and binding) of quality paperbacks is almost as great as that of hardbacks. (Only the fact that they can be sold in larger volume and carry a reduced royalty and often a lower fixed cost makes it possible, therefore, to sell such paperbacks profitably.)

Smyth-sewing is more expensive than perfect binding. Case binding varies in cost with the cover materials employed, with high-grade cloths like buckram involving far greater expense than plastic or impregnated paper substitutes. Little luxuries like top stain and head- and footbands also add to the budget but do enough to dress up a book so that they are usually employed in quality production. Two-color jackets or covers are cheaper than three-color and certainly far less expensive than four-color process covers. Lamination of covers is more costly than the application of a varnish while on the press; however, the development of coated coverstocks with high ink absorbency now often makes even the application of varnish no longer necessary.

As a compromise measure some publishers succumbing to the temptation of overprinting a title's initial run hold some of the printed sheets, binding only a portion of them. While this method may have some advantages over binding up an excessive inventory in its entirety, it may be better still not even to print the extra sheets. To begin with, sheets that are held flat on skids (i.e., stacked on movable platforms) are often damaged in transit or storage. If they are partially bound (folded, gathered, and sewn with endpapers attached) the largest portion of the binding cost will have been incurred anyway and little saving realized.

In the terminology of the trade as defined in AAP Surveys, fixed or nonrecurring manufacturing costs (typesetting, artwork, negatives, and/or plates and binding dies) are known as "plant costs." Those that recur in reprinting (paper, printing, and binding) are called "running costs." (Offset plates that are used only once for a particular printing are considered to be running costs; deep-etched plates that can be used repeatedly are classified as plant costs.)

### Scheduling

The production of a book from edited manuscript to finished product may take as long as a year. Trade books usually take no more than seven or eight months, but complicated texts, professional and scholarly works necessarily consume more time. There is the exception of the "instant" book of course: a topical work on a "hot" subject which can be manufactured on a crash basis in one or two months. To do so requires very special and costly arrangements, however, which would not be possible except under very special circumstances.

Why does it take so long? Because of the series of cumbersome steps that must be taken before the book is ready for sale. The process begins with the designing of the book and often, the ordering of sample pages from the compositor. The design must be reviewed and approved, decisions must be made regarding processes and suppliers, and a definite schedule must be prepared. This schedule will allow for the time needed to set the text and prepare any missing illustrations, for first proofs to be read by editors and author, for corrections to be made by the compositor, for pages to be made up, for page proofs to be read by editors and author, and for the index to be prepared. Only then can the type be locked up in forms or reproduction proofs furnished. Negatives and plates need to be made, arrangements for paper must be completed, all before the presses can roll. Press time itself is not always easy to come by, particularly if one has in mind to use certain equipment and there are long waiting lists for some presses. Finally books must be bound and jacketed. In the case of trade books, an allowance of up to two months must be added before publication date to permit the distribution of review copies and allow shipments to reach bookstores.

It is a lot easier to prepare a schedule, furthermore, than to keep one. When the manufacturing timetable is first formulated, the production department will agree with the editor on the specific dates by which proofs are to be furnished and returned. The editor in turn will advise the author and elicit a commitment from him regarding these dates. Predicated on these firm promises, press and bindery schedules are set and manufacturers reserve time on their equipment for the title in question. Far too often, however, editors and authors fail to live up to their commitments. The result is that the book loses its turn on the manufacturer's docket, must be rescheduled, and a delay of days in returning proofs can lead to a delay of weeks in getting on a printing press or into a bindery.

Some editors and authors appear to have little sense of time and to remain insensitive to the pleadings of production and marketing managers about the absolute necessity of keeping schedules. Authors particularly, though they may be vocal about what they regard as the unconscionably long periods it takes to move their manuscripts into print, fail to realize that their own sins of commission and omission are often the chief instruments of demolishing a carefully worked out timetable. The bane of a publisher's existence is the author who insists on rewriting his book in proof. Though his contract usually specifies that any alteration costs in excess of 10 percent of the original setting expense will be charged to him, he may ignore this item and make such extensive changes that the time required to correct— really to reset—his proof is totally beyond any reasonable allowance that can be built into the schedule.

There are other reasons why schedules fail, such as delays in receiving ordered paper or binding materials, failures by printers and binders to meet their commitments, and, sometimes we fear, even inefficiency on the part of production people themselves. In any case, sales departments and booksellers tend to view announced publication dates with skepticism, and delays often have unfortunate effects on promotion plans and on the market success of the books in question.

If industry performance on routine schedules is sometimes less than enviable, the virtuosity, skill, ingenuity, and determination of publishers who produce instant books is therefore all the more admirable. Such events call for total rapport between author and editor, superlative planning by the production manager, perfect coordination of the manufacturing process, and all the cajoling and sweet-talking of suppliers that may be needed and that long-established and valued personal relationships make possible. Sometimes the editor takes up residence at the typesetter's to work on proofs as they come off the machines and to check any necessary changes with the author by telephone. A special emissary from the production department may stand by the presses as the book runs to lend moral support and to emphasize the stake the house has in the crash program. The process is costly—but it works. And perhaps it teaches us something about ways in which even normal schedules could be improved.

### Imports

Not every book published in this country is manufactured here. We alluded earlier to the occasional desirability of printing certain books, notably those with process color plates, abroad. In addition economies can be achieved by joining a foreign publisher in his press run (sharing rather than duplicating his fixed manufacturing costs, in other words) thus making even a small import economically feasible. Many trade, professional, and scholarly publishers import titles which have been printed for them abroad, sometimes acquiring fully bound and jacketed books, at other times sheets which are then bound stateside.

Importation may affect copyright, however. If the author of an import is foreign, no special problem arises. However if the author is an American or domiciled in the United States, the current copyright law limits importation to 1,500 copies and the term of copyright to five years (under what is known as an "ad interim" copyright arrangement). Should a publisher require further supplies or wish to retain copyright beyond the five-year period, additional copies would have to be manufactured in the United States.

### Production Systems of the Future

Technology now available and some that is being developed promise to have a major impact on the methods employed in editing, book design, and production during the coming years. What is likely to develop, according to Paul Doebler, consultant with Thomas P. Mahoney Associates and editor of the production section of *Publishers Weekly*, is the use by publishers of what he calls "Write-Edit-Compose" systems: computer-based installations that encode the author's manuscript at an early stage—perhaps by having the author himself or the typist who retypes his rough draft use the appropriate typewriter equipment. This encoding (on magnetic tape, paper tape, or disc) could then be displayed on an editing terminal equipped with a video screen or a print-out device and permit the editor to make whatever changes and corrections may be necessary. Hard copy of the edited manuscript would then be shared with the author whose final changes would also be entered through the terminal.

The same terminal could be used by the designer to "mark up" the manuscript, specifying font, spacing, measure, justification, indentations, character treatment, headings, etc. Utilizing another type of terminal equipped with a video screen, the designer could make up pages by displaying blocks of type following his setting instructions and integrating them with illustrations whose outlines would be shown on the screen according to specified size. This method would simplify page makeup immeasurably, eliminating the labor entailed in cutting up galley proofs and pasting up a dummy. By simple electronic commands, type elements could be rapidly shifted, measure of setting adjusted, and depth of page altered.

The end product of the process—the fully edited, typeset, paged manuscript on tape or disc—would then be sent to the compositor and fed into a photosetter for printing out the text. Illustrations would be stripped together with the type in negative as is the practice now. Should a proof be needed at any stage of the process, a printout of the text could be supplied almost instantly.

The economics, speed, and mechanical advantages of such a process are obvious. Publishers of elhi materials who prepare major portions of their manuscripts in-house already would find it particularly advantageous. Where temperaments incline to be disposed against automation, some obstacles might be encountered, and some editors and authors may prefer to continue working with hard copy. Because of the system's flexibility this is possible without sacrificing the advantages of the process—the delay of actual typesetting until after the copy is fully edited, specked, and paged.

Another, far more modest development would be particularly applicable in the case of technical, scientific, and scholarly books and is, in fact, already being used by some publishers in these fields. It involves the preparation by the author, or by a typist under his supervision, of cold-type, camera-ready copy of his monograph. Since composition costs in these fields represent the major production investment by the publisher, this makes possible the publication of books that might otherwise not be released and puts others that might have been unprofitable in the black.

In such arrangements the author's manuscript is edited and, once the final version of the text is agreed on, typed on specially diagrammed sheets with a typewriter and ribbon furnished by the publisher (unless the author already has access to suitable equipment). The publisher also provides full instructions on the requirements that will make the resulting text suitable for reproduction.

Although some scholars oppose cold-type composition and think of it as second class, others have come to realize that their purposes and those of the publisher are greatly benefited by such an arrangement and that it provides an answer to the growing impasse created by shrinking markets and the threat of photocopying. Since a great many formal and informal publications in scholarly and scientific programs are today set in cold type, the process is gaining increasing acceptance within the disciplines themselves.

Somewhat related to this approach, and applicable in the same fields, is the possibility of increased "on-demand" manufacture. This method, employing Xerography or similar duplicating processes in preparing single copies from microfilm originals, is already being used in issuing out-of-print books and academic dissertations. The major advantage here is that one need not invest in an inventory at all but need supply only what are in effect guaranteed sales at prices that cover costs and engender profits. One could conceivably combine cold-type composition by the author with on-demand manufacture to achieve ways of issuing books in very specialized fields that on the one hand would guarantee their dissemination while on the other would keep their publishers from suffering bankruptcy.

# Chapter V.

# How Books
# Are Marketed

No matter how carefully selected, meticulously edited, or attractively produced a book may be it will not achieve its purpose nor will a publisher achieve his goal unless the book reaches its intended consumer. What the publisher does in marketing and distributing his product is as vital to his success as his editorial and production efforts.

In discussing the industry's divisions and their activities we have already identified the publisher's principal marketing concerns: his customers (individuals, libraries, schools, institutions, industry, government) and his distribution channels (retail stores, mass market outlets, wholesalers, jobbers, and book clubs). Now we must examine these in greater depth, along with the publisher's main marketing tools: sales representation, direct mail, space advertising, and publicity. We must also look at international markets, the selling of subsidiary rights, and such peripheral activities as the promotion of remainders and "special" sales.

Unfortunately the general segment of the book industry has not engaged in a great deal of market research, and what one can judge of consumer interests and behavior is therefore often largely conjecture based on the experiences of booksellers, libraries, and publishers themselves. There are indications that general publishers, stimulated by the example of their educational colleagues and led by a few houses more business-oriented than the rest, are becoming converts to the advantages of sound research and market analysis. It may therefore soon be possible to document thoroughly certain facts which we can now only surmise.

## RETAIL OUTLETS

### Bookstores

When the trade speaks of bookstores what it really means is a diverse group of outlets which range from shops that carry books exclusively to those which handle them only as a sideline. Even among stores which place primary emphasis on books there is a bewildering variety in size, type, quality, and specialization.

A few are fully stocked stores in which one is likely to find the most important new hardbound and softbound books and at least a respectable selection of older books in print. These outlets are likely to be fairly large, with an annual sales volume of $400,000 to $500,000, and to be located in affluent suburbs or in high-traffic urban shopping areas.

More numerous are stores that carry a limited range of titles, placing emphasis mostly on new hardcover books of wide general appeal in addition to sizable displays of popular paperbacks and, perhaps, an enticing selection of remainders. Such stores are characteristically in the $300,000 to $600,000 range and are also located in high-traffic urban or suburban shopping centers.

Even more common is the small store (less than $100,000 in annual sales) which confines itself largely to best sellers, cookbooks, Bibles, dictionaries, gift books, greeting cards, stationery, and other sidelines. It, too, is usually found in a high-traffic location, urban or suburban. There is a growing number of stores of various sizes specializing in mass market and quality paperbacks, with inventories that range from the largely popular to the more diversified and sophisticated. There are book departments in department stores and stationery stores with book sections. There are college stores that carry a selection of books far beyond that required in courses and which double as general book outlets in their communities.

There are stores specializing in religious books, technical books, rare books, secondhand books, and remainders, many of which carry general books in addition. There are bookstores attached to museums and historic sites with title selections tailored to their particular clientele. There are hobby stores, office supply dealers, and art supply stores with small book departments.

When the R.R. Bowker Co. lists over 12,000 "book outlets of all kinds" in the United States such stores as we have described and others similar to them are included. Bowker notes that 6,700 of these handle new books; 900 are department store book departments; 2,900 are college bookstores; 7,300 handle paperbacks; 1,700 carry law, medical, technical, and scientific titles; 4,000 sell religious books; 3,000 handle juveniles; 1,300 are rare book dealers; and 1,000 are secondhand dealers.

Since Bowker does not classify these dealers by size it is difficult to assess their specific role in the distribution process. It is obvious, however, that most of them are small, with annual book sales of $75,000 or less. The American Booksellers Association which does classify its members by size, reports the following breakdown of 4,000 stores (including 100 foreign outlets) covered by membership: 600 are variety stores with which books are mostly a sideline, netting them some $20,000 or less annually; 2,000 are small bookstores with volume up to $100,000; 250 are medium-sized outlets (annual sales between $100,000 and $250,000); and 200 are large stores with sales in excess of $250,000. The balance is made up of 500 college stores, 500 branch stores of chains, and 48 book departments in department stores.

The ABA data reveal the considerable importance of the chains in the retail book field. The Walden Book Co. operated 400 branches, and enjoyed sales of $100 million, in 1972. Its stores, each of which usually holds 3,000 square feet of selling space, are situated in prime locations. Walden is embarked on a vigorous expansion program which projected the opening of 64 additional stores in the fall of 1973. Dayton-Hudson, which owns 21 Pickwick Book Stores in the West, and some 80 B. Dalton Booksellers located in shopping centers in other areas, is also expanding. Dayton-Hudson anticipates a first-year sales volume of $300,000 from every new branch. Another notable chain is operated by Doubleday, and Kroch's & Brentano's has several branches in the Chicago area.

It is interesting to note the geographical distribution of ABA member stores. There are, for example, 553 in California, 372 in New York, 176 in Massachusetts, 175 in Illinois, 169 in Florida, 122 in Michigan, 52 in Wisconsin, 44 in Arizona, 16 in Hawaii, and 9 in South Dakota. As one would expect, booksellers congregate in well-populated areas.

The fact that 500 college stores are members of ABA attests to the fact that they are significant general book outlets; I estimate that in 1972 some $60 million of a total $525 million in college store book sales were generated by titles not related to course work. However, the principal purpose and activity of college stores is to market educational materials; accordingly they have a trade association of their own, the National Association of College Stores (NACS), which numbers 2,000 members. (To the extent that college stores sell general books they fit into the present discussion. Their course-related sales will be covered in a later section dealing with the marketing of college textbooks.)

The available evidence suggests that on the whole serious American book buyers are not happy with the outlets that serve them. Although no formal study has been undertaken in this area, the conclusions reached in such assessments as *The American Reading Public* (edited by Roger H. Smith, R.R. Bowker, 1964) and in articles which have appeared from time to time in the book review media and in *Publishers Weekly*, are that most booksellers do not maintain a sufficiently varied inventory to satisfy their customers' demands. When compared to the great European booksellers, we are told, most American stores do not measure up.

Exceptions are of course cited: the Harvard Coop, Yale Co-op, Kroch's & Brentano's bookstores in Chicago, the Pickwick Bookshops in Los Angeles, and Scribner's and Brentano's in New York, among others. At the same time critics point out that some of the great bookstores of yesteryear have disappeared and others have suffered a marked decline. Some commentators admit that quantitatively the retail book field is on the upswing: the opening of new stores by the chains and some independent outlets are making books more accessible in many places. But, they complain, the quality of these new stores is often low and their selection poor. While some additional copies of good books are being sold, the prime beneficiaries seem often to be the best sellers—prosperity is concentrated on a few titles. What can this accomplish for learning, literature, and culture or for the hard-core book buyer whose tastes are not being satisfied?

**Booksellers and Their Patrons**

To understand these complaints we must realize that there are really two types of general book consumers: the genuine book addict who purchases books regularly and the occasional buyer who only infrequently and unpredictably spends money on books. The steady book buyer may feed his habit for one or more of several reasons: professional need, interest in current affairs, intellectual curiosity, entertainment, a hobby. An accountant, for example, may buy books on computer applications in auditing for professional reasons, titles on the Civil War to satisfy an interest in history, and books on model railroading in connection with his hobby. The occasional buyer, on the other hand, may only be attracted to a book because "everybody is reading it," or because he has a few hours to kill on a plane, or wants to take a gift to a friend in the hospital. People who buy cookbooks, dictionaries, or atlases, furthermore, may not be readers at all; what they are really buying are home furnishings.

In a way it is a great deal easier to cater to the occasional book buyer than to the addict. There are not many best sellers and not too many cookbooks and gift books to identify, select, and keep in stock. Nor need a retailer know much about books or be well read to serve the best-seller buyer. Not so if he wants to earn the respect and confidence of genuine book buyers. To do this he must know books, not only important current productions but the great and successful books of the past. He must have a broad knowledge of the world of learning, art, and culture, if only to know what references to consult to help an inquiring customer. And since personal relationships are highly important when one wishes to capture and retain a steady patron, the bookseller must display sufficient sparkle to entertain and beguile his customer. The reason book buyers value the experience of patronizing certain shops is not only that they find the selection good and the service competent but that they feel understood and have a genuine rapport with the staff.

Bookselling, then, is a profession; running an outlet for best-sellers and cookbooks is merely a business. The rewards of professional bookselling involve pride in knowing one's field, helping people to satisfy their tastes and interests, and enjoying their respect and gratitude in return.

The professional bookseller faces formidable odds in pursuing his objective. His customers are a cultural minority. To attract them—along with the best-seller purchasers whom he cannot ignore because they will give him a substantial amount of business—he must locate himself in a heavy-traffic area where rents are often disproportionately high considering his modest list prices and low stock turnover. There are far too many books published, placing a staggering burden of choice on his shoulders. Many of the publishers from whom he buys have chosen to travel the easy road by emphasizing best sellers—or potential best sellers—to the detriment of other, more solid titles on their lists. When he buys the less glamorous titles, therefore, he must often do so with little help or support from the publisher. Delivery is usually very slow; stock orders may take weeks, special orders sometimes months.

Still—even from an economic standpoint the professional bookseller enjoys certain advantages over his less knowledgeable, less "bookish" colleague. While he has to work harder to obtain and manage a diverse and balanced inventory, he cultivates a stable clientele and builds and maintains a steady sales volume. When he recommends a book, his customer listens. When he is out of a title, his customer may be willing to take another book instead. After all, the patron is a *reader*: reading is a regular occupation with him, a source of deep satisfaction, a cultivated habit. When he goes to visit his friend the bookseller he may have something specific in mind, or he may not—but rarely will he leave without a purchase under his arm.

One can *browse* in a genuine bookshop—something impossible to do in a best-seller parlor. And browsing for the book addict is inevitably the introduction to buying. The reason why so many bookshops incur the wrath of true bookbuyers and have long ago lost their patronage is that their shelves hold so little attraction for the browser—no variety, no depth, no discrimination, no appreciation for the world of books.

One reason why even well-meaning bookdealers often fail to satisfy their best potential customers is that they do not know enough about their profession. They have no background or training when they enter the field; they have never even worked in a bookstore prior to going into business. The American Booksellers Association has sought to remedy these conditions in a number of ways: by sponsoring a booksellers school (jointly with NACS), by publishing a *Manual on Bookselling* and cassette-tape training programs, by compiling a "Hardbound Basic Book List" and a "Paperbound Basic Booklist" to aid dealers in selecting a well-rounded staple stock, and by sponsoring an annual convention and trade exhibit that provides booksellers with the opportunity to plan their requirements for the year ahead.

But even these aids are of little help when booksellers are badly undercapitalized—as many are—or when an elderly couple opens a bookstore in "active retirement," not realizing what a demanding, time-consuming, complicated endeavor bookselling really is. Perhaps if more people planning on opening bookstores investigated the requirements in advance—ABA and NACS offer helpful information there too—there would be fewer bankruptcies and more satisfactory bookshops. G. Roysce Smith, executive director of ABA, believes that no bookstore is viable today unless it is begun with a minimal investment of $100,000 which includes the cash required for a starting inventory. A good store can count on turning over its inventory about three times a year (3.3 was the average reported in 1968) while some stores have a rate of turnover as high as five times a year and others as low as twice a year. Some of the country's best bookstores are in the low category; they carry a wide selection of titles which do not sell very rapidly in aggregate. Yet these stores are quite successful financially while maintaining a first-rate reputation.

## How Publishers Market to Bookstores

Most books sold by bookstores are published by trade publishers and with some exceptions the practices established by trade houses are followed by other industry segments—mass market paperback, religious, and scholarly publishers—in attempting to reach this market. Trade publishers cover their major bookstore customers primarily through personal sales calls, supplemented by mailings of catalogs and brochures—particularly to stores which because of their small size and out-of-the-way location cannot economically be covered in person. Publishers also advertise in the trade media, such as *Publishers Weekly*.

Large houses can justify maintaining their own sales force. Smaller houses either arrange to have their books distributed by larger houses or they engage "commission men," salesmen in business for themselves who may represent as many as sixteen publishers. Sales territories vary in size and scope depending on a publisher's circumstances, but commonly the country is split up into "primary" and "secondary" areas, with the primary territories embracing the important stores in large metropolitan centers such as New York, Los Angeles, Boston, and Chicago, which require more time to cover and demand more experience and skill on the part of the traveler. Secondary territories are usually laid out by regions: New England, the Middle Atlantic States, the mid-West, the far West, the Southwest, and the South. A commission man may cover a regional territory, primary as well as secondary accounts, by himself or with the help of assistants. A house staff may number as many as a hundred men nationwide, with several working in each region and with primary and secondary accounts assigned to suit the ability and effectiveness of individual representatives.

The frequency with which an account is visited depends on the size of a publisher's list and the importance and volume of the store. As there are two principal publishing seasons, spring and fall, most accounts are visited at least four times yearly: once in advance of each season to solicit orders for forthcoming titles, and once during the season to take reorders and check stock. In recent years publishers have scheduled books for publication also during the summer which has led to some adjustments of sales schedules. In primary territories sales calls will be far more frequent, as often as monthly for major accounts. Chain stores do much of their buying centrally and require special attention.

To prepare the salesmen for their task publishers engage in a time-honored ritual: the sales conference. All the representatives meet with the sales manager before seasonal trips and are given information and pep talks on forthcoming books. Editors often make presentations, authors are occasionally invited. The after-hours frolicking associated with these occasions makes them bearable, though not necessarily more effective; some representatives have difficulty staying awake while they are being assured that every book on the list is first-rate and will sell superbly if only the salesman will apply himself to promoting it. Each man is given a sales kit consisting of jackets or covers, sample pages, illustrations, etc. (Too often jackets or covers are not ready on time, which can prove to be quite a handicap to the man on the road.) Backlist titles are sometimes discussed though not usually with great intensity or enthusiasm. Some houses assign quotas for total sales or individual new titles to their representatives, but as these quotas are sometimes very unrealistic they are not always taken too seriously. Some houses make galleys of outstanding titles available to their salesmen; it is not certain that they are always read.

The sales tool most men find indispensable is the seasonal catalog. Even though copywriters sometimes substitute glowing adjectives for solid information, catalog blurbs usually give a summary of the book's content, information about the author, and some indication of the prospective market for the title. A good salesman knows his accounts and is aware that he is effective only if he recommends to them titles which they can really sell. If he consistently recommends books that prove themselves by their performance, he will gain the confidence of his customers and will be able to make his recommendations heard over the years.

Buyers often complain that salesmen understand neither their store nor the books they are selling and often prove naive and untrustworthy in their recommendations. They are also often accused of being long-winded. It is obvious that most books published cannot be acquired by most bookstores: there is simply too little shelf space and cash available to make it possible. Furthermore, a salesman who insists on making a full presentation on every title in his catalog will soon lose the buyer's attention: the poor individual simply cannot command the required time and energy. So a good salesman must "highspot," discussing only those books on his list which the store is likely to find successful. Every good sales manager knows this; so does every head of house. Still—most sales conferences insist on tiring, detailed discussions of every title on the schedule, and publishers continue to contract for books their representatives are unable to place in the market.

The terms which publishers extend to booksellers vary a good deal from house to house so much so that the American Booksellers Association annually publishes the *ABA Book Buyer's Handbook*, a loose-leaf guide designed to keep its members abreast of an unbelievably complicated mass of discount schedules and returns policies. In general, however, trade books in quantities of five or more assorted copies are sold to retailers at a discount of 40 percent off the list price and publishers offer larger discounts on quantity purchases—such as 42 percent on 50 assorted and 43 percent on 100 assorted books. Most trade houses will accept returns of unsold books within a year of purchase or publication date, although some make returning books difficult by attaching complicated requirements and extensive paperwork to the procedure. Dealers normally pay all transportation costs, incoming and returning. Many a salesman tries to convince the hesitating buyer to purchase a new book in quantity by assuring him that "it will be all right—you can return it if it doesn't sell." Many buyers believe him, too, forgetting that a book that does not sell is taking away shelf space and inventory money from one that might sell and that returns are therefore very costly. If booksellers were to measure the true cost of handling unsold books (the space, personnel, and overhead expenses actually incurred by these titles while sitting on the shelf), they would be far less willing to buy titles on which there was even a chance of heavy returns.

At the same time booksellers might learn to appreciate more what even a slow but steadily selling basic stock inventory can do for them. Fortunately there are still some publishers and booksellers who are convinced of the economic and cultural advantages of a good backlist and the salesmen of such publishers carefully check stock when they visit their customers to make certain that missing titles are replenished. Particularly publishers with paperback series are alert to this opportunity. A well-managed store, furthermore, maintains effective inventory control, a requirement that can be met with increasing facility in this computerized age.

Yet the book industry as a whole, which has had as ready access to computers as have the many other industries which have successfully dealt with their distribution problems, has failed thus far to develop a system that would effectively link retail inventory control with publishers' order processing and shipping procedures. What could be more logical than to introduce a standard stock control and order form for retailers which would be machine readable (utilizing the International Standard Book Numbering System already in existence) and which would help make all inventory control, billing, and shipping documents compatible within the industry—a feat that could be accomplished no matter what computer equipment an individual retailer and publisher might now be using? Instead publishers and their customers continue to operate in chaos, each using a different form, a different method, and a different approach to these necessarily common processes.

Nowhere is this failure of the industry to deal effectively with its ordering and fulfillment problems more troublesome than in the processing of special orders. Obviously if a bookseller cannot stock everything published he will have to special-order a great many titles if he hopes to keep his customers happy. These days it seems that to accept a special order may be the quickest way of making a customer unhappy. Shipments, even status reports, appear to take weeks if not months to process. Customers complain that they have placed special orders, for which they may even have paid in advance, only to learn four or five weeks later that the book is out of print or out of stock at the publisher. Such orders are also usually very costly for bookseller and publisher to deal with—labor, machine time, and materials exceeding the gross profit margins of the transaction. Although ABA sponsors the Single Copy Order Plan (SCOP) whereby special orders are prepaid by booksellers and in return are given a "trade" discount (40 percent) rather than the usual "short" (20 percent) discount applicable to single books, this plan has not significantly improved publishers' service, promptness of delivery, or the economics of the special-order process. Industry-wide consolidation of some sort—cooperative arrangements with regional service depots, for example—appears to be the answer. Although a number of plans have been forwarded, the industry has thus far failed to take action.

If publishers are not very effective in selling or delivering their books to stores they do try to give retailers some support on the titles they buy. Publishers' general publicity and advertising efforts, resulting in national review coverage, the appearance of authors on TV, and similar exposure, are mainly designed to benefit booksellers. (The ABA recently inaugurated the *Newswire*, "a comprehensive weekly listing of forthcoming publicity about books and authors, helping booksellers prepare themselves for public demand.") Publishers also offer dealers cooperative advertising (i.e., the publisher pays for 50 or 75 percent of an ad which is run locally over the bookseller's name) and they arrange for authors' autographing parties in leading stores.

While publishers other than trade houses will generally follow trade practices when marketing to bookstores, publishers of professional books are the exception for they have had to develop policies that reflect the special circumstances of technical, scientific, business, medical, and other professional books. As such books are usually addressed to quite limited and specific audiences and represent very substantial editorial and manufacturing investments by the publishers, they are higher priced than trade titles and are offered to dealers at "short" discounts of 20 to 25 percent. Professional publishers whose lists lend themselves particularly to retail distribution often offer dealers a special "agency" plan whereby the retailer can earn a better (though still short) discount of 30 to 35 percent on the most salable titles provided he agrees to keep a reasonable selection of them in stock at all times.

Discounts are an emotional issue in the book trade. For years booksellers have complained even about trade discounts which they claim are inadequate (as they no doubt sometimes are) and have shown themselves reluctant to stock books offered at short discount. As a result, many stores that could enjoy success with professional books do not carry them, depriving themselves of good earnings and their customers of a service that is sorely needed.

The economic argument booksellers use against short-discount books does not hold water. What matters in retailing is the dollar yield of a transaction; discount is only one factor contributing to profit—list price, turnover, and applicable operating cost are at least as significant. If in a week's time I can sell two copies of a five-dollar trade book on which 40 percent discount allows me a margin before transportation and operating expenses of $4.00, I am not as well off as I am if during the same period I sell one professional book listing at $25.00 at a 20 percent discount, which makes my margin before costs $5.00! If, as is likely, in addition I have heavier returns and higher personnel, storage, and promotional costs on trade than on professional books, and am receiving an agency discount on the professional titles, I may find that I can actually make more money on specialized books at short discount than on trade books at full discount. (See "How to Make a Profit in Bookselling" by John P. Dessauer, *Publishers Weekly*, April 2, 9, 16, 1973.)

Not every bookstore can count on a sufficiently large professional clientele to succeed in this area, of course, just as some dealers cannot command enough patrons to support a well-stocked bookstore. One must have a solid and congenial population base to succeed as a real bookseller. Nevertheless many opportunities for such ventures are lost today mainly because dealers lack the skill and resources to make them go.

**Mass Market Outlets**

It is difficult to determine exactly how many mass market outlets exist in the United States. There are the 90,000 outlets served by magazine wholesalers, most of which are newsstands and drugstores but which also include bookstores, department stores, and college and school stores. In addition there are the chain stores, such as Woolworth's and Grant's, which usually buy directly from publishers. In all, there are probably 100,000 retail locations at which books are sold and of these some 93,000 are exclusively mass market outlets as distinguished from traditional trade stores.

These mass outlets are cultivated by paperback and certain children's books publishers. Field salesmen are used even in territories where wholesalers effect the actual distribution; publishers feel they must supplement wholesalers' efforts to ensure that their books receive the proper exposure. Such coverage is of a service nature: checking stock, making certain that important titles are effectively displayed, ascertaining that the wholesaler is supplying inventory when needed. Needless to say, field men are likely to concentrate on leading best-selling titles; their pinpointed efforts cannot practically be spread to an entire list—even if there were enough room in the stores to display all the books on the list.

In addition to those served by wholesalers, there are mass outlets to which publishers sell directly, such as variety, five-and-dime, drugstore, and supermarket chains. These operations usually buy centrally, are highly selective, and because of their considerable purchasing power receive favorable discounts and terms. It is customary throughout the mass market for the publisher to furnish display racks or rack allowances to house his books, and featured titles are often shipped in prepacked display cartons known as "dump bins." The chains frequently prefer to buy such package arrangements, highspotting titles rather than attempting to offer their customers a wide variety. Given the nature of these stores and the way they must normally operate, this approach makes sense for both chain and publisher.

## BOOK CLUBS

Experts on retail merchandising often refer to the present era as the age of direct marketing. Indeed the various techniques of reaching the consumer directly—personal visits, mailings, telephone selling—have been greatly perfected within the last decade. A number of factors are contributing to the advance of direct marketing: increased affluence which is making the indulgence of specialized tastes more feasible and is increasing the consumer's purchasing power; the movement of affluent consumers to the suburbs resulting in more home-centered life-styles; and, finally, the sheer convenience and comfort of shopping from one's armchair.

Not that direct selling, particularly in rural areas, is a new concept. Some of the most successful retailing enterprises in the United States, such as Sears Roebuck and Montgomery Ward, have grown to size and eminence by employing, even inventing, some of the direct marketing methods in use today. The direct selling of books enjoys a similar time-honored tradition: companies such as Doubleday pioneered direct mail to the consumer early in this century, and, for decades, encyclopedia publishers have employed sales representatives to call on homes.

When the Book-of-the-Month Club and the Literary Guild were founded in the mid-twenties they became instantly successful. Even then many people interested in books did not have ready access to bookstores or were unable to find what they were looking for in their local book outlet. Even then too many books were published, making it difficult for a reader to learn about new titles and to make satisfying choices from the flood. The clubs promised to advise their members about the newest and best and to choose on their behalf. They also offered inducements: free books and substantial savings on selections.

Fundamentally the attractions of book clubs are still the same today, and subscribers still look to clubs for information about significant new books and for the opportunity to buy them conveniently at attractive savings. But the scope and complexity of book clubs has grown. Members are no longer satisfied to accept without question a single monthly selection or even a single alternate: they want a wider variety of titles from which to choose. Also, in response to the steady trend toward specialization book clubs have become diversified and many now cater to special classes of readers or to subject interest groups. Furthermore, the book club vehicle has proved to be adaptable to the professional market as well and a substantial number of clubs now cater to peoples' work interests.

The Book-of-the-Month Club and Doubleday's Literary Guild appeal to the broadest consumer market, as does Doubleday's Bargain Book Club and the Reader's Digest Book Club. There are "egghead" clubs, such as Readers' Subscription (Harper & Row), which cater to a more intellectually oriented reader. Specialized consumer clubs include American Garden Guild Book Club (Doubleday), Americana Book Club, Antiques Book Club, Arts and Crafts Book Society (Prentice-Hall), Book Club for Poetry, Catholic Book Club, Chilton's Foreign Language Book Clubs, Classics Club, The Commentary Library, Conservative Book Club, Cookbook Club, Detective Book Club, the Ecological Book Club, Evangelical Book Club, Golfer's Book Club, History Book Club (Harcourt Brace Jovanovich), The Limited Editions Club, Military Book Club (Doubleday), The Movie Book Club, Nostalgia Book Club, Outdoor Life Book Club (Popular Science), as well as several clubs for children and students.

In the professional area are a number of clubs operated by McGraw-Hill (Chemical Engineers Book Club, Civil Engineers Book Club, among others), by Macmillan (including Behavioral Science Book Service, Investors Book Club, Library of Contemporary Education, and the Library of Science), and by Prentice-Hall (among them Books for Accountants, Builder's and Contractor's Book Society, Electronics Book Service, Lawyers' Book Club, Management Book Institute, Real Estate Book Institute, Salesmen's Book Club, and the Secretary's Book Club).

While the terms of membership and operating methods of clubs vary widely, there are some common features: members are enticed to join by offers of free books or of books at nominal cost, in return for which they commit themselves to the purchase of a minimal number of books for a specified period. After the member has fulfilled his obligation he is encouraged to remain in the club by offers of additional free or nominally priced books every time he makes a further purchase. Most clubs work on a shorter cycle rather than on a full calendar month, giving them up to fifteen instead of only twelve selection periods a year. In advance of each cycle the member receives a brochure announcing new selections, alternates, and other available books together with a notice that the prime selection will be shipped to him automatically unless he advises the club by a certain date that he wants another book instead or no book at all.

This device, which assumes that the member agrees to accept a selection unless he specifies otherwise, is known as "negative option" and has recently come under fire from some consumer groups and the Federal Trade Commission. So far, however, book clubs seem to have persuaded the government that the negative option practice, while subject to abuses that should be corrected, is fundamentally sound and necessary if book clubs are to survive. The clubs argue that they cannot plan their printings and distribution, and therefore operate efficiently, unless they can establish in advance how many members will accept a selection or alternate. Without the device of negative option many members will not respond on time or will not respond at all to selection announcements. Clubs admit that errors have been made and that members have received unwanted books; that it is a nuisance for the member to ship the books back or to have to refuse them; that it is a nightmare for him to be dunned repeatedly or even threatened with legal action for not paying for books he never wanted or had returned. Clubs acknowledge that computerization has created new unforeseen problems in membership service and that service personnel are often careless and indifferent even to members' angry or pleading letters. They agree that better controls must be instituted to prevent such occurrences. In other words, the FTC probings have had a beneficial effect in making clubs more conscious of and conscientious about the difficulties they are causing their members by their inefficiency.

On the other hand, the economic argument advanced by book clubs is fundamentally sound for they can prosper only if their members buy a sufficient number of books. A club must balance its investment in a member—the advertising cost of acquiring him, the cost of books in his introductory offer, and the cost of books purchased, as well as the cost of serving his account—against the income realized through his purchases. A member who quits prematurely without buying the agreed-upon number of books may well create a loss for the club. Conversely a member who remains active for many years and is faithful in buying titles, is a great asset. Experience has shown that professional and specialized consumer clubs enroll members at smaller cost, retain them longer, and sell more books to them than do general consumer clubs. On the other hand, general consumer clubs enroll many more members and benefit from the economic advantages of large size and volume production.

All book clubs enjoy certain cost advantages. When they contract for the rights to a title they usually arrange to print an edition from the publisher's plates, even joining the publisher's press run in some cases. Thus they avoid all plant and editorial expenses and need only defray the running costs of their edition. Some clubs economize considerably in preparing their printings, furthermore, using cheaper paper, narrower margins, and less costly bindings than the publisher (often to the distress of members who are not enthusiastic about such skimping on the book's design).

Book clubs pay the publisher a royalty on their sales—usually 10 percent of the club price on books sold and 5 percent on copies given away—and the larger clubs offer substantial guarantees, running as high as $100,000 on major titles. Smaller or more specialized clubs will usually pay a guarantee corresponding to anticipated royalties from the initial distribution of their edition.

Recruiting of new members is carefully planned and the results of campaigns are imaginatively analyzed. The major clubs, who advertise regularly in newspapers and magazines and make promotional mailings, have compiled records not only establishing the number of members a certain promotional effort has produced but relating the members' performance and productivity to the medium through which he was obtained. Book clubs are thus able to evaluate the effectiveness of various promotional approaches and to plan their investment in ads and offers with genuine skill.

Important though book clubs are in the general distribution pattern of the industry, and although their significance and effectiveness promises to grow further during the coming years, they cannot be expected to take up the general slack or make up for the deficiencies of bookstores. By their very nature book clubs must be selective; even specialized and professional clubs whose appeal to members lies largely in their ability to announce and supply the outstanding books in their field, cannot claim to be exhaustive in their coverage or to be able to list even a majority of titles in their respective areas. In fact, because book clubs can only take the cream off the top, they are less well equipped than other channels to solve the pressing problem of bringing thousands of good books to consumers who badly want or need them.

## MAIL ORDER

Some distinctions must be made at the outset of a discussion of mail order bookselling. First—some books are designed and published primarily for marketing by mail to the general consumer (and are defined in AAP terminology as "Mail Order Publications"). Many other books, notably professional and scholarly titles, though widely sold by mail are not specifically and predominantly so planned. Second—quite a few retail bookstores and mail order houses market books by mail just as publishers do. However, because the retailers' method and approach are very similar to that employed by publishers, we shall not discuss their activities separately.

## Mail Order Publishing

Mail order publishing has a mystique all its own. Invented by mass magazine publishers, it deals in numbers that leave the traditional trade-book publisher breathless: mailings in the millions, sales in the hundreds of thousands, prices that often hover around $30 for single books or a hundred dollars or more for series or sets. Editorial and plant investments are staggering. It is a game for big operators which in its own way has revolutionized the industry as much as the paperbacks have. And we have barely seen its beginnings, with much of the potential of the new technique as yet unrealized.

Like book club selling, mail order publishing is limited to widely popular subjects and requires a big price tag or multiple purchases by consumers for financial success. Its leading practitioners, such as Time, Inc., Reader's Digest, Meredith, Newsweek, Playboy, and American Heritage (McGraw-Hill), plan and create their own products, usually after careful market research. However, before actually launching the writing of the text and assemblage of illustrations—normally done by an in-house staff supported by outside experts—a beautiful brochure is prepared, featuring sample mock-up pages and color plates from the proposed book. This brochure, with covering sales letter, reply order card, and an occasional gimmick or two, is test-mailed to a representative list of prospective purchasers and the replies are carefully analyzed. The test serves not only to establish the likely acceptance of the product but the effectiveness of various promotional approaches: advance price savings, different types of brochures, order forms, stamps to lick instead of signing cards, etc. The test, or "split test" when more than one promotional approach is being tried, will determine whether or not the book will be published as planned or modified, and how it will be promoted to its full audience.

Publishers rely primarily on the circulation lists of their own magazines and on the buyers lists of previous products to reach that audience. Promoted are either "continuity programs" (sets or series which the customer agrees to receive a volume at a time with the option of discontinuing any time he wishes), or single titles, or catalog sales (i.e., titles selected from mailings in which the publisher advertises his entire or partial backlist). Continuity programs differ from book club arrangements in that they do not require a membership commitment.

Mail order publishing is less than two decades old, still in the exploratory and formative stage, still subject to many surprises despite careful planning. Conditions in the general consumer market seem to affect its fortunes more than they do other books—which is hardly surprising when we consider that the appeal of mail order products goes far beyond a hard-core book readership to people who probably are being sold books for the first time.

As they do not have the book buying habit and as the price tags of mail order publications must necessarily be steep, these consumers fall readily by the wayside when the economy turns sour.

But in good times the sales and profits of this new publishing genre have been phenomenal. Like the book clubs before them, mail order ventures have created new readers, new lovers and buyers of books. They have also demonstrated once again that books have an intrinsic aesthetic appeal, an attraction for the eye as well as the mind, and that the desire to build a handsome library can readily be awakened in people when the means and marketing methods are available.

**Mail Order Selling**

The secret of all good marketing is to bring product and buyer together with a sound understanding both of what one is selling and of the consumer to whom one is trying to sell it. Direct mail is one of the most effective tools in book promotion, but it is costly and demanding and mistakes come quickly home to roost. Unless one has correctly sized up one's product, identified clearly who its customers are, and determined how they can best be reached, one may quickly face disaster in the mail order business.

A look at the economics of direct mail bookselling will demonstrate this fact. On a mailing to a general consumer list promoting a book with a subject of wide interest (an instance characteristic of the mail order publishing operations just described), a return of 1.5 to 2 percent is considered average. This means that for every 1,000 pieces mailed 15 to 20 orders will be received. The cost of such a mailing will depend on the type and number of inserts included in the package and the nature of the mailing list used. The expense of printing the brochures, sales letters, and order cards, of stuffing them into envelopes, of utilizing a mailing list and addressing from it, of bundling, post office delivery and postage (at third class bulk rates), can run some $250 per thousand pieces. If the returns received from a 1000-piece mailing are 2 percent, and the list price of the book is $30, a gross income of $600 will be realized. This will leave a margin after mailing expenses of $350 to cover the manufacturing cost and royalty on the books (perhaps $120) and general operating expense (possibly $140), and allow the mailer a pretax profit of $90.

Suppose, however, that the return were to be only 1 percent, or 10 orders per 1,000 pieces mailed. Income would then shrink to $300, leaving a margin after mailing expenses of only $50. Although book costs would also go down (to $60) and operating expense would likewise be lower (conceivably $100—some operating expense won't go away simply because not enough books are sold), the mailer would show a whopping loss of $110. He would encounter somewhat the same problem if the book promoted were only half as expensive, carrying a list price of only $15, even if he enjoyed a return of 2 percent. If, on the other hand, he could increase his return rate to 4 percent, he could show a profit even on the fifteen-dollar book (probably close to $50) while on the thirty-dollar volume he would better than double his profit over the 2 percent return because his operating costs would not quite double along with sales. (One way he might be able to achieve a higher return would be by promoting several books simultaneously thereby increasing not only the number of responses but, hopefully, the income per response as well.)

If rate of return and list price are vital factors, costs are no less so. If the mailer were promoting professional or scholarly titles, for example, and did not require expensive color brochures, fancy order cards, or gimmicks, but only a simple, modest announcement letter, mailing expense per thousand might be reduced to $150. Assuming the list price of the book promoted to be only $20 in such an instance, with a 2 percent return, the publisher would show a gross income of $400, a margin after mailing expense of $250, with book costs possibly of $80, operating expense of $120, and a profit of $50. Should he realize only a 1 percent return or be dealing with a title listing at only $10 he would, of course, find himself in the loss column.

Some points about direct mail become therefore obvious: books or series must be sufficiently high-priced to support the mailing cost required to promote them. Mailing lists must be carefully chosen so that they will yield a sufficiently high rate of return. Mailing packages (i.e., brochures, covering letters, order cards, other enclosures, even envelopes) must be effectively prepared in order to do the required selling job as economically as possible.

Many direct mail practitioners place the choice of the proper mailing list at the top of their requirements. There are many sources for such lists: magazines sell address lists of their current or expired subscribers; publishers, like American Heritage, make available buyers lists of their titles; and in the scholarly and professional field there are learned societies whose membership rosters are obtainable. The Association of American University Presses maintains the Educational Directory, a list of teaching faculty in higher education classified by discipline and rank. R.R. Bowker markets mailing lists of booksellers, libraries, and schools. There are many list brokers who represent owners of mailing lists and who are only too anxious to assist the mailer. A directory of such brokers and other mailing list sources appears in *Literary Market Place*.

On highly specialized items, such as certain professional works, a good mailing list may be the best if not the only entree to a very precise and very limited market. The mailing itself may be small, but the rate of return can be very high. Also, in specialized mail order one often encounters a phenomenon known as "echo," i.e., orders from bookstores or from libraries in addition to those arriving directly in response to the mailing.

Some of the customers to whom the promotion was addressed simply prefer to order through a bookstore or they recommend the book to the company, laboratory, or academic library with which they are affiliated.

Publishers who regularly promote by mail often find it advantageous to develop mailing lists of their own. This provides them not only with a strong marketing tool but also with a source of income: addressing on good mailing lists can be sold for $25 or more per thousand. Maintaining a mailing list is a demanding chore, however; address changes in our mobile society are almost constant and list owners must regularly employ a "list cleaner," i.e., a service reporting address changes provided at nominal cost by the post office. To keep a mailing list effective also requires periodic elimination of nonbuyers; even though a purchaser was placed on a list originally because he bought a book may not mean that he will continue doing so regularly. Some publishers, particularly those who specialize in general consumer mailings, have found the necessary record keeping too costly, however; they prefer to retire the entire list after two or three years and start all over.

What one mails to the customer—the mailing package—is at least as important as the list to which it is mailed. Brochures are basically of two kinds: self-mailers, which require no envelope but can be addressed directly, and enclosures, which must be inserted in envelopes (or occasionally in a self-mailer). Generally, promoters of books have found enclosure mailings to be more effective, albeit more costly than self-mailers, particularly in attempts to reach the general consumer. For trade mailings (to bookstores and libraries) self-mailers are often quite satisfactory.

The character of a mailing package changes significantly with the type of person to whom it is addressed and the product being promoted. Mailings on expensive, colorful books to the general consumer will feature elaborate, color-illustrated brochures with strongly "pitched" copy rhapsodizing about the product, accompanied by long, glowing sales letters, order cards with pictures, and reply envelopes. Good direct mail copy does not rely solely on adjectives or superlatives, however; even the most enthusiastic sales piece should be long on information, description of content, facts about the author, data on illustrations, binding, etc. Facts, not words, sell books. While the words should be lively, clear, and persuasive, they are not likely to succeed if the substance they present is vague and abounds in generalities.

When a technical handbook is promoted to a professional audience the mailing package can be modest, even spartan in appearance and yet be very effective if it features the information the customer will find persuasive: as much specific detail on the book as possible, including, perhaps, sample pages, and solid data on the author. In mailings to scholars and academicians simple, mimeographed announcements have sometimes produced better responses than elaborate brochures; scholars incline to distrust what they regard as "slick" sales approaches, but they will respond solidly to announcements that are factual and resemble in appearance the mailings they receive from colleagues or scholarly associations.

Some aspects of direct mail practice, such as the virtue of enclosing sales letters with brochures, are the subject of controversy among practitioners. Tests show that covering letters are very effective in general consumer mailings; the evidence is less conclusive where promotion to scholars or professionals is concerned. (These days the ultimate in sales letters is the computer-addressed and personalized letter in which the name of the recipient may be repeated several times throughout the text.) Another subject for never-ending debate is the virtue of promoting a single book as against several in the same mailing. Tests have indicated that mailings devoted to a single title are more effective in promoting that book than mailings diluted with other announcements; other tests show, however, that the total number of responses and the return per response is often greater when several books are offered for sale. The objective of a mailing and its audience require careful analysis, therefore, before a decision is made regarding the use of single or multiple insertions. If a truly important new book is being established in its market, a book which by its substantial list price can make the mailing pay on its own, it is probably wiser to confine the effort to that one title rather than scatter one's shots by including other books. If, however, the title is part of a series, or if its price is too low to ensure a profit on a single insertion mailing, then the better part of wisdom may be to do a mailing featuring the entire series or other books in the same subject area. This is probably true whether one is dealing with a general consumer or a specialized audience.

In any case, direct mail today is the most underused marketing technique in the book industry. While some of the publishers we have cited have developed the technique to the level of a fine art, many others, even in the professional and scholarly area, and certainly most trade-book publishers, have far from exploited the opportunities available to them through direct mail selling. Many books and series, particularly in the trade book field, would lend themselves ideally to this promotional approach if their publishers would only utilize it.

## LIBRARIES

Like retail outlets, libraries are a heterogeneous lot. There are public libraries, sponsored and supported by cities and towns, some of them organized into large systems with several branches. There are state, county, and regional libraries. There are federally sponsored libraries, notably the queen bee of all, the Library of Congress, but including also libraries attached to government departments and military installations. Educational libraries embrace those of colleges and universities, and of public and private elementary and high schools. And then there are "special" libraries: business, industrial, professional, music, art, and historical collections, many in the hands of learned and cultural societies.

Bowker maintains lists of these libraries classified by type and in some cases by the size of their book acquisition budgets. For example, of 8,783 public libraries in the United States, 952 have annual funds for purchasing books of $25,000 or more; 992 dispose of funds between $10,000 and $25,000; 1,048 command between $5,000 and $10,000; and 2,592 have resources between $1,000 and $5,000. It is immediately apparent that very few of these libraries were in a position to consider purchasing even the bulk of the 27,000 new titles published in 1972; the assurance with which authors and agents sometimes approach publishers, ready to guarantee a big core market for their titles ("every library will buy one, of course") has precious little foundation.

There are, furthermore, only 1,667 four-year college and university libraries, and of these only 976 command a book budget of more than $25,000, only 381 can purchase between $10,000 and $25,000, leaving 310 whose annual book acquisition amounts to less than $10,000! Bowker lists give no budget breakdown for 1,078 junior and two-year college libraries.

A bright spot in the picture is the existence of the 40,936 elementary, 17,455 public high school, and 9,264 junior high school libraries most of which came into being during the 1960s under the stimulus of large federal grants. Although the continuation of federal largesse in this area is in some doubt, the concept of the library as an integral part of the school and of the pedagogical process has been firmly established and its advantages have been demonstrated. Not only is this a step forward for education, it also is an important advance for the cause of books which children are now accustomed to using and enjoying on their own initiative at an earlier age.

Of 7,733 special libraries, 3,375 are technical and scientific, 2,393 are business, 860 are law, and 1,967 are medical libraries. Some collections house volumes in more than one of these categories.

Libraries of all kinds purchased an estimated $448 million in books during 1972, therefore representing some 14 percent of the total U.S. consumer market. As John Berry, editor of *Library Journal*, points out, however, libraries absorb a significantly larger percentage of books which are published in quantities under 5,000 copies; in fact, were it not for library consumption, most such books would go unpublished altogether. His point is borne out by the sale of, for example, university press titles, where the library market is over 36 percent, of professional books where it is over 21 percent, or even of trade books where it is over 20 percent.

Significantly a very large portion—apparently some 76 percent—of book sales to libraries are channeled through wholesalers and jobbers, which is understandable when one considers the acquisition problems libraries face. To place thousands of orders with individual publishers, process a multitude of small shipments, and pay myriads of small bills, adds significantly to administrative burdens. Since jobbers are able to simplify and consolidate these tasks their services are indeed welcome. Furthermore, there are certain record-keeping and bibliographic steps which jobbers offer to libraries as part of their contract: cataloging, supplying a checkout card in the book, marking a shelf number on the binding. Since jobbers give contract discounts in addition (usually 33 1/3 percent on trade books, 20 percent on short-discount titles), discounts which are larger than the 10 to 20 percent library discounts many publishers would allow, it is hardly surprising that libraries generally prefer to deal with wholesalers rather than with publishers directly.

The publishers' efforts in reaching libraries, by mailing catalogs and brochures, through personal sales calls, by attending library meetings and conventions, and by sending sample books for examination, are often aimed at obtaining orders through jobbers as much as at receiving them directly. In fact, many a publisher who relishes the task of processing a host of individual orders and shipments no more than the library does, is only too delighted to see the order he has solicited filled through the wholesaler.

The criteria libraries use in acquiring books are often quite discouraging, however. The largest public and academic collections, which have the potential of acquiring nearly every title published, often do so without eliminating the chaff from the wheat. Whether this practice is motivated by a desire to represent all available materials or results simply from unwillingness—or inability—to examine books, announcements, or reviews with care, the results are the same: glut. Often such a library will make arrangements with a jobber to supply practically all books published "on approval," giving the library the option to reject unwanted materials, an option rarely exercised.

Medium-sized and small libraries are forced to be selective by the very limitations of their budgets. Unfortunately, as John Berry notes sadly, the selectivity, particularly in public libraries, is often based on considerations other than quality. In nonfiction, for example, subject matter seems to count as much as competence; if the book treats an "interesting" topic it may be ordered whether it covers the subject adequately or not.

The desire to avoid controversy is often a motive for indiscriminate acquisition. The public library as a community-service institution is obligated to represent various viewpoints on controversial issues. Since one way of making sure that one has represented several viewpoints is by purchasing a broad range of books on a given subject, librarians often resort to this approach.

Fiction and children's books seem to fare better in public libraries than nonfiction when it comes to discriminating choices. In these areas the review media—*Library Journal, School Library Journal, Publishers Weekly,* Virginia Kirkus Service, and *Choice* and the *Booklist* (both published by the American Library Association), as well as general consumer review media play an important role and carry a good deal of weight. School libraries, also, appear to show better judgment in the selection of juveniles. Children's book publishers rely heavily on the sampling technique to expose librarians to their titles; sometimes as many as 500 copies of a book are sent to individuals and committees who make choices in public and school libraries. In some regions such purchases are now made on a systemwide or countywide basis and staff reviewers may even issue written reports for the benefit of their colleagues. Exhibits at library meetings also play an important role, as do the showrooms of jobbers where librarians can browse through the newest titles on display. A recent tendency to decentralize buying decisions and allow greater autonomy to individual librarians is creating logistic problems for publishers, however. It is becoming increasingly difficult to send samples to the growing number of people involved in the decision process and even more difficult for sales representatives to visit them.

Intelligent selectivity appears to be at work also in the medium-to-small academic library where the librarian relies on the faculty to make recommendations or is guided by reviews in scholarly journals (even though these may not appear for up to two years after the book is published). In some colleges arrangements are made allowing each academic department a share of the library budget, and money is spent at the discretion of the department chairman in consultation with his faculty.

The acquisitions problems librarians are experiencing are only a reflection of the more serious underlying difficulties which are besetting libraries these days and which can be simply summed up in one word: money. True, there are some difficulties in obtaining competent and qualified staff, and the policies of some library administrators are less than totally conducive to creating irresistible meccas for book lovers. But such problems pale beside the financial difficulties, such as threats of curtailed federal funding and rising costs. In some cases the cost of processing a new book can equal the price of the book itself, according to John Berry, and personnel expense represents more than half of the total budget of most libraries, while journals are absorbing an increasing portion of the shrinking acquisition dollar, at the expense of books. Now a movement sponsored by authors organizations hopes to exact royalties from libraries for book use by patrons—a practice current in Australia and some Scandinavian countries—which would further add to the already critical budget burden.

The cost problems could be eased in many instances through greater efficiency of operation, including the use of new automated techniques. Unfortunately vested interests often oppose such improvements: many people would lose their jobs and administrators would see their empires reduced if they were implemented. Commercial services, prepared to perform cataloging and other vital tasks at less than current internal cost, have often been unable to make inroads because of the resistance of the present library establishment.

But time has a way of catching up with reality, and there are signs that in many places the demands and interests of library patrons are changing the pattern. Libraries, according to Berry, have become more alert to their social and community responsibilities, and librarians are often finding themselves in the front battle lines for social change. In inner cities experiments with new techniques designed to benefit the user are revolutionizing traditional approaches. (The Langston Hughes branch of the New York Public Library in Queens is run by nonprofessionals, offers a wide selection of occupationally oriented material, and uses new devices, such as colored tapes instead of numbers, for subject identification.)

Many public libraries now offer audiovisual and other nonprint items for enjoyment by their patrons. Some are operating bookstores. Many are becoming important community social centers, even providing counseling for people who require orientation and help on routine living problems. In many places uncertainty by younger library professionals about their role is raising such basic questions as: what services should a library perform today, who is our constituency, what do we owe to the community?

In the academic world, too, key questions about the role of the library in the educational process and that of the librarian in the academic community are being asked. Unions which have organized large numbers of librarians in recent years are contributing their share to rejuvenating the profession. And as the librarian's image changes from the underpaid and uninvolved to the socially alert and economically competitive, the library, too, is undergoing a metamorphosis. One hopes that new purpose and new sophistication will lead not only to greater efficiency and improved service but also to increases in the quality and range of library holdings of books— still their most basic commodity.

## WHOLESALERS AND JOBBERS

### Wholesalers to Bookstores

Most industries faced with the complexity of product and the delivery problems characteristic of the book field have developed viable wholesaler networks to service their retail outlets. Strangely enough this has not been true in the book industry. While there were once adequate wholesale facilities—prior to World War II the American News Company, with branches in principal cities, as well as a number of independent companies, such as Baker & Taylor and A.C. McClurg, were active in serving retail stores—in postwar decades this facet of the industry declined. Now there is evidence, however, that current growth in bookselling is once again awakening wholesalers' interest in catering to bookstores.

Baker & Taylor, the nation's largest supplier of books to libraries, curtailed its bookstore business considerably during the postwar era. But in 1973 they announced that they would once again expand their bookstore service facilities. Ingram Book Co. of Nashville, Tennessee, created a good deal of attention, and gained a great many retail customers during the same year, by introducing effective automated systems for advising bookstores of titles available in Ingram's inventory, as well as apprising them of promotional appearances by authors, important book reviews, and lists of best sellers. A number of smaller firms which had provided wholesale services to booksellers in certain metropolitan regions all along were expanding their activities.

This was good news for publishers and bookstores alike. Rarely can a store manage to buy in advance a sufficiently large inventory of a successful new title to meet the entire demand; even more rarely can a publisher hope to ship all reorders for such a title promptly enough to keep all stores adequately supplied. The situation is aggravated when the bookstore is located at some distance from the publisher: it is not unusual for a bookseller in California to wait up to six weeks for a reorder of a bestseller published by a New York house.

If a good wholesaler in the region stocks such a title, however, and is efficient in serving his customers, stores can be more readily supplied in cases where the need for rapid service is critical. Wholesalers can also be helpful by stocking the most commonly ordered backlist titles of leading publishers—staples which a store hates to be out of and knows it will lose sales on unless it can obtain them on rapid reorder.

Needless to say, most wholesalers are not able to maintain an inventory of the nearly half million titles in print. They may therefore not be able to furnish immediately certain less popular titles on special order but would in turn have to order them from publishers. Still, they might be able to render an important service even here by "funneling" such special orders— consolidating orders to publishers on the one hand, and consolidating shipments and invoices to retailers on the other—thereby substantially simplifying the process for both their suppliers and customers and reducing their costs.

Theoretically wholesalers can show a profit as middlemen because publishers give them a favorable discount based on the large overall sales volume they generate, while retailers can accept a shorter discount from them because of the more rapid service they give and the lower transportation costs they charge. Because each adds to his sales volume, both retailer and publisher are ahead even if each deals on a less profitable basis with the wholesaler than they would directly with each other; a book sold at a slightly lower gross profit still adds more to the retailer's or publisher's income than a book not sold at all.

When the publisher gives the wholesaler the customary discount of 46 to 50 percent on fast-selling trade books, and the retailer is extended only a 33 1/3 percent discount by the wholesaler, the latter can probably show a profit provided his costs are under control. The matter is less certain where special orders are concerned. Many titles on special order are published at short discount and the wholesaler may therefore not be able to realize a sufficient margin to be able to handle them profitably. Nor may publishers be able to increase their discounts sufficiently to pay the wholesaler a living wage.

As the reentry of major wholesalers, such as Baker & Taylor, into the retail service field is a rather recent development it is not yet possible to measure its effectiveness in solving the industry's most crucial problem of delivering a wanted book to the customer who wants it. One hopes that wholesalers will be able to provide the badly needed solution. If not, the industry must find other ways to come to terms with this most critical issue.

In any case, even if its benefits are ultimately confined to the more rapid and efficient delivery of fast-selling trade books, the renewed interest of wholesalers in serving bookstores is a significant and most welcome development.

### Mass Market Wholesalers

Because mass market paperbacks and juveniles are sold not only through mass market outlets but also through bookstores, the wholesalers discussed above who now cater to booksellers are increasingly stocking such mass market titles and making them available to their customers. In doing so these wholesalers are applying their trade book policies, particularly their trade paperback policies, to such distribution.

When it comes to wholesaling mass market titles, however, the lion's share of the business is consummated by nearly 600 "independent" mass market wholesalers (traditionally called "independent" to distinguish them from branch outlets of national wholesale chains), whose primary business is the distribution of magazines. Publishers deal with them directly or through a national magazine distributor. Discounts extended to these wholesalers run from 46 to 55 percent depending on the line or the publisher; sometimes regular discounts are supplemented by incentive arrangements enabling the wholesaler to earn a better profit if he promotes and sells books more vigorously and successfully.

Some wholesalers are extraordinarily efficient and enterprising. Charles Levy Circulating Co. of Chicago, for example, not only serves outlets of all types in its metropolitan area, but a subsidiary, Computer Book Co., very ably operates leased book racks in national store chains such as K-Mart and J.C. Penny. There are wholesalers whose inventory is representative of what is best and most in demand in the field; they serve effectively newsstands, supermarkets, chain stores, drugstores, bookstores, and schools in their territories.

Significantly many of these wholesalers have opened affiliated retail outlets—among them some of the best-stocked and best-managed book-stores in the country—which carry not only magazines and mass market paperbacks but quality paperbacks and hardcover books as well. Some 500 such retail stores were in operation in 1973.

Many wholesalers employ expert field men who serve outlets from trucks that carry selective inventories and whose knowledge of books and of their customers leads them to maximize their merchandising opportunities. In other cases experts work within wholesalers' warehouses, carefully assembling shipments for their outlets on the basis of past sales records and returns. Whether the method employed is "book truck" or "prepack" (to use the industry's nomenclature), what makes a wholesaler effective is the expertise of his staff and his commitment to book distribution. Such a wholesaler can also be counted on to control his inventory with care, to reorder regularly titles that sell well, and to remove from sale promptly those that are not moving. When the publisher consults him in preparing allotments of new titles, he can be relied upon to make intelligent and discriminating judgments.

Not so in far too many other cases. Many wholesale agencies have no book-buying expertise nor any staff available that can serve outlets intelligently. Too often books are received at wholesalers' warehouses and shipped to outlets without understanding of their sales potential. Since more books are published than there is room for, this often means that even the best and most salable books are not given a chance; sometimes they are not even unpacked and are returned to the publisher "live" (i.e., in the original cartons, untouched). Publishers try to help matters by sending field representatives to the agencies to help sort out at least the titles with the biggest potential and make certain that they receive exposure. Special displays, dump bins (i.e., combination shipping cartons and display units), posters, streamers, special discounts, and other means are employed by publishers to take a title out of the ordinary and give it visibility within the maelstrom. The problem is—for how many titles can this be made to work? A dozen or two a month? In 1972, 2,200 titles were published, or nearly ten times as many as could reasonably be featured through special promotion.

The automatic shipping of new releases by publishers, which is standard practice, does not help, although one wonders what alternative publishers could employ in the case of agencies that lack book-buying expertise. In the hands of a responsible publisher the automatic allotment system—whereby the publisher or national distributor determines what titles and what quantities a wholesaler will receive without necessarily consulting that wholesaler—may even have occasional advantages. The publisher presumably knows more about a forthcoming title than his customers do. But in the hands of a publisher who does not hesitate to flood the market—no matter how destructive the practice may be for the field as a whole—just to capture a share of it, whether justified by his title's intrinsic salability or not, the system can become a dangerous weapon and invitation to chaos.

The worst of the problem is that a wholesaler who does not have a qualified book buyer on his staff has no argument or defense against the indiscriminate flooding of titles to which he is subjected month after month. If he is already inefficient in distributing books, the system will make him even more so and the efforts of publishers' field men, concentrated as they must be on a few extraordinary titles, will act as no more than a palliative. In the meantime publishers, authors, and the public continue to suffer.

This is a problem which the industry as a whole will sooner or later have to tackle on a cooperative basis. Certain wholesalers must be offered opportunities to learn more about book distribution and be given access to book-buying expertise. Independent central buying offices that wholesalers could make use of for a fee—somewhat like department store group buying offices—seem one possibility. In addition methods must be found to enable wholesalers to assess the potential of the outlets they serve and match that potential with available books.

Efficiency in buying and distributing mass paperbacks would make the wholesaler more independent of the publisher, would give him a greater voice in his own book distribution efforts, and would result in the far greater success of good titles in the marketplace. It would also result in the more decisive failure of unsalable titles and even, perhaps, in the elimination of some publishing imprints that are more opportunistic and less responsible than the rest and whose only chance for survival lies in the continuation of the present chaos. Anyone sincerely interested in the future of the book industry, particularly wholesalers who now so often stand no chance at all to make a decent profit on their book operations, would benefit greatly from this development, as would responsible publishers and authors.

### Library Jobbers

A sign of the continuing shifts in traditional patterns in the industry is the fact that it is possible to encounter the same cast of characters among wholesalers who serve retailers and among those who supply libraries and schools. We have already mentioned the reentry of Baker & Taylor into the bookstore service field; now we must note that several wholesalers who originally began as middlemen to bookstores have over the years broadened their activities to include schools and libraries as well. Bookazine Co. and

Dimondstein Book Co., both in the New York area, are examples of this trend.

The role of the library jobber is often more extensive than merely to supply books. What libraries require as much as or even more than books is service. So jobbers offer a great many services: cataloging, approval plans, out-of-print search, and above all the ordering and processing of books from publishers with all the correspondence, checking, and follow-up this entails. The library enjoys the simple life: one source, one invoice, only one supplier to complain to. The jobber must deal with hundreds of publishers on thousands of titles; just to identify titles and authors correctly and address orders to the proper publisher in each case can be a herculean job.

To cement their relationship with their library customers jobbers often arrange for exclusive contracts and as part of their terms offer an attractive discount—usually 33 1/3 percent on trade titles, somewhat less on short-discount materials. It has never been clear to me how such a discount can be justified. A library is, after all, a consumer and does not resell books. It certainly does not need such a discount in order to survive. No doubt the motivation for offering the discount originally, shortly after World War II, was to be competitive with publishers (who then and now offer 10 to 20 percent to libraries), with booksellers, many of whom at one time supplied libraries, and even more with other jobbers. In any case, I believe it was a serious mistake which has hurt the industry because it has curtailed some of its income without justification. Publishers aided and abetted the scheme by continuing to give wholesalers, who were then abandoning their retail customers for the library business, the same large discounts which they had extended to them as middlemen reselling to bookstores. Without this permissiveness by publishers, wholesalers could never have offered the special contract terms to libraries.

Now that libraries are in bad budget straits seems hardly the time to suggest a change in the discount jobbers should extend to their institutional customers. However, the structure remains a strange anomaly in the American book distribution system. One of its most unfortunate consequences has been that it has put bookstores, which used to be the principal book source for many libraries, out of the business of supplying institutions, thus making it even more difficult for many good bookstores to survive.

Among library jobbers are those who work more closely with academic libraries, such as Richard Abel & Co., and others who are more extensively involved with public libraries and schools, such as Bro-Dart and Campbell & Hall. A recent development of some interest is that the increasing demand by schools for paperbacks has begun to sway some jobbers from their once exclusively hard-cover positions, so that even Baker & Taylor, the largest wholesaler of them all, announced during 1973 that they were expanding their inventory to include mass market paperbacks. Similarly,

Baker & Taylor and Bro-Dart indicated their entry into the audiovisual materials field, an area in which all their school and library customers have an avid interest, and which until they began their services had been generally left to jobbers and wholesalers who specialize exclusively in audiovisual materials.

Book wholesalers and jobbers serving libraries, schools, and bookstores are listed in *Literary Market Place*. Information regarding independent magazine wholesalers is available from the Council for Periodical Distributors Associations, 488 Madison Avenue, New York, N.Y. 10022.

## ELEMENTARY AND SECONDARY SCHOOLS

Since we have already discussed marketing practices relating to school libraries, the present observations on the schools as publishers' markets will be confined to their acquisition of materials for classroom use. Here we will remember that 23 states currently engage in some form of state adoption whereby districts are limited in their choice of titles to those approved by a state board. Such adoptions are usually made for a period of five years after which new and formerly adopted materials are again submitted and a new adoption list is prepared.

Because state adoptions mean a great deal to school publishers—even though the system is generally on the wane and the trend is toward increasing autonomy by local districts—much title and series planning revolves around the five-year adoption cycle. Often when a major state adoption is up for consideration publishers will schedule the development of a new title or series to coincide with it. This means that they must have the materials ready for demonstration purposes the preceding fall. States usually make available a list of official evaluators, and publishers then arrange for presentations of their product which may include appearances by authors and by "consultants" (i.e., teachers retained by the publisher to demonstrate the materials).

A publisher whose title is selected for adoption is thereby granted a hunting license to seek out local districts and persuade them that of the four or five competitive titles chosen by the state his is the most meritorious. As adoption lists are usually released by the first of the year, this gives the publisher some three months (January to March) to make local presentations. Salesmen contact superintendents and advisory committees in the districts, leave samples of books behind them, and make appointments for formal presentations to be made before school authorities and/or their advisors. The distribution of free sample copies is one of the publisher's most important promotional devices; it is not unusual for a publisher to give away 20,000 copies of an important title during a single year.

The sales presentations themselves, in which consultants usually participate if the materials are on the elementary level, while normally the salesmen alone will conduct them if secondary level items are under consideration, will emphasize the pedagogical features of the titles submitted and may offer data on field test results. In addressing teachers, emphasis is usually placed on the ease with which the materials may be used in the classroom; when approaching superintendents and school boards, validation is made much of and accountability is stressed.

Since both salesmen and consultants are for the most part former teachers who speak the language of the schools and are thoroughly familiar with the problems and attitudes in vogue, the presentations usually assume an insider's, colleague-to-colleague air.

The role of salesmen, and even more that of consultants, does not stop with this presentation. If the district decides to select the product, particularly if it is on the elementary level, consultants will return to demonstrate to teachers how the product should be used. In fact in many districts such demonstrations are required and without them a purchase contract would not be awarded to the publisher.

In nonadoption states the technique of selling to local districts is much the same except that publishers do not have the advantage (or suffer from the impediment) of a special state adoption list. The field is totally open and the publisher must make his way with sample copies and persuasive demonstrations. The way may have been paved for him by favorable advance comment on a title within the profession, by reviews in pedagogical journals, or by evaluation services. The reputation of authors will have an impact, as will friendships with superintendents and evaluators cultivated over many years by salesmen and consultants.

Publishers do some advertising in magazines for educators but this does not produce massive results; rather it serves to alert prospective buyers to the existence of a product thus preparing the way for other sales efforts. The same is true of mailings to teachers and exhibits at teachers' meetings.

As school publisher Charles W. Pepper observes, from the publisher's standpoint district-level selling and selection is the most advantageous. State adoptions, despite the bonanza they create for a few winners, leave nothing for the losers; the hit-or-miss character of the adoption system tends to concentrate success or failure too much and offers too little opportunity to the average title or publisher. On the other hand, the current tendency in some areas to localize the selection process even below the district level and to allow every teacher to select materials for his or her classroom, is equally hazardous for the publisher because it makes the cost of marketing his product prohibitive. Who can afford to furnish a sample book to every teacher or to invest in a personal sales call on every classroom?

According to estimates by the U.S. Office of Education, there were 2,318,000 elementary and secondary classroom teachers in the United States in 1972. The number of schools, last reported for 1971, was 64,020 public elementary, 23,572 public high, and 1,780 combined public elementary and secondary schools, organized into 17,995 school districts in the fifty states and the District of Columbia. In addition there were 14,372 private elementary and 3,770 private secondary schools. It takes little imagination to conclude that selling to every teacher would be beyond the realm of possibility even if publishers were much larger and much wealthier than they really are. Even to cover all schools individually would be a staggering task. Ultimately the district-marketing approach is the most economical and most efficient because it is the one in which the taxpayer is least likely to have to pay excessive prices for materials just to cover their abnormally high cost of selection.

Whether they quote on a state or district level, publishers must guarantee firm prices on their products for the life of the purchase contract. Nominal discounts are given, but everyone realizes that for practical purposes the price of the product is the price at which it is billed to the purchasing school. Transportation is usually paid by the purchaser, although publishers have sometimes agreed to prepay shipping costs in exchange for reduced discounts.

In some states publishers are required to ship books to designated official depositories, usually private firms operating under state contract charged with housing adopted materials so that schools can readily draw on them as they are needed. Arrangements by publishers with such depositories usually involve a consignment of inventory (i.e., placing the stock in the depository, with books paid for only when actually sold) and a charge by the depository for the warehousing and shipping services provided.

## COLLEGES AND UNIVERSITIES

The adoption process in higher education shares some characteristics of the elhi-level procedures but there are substantial differences as well. On the college level, marketing efforts are also directed at the faculty: salesmen call on department heads, professors, and instructors. In some cases, particularly those involving basic freshman and sophomore courses, books may be selected by a departmental committee. In most other instances, however, the instructor teaching the course decides what materials he will use. In fact, the general trend is toward increasing autonomy by individual teachers with diminishing interference from the departmental administration.

Instructors or departments very rarely do the purchasing, but leave the chore to the institutionally or privately owned bookstores serving the campus. Ideally professors should make their choices of books several months in advance, for example by April for the following fall term. Local bookstores are then notified of the titles that will be required or recommended, along with estimates of the number of students expected to enroll in the course. It is then up to the stores to acquire sufficient stock by ordering from publishers or buying back used books from students.

It is a good system in theory. Unfortunately too many things can go wrong with it in practice. To begin with instructors and departmental committees often make up their minds late. Despite constant urgings by bookstores to advise them of their choices early, professors have been known to delay determining their requirements even until after their courses have begun. If the store does not then produce the needed books almost overnight, the professors are often peeved. Frequently books are adopted that are out-of-print, that are published abroad and it takes months to import, or that are published by obscure publishers which are difficult to locate and even more difficult to deal with.

Additional problems are created because professors are often very inaccurate in estimating enrollment in their classes. Predictions that scores of students may take a course may turn out to be only 60 or 40 percent correct. If the store has ordered stock to fill the initial prediction, it will be forced to return a large quantity of books to the publisher at considerable cost and inconvenience. These difficulties are enhanced by the tendency of many students not to buy the books their instructors adopt. Instead they will share, borrow, or steal copies or consult them in the library—if they can find them there. Because the trend is toward the use of ever greater numbers and a greater diversity of books, the combination of professorial tardiness, inaccuracy in prediction, and the unreliability of students in purchasing has placed a staggering burden on college bookstores and publishers. In 1972 returns in many cases represented more than 20 percent of books shipped, a startling total when one considers that the college-textbook market is supposedly governed by faculty decision and in theory at least should not be subject to impulse or speculation.

Publishers and bookstores have joined in efforts to orient the faculty toward greater promptness and accuracy. There are indications that these efforts are bearing fruit. What can be done to persuade students to buy the required books is less clear and no good solution appears to be in sight. Many students take a rather hostile attitude toward bookstores, apparently regarding them as suitable targets for mischief. Some college stores now report pilferage rates in excess of 3 percent of sales despite often elaborate security measures. It would be unfair to generalize and suggest that today's college students are less honorable than their predecessors; yet it is alarming that a large portion of today's student body seems to have developed remarkably relaxed standards regarding the propriety of "ripping off" college stores.

Despite all, the stores attempt to deal effectively with their many problems and many have developed good techniques for acquiring and marketing course materials. Their trade association, the National Association of College Stores (NACS), has played a significant role in making its members more efficient. For example, when it became apparent some years ago that paperbacks would be used increasingly in course work, NACS founded a wholesale enterprise that makes available to its members most of the steadily demanded trade and college paperbacks. NACSCORP, as this operation is known, stocks its inventory in a warehouse adjoining the Association's new headquarters building in Oberlin, Ohio.

College stores have learned to capitalize on the demand for used books. Why let students themselves do all the profitable trading? Through NACS, lists of available used books are circulated among the stores, enabling them to buy surplus stock from each other. There are also a number of wholesalers in the field who purchase surplus used books from stores or, through the stores' facilities, directly from students, and who conduct a brisk and profitable trade with retailers. The frequent changes in text adoptions, whereby even some of the big basic course textbooks may be dropped after a year or a semester (or trimester or quarter where schools are on shorter cycles), have made the wholesale and intraretailer exchanges of used books a sizable business.

For many years the college store field consisted largely of two types of operations: the institutionally owned store, often functioning at a loss and subsidized by its owner, and the privately owned and usually profitable store. Recently a new entity has been added: the leased store operated by a private entrepreneur for the college, involving financial arrangements satisfactory to the institution and designed to be profitable for the operator. Many of the leased operations are parts of chains which also conduct a lively used book business; some of them, in fact, are affiliated with the wholesalers of used books as mentioned above.

Publishers, always wary of a strong used book market, are concerned about this development. They are apprehensive about the economic power which is being concentrated in the chains and which they fear will become dominant in the field if the present trend continues. Used books have, however, always been part of the college textbook scene. By the very nature of things demand for them always exceeds supply (many students do not sell their books, and some books simply wear out after passing through two or more owners). Used books are apparently a necessary evil, an irradicable nuisance from the publisher's point of view. The growth and prosperity of the leasing chains, furthermore, may actually turn out to be a boon for the industry. By bringing effective merchandising and management techniques into the picture in many places (where such expertise may previously have been lacking), they may be contributing to the long-term health of the college book field.

Traditionally textbook publishers have extended a 20 percent discount to college stores. The stores complain that they are unable to survive on this discount. They emphasize that their interest in handling used books is stimulated by their ability to show a much better profit on them. Stores usually buy books from students at 50 percent of list price and sell them at 75 percent, thus giving them a substantially larger dollar yield on the transaction and on their investment than can be obtained from the sale of new books. Recently some publishers have increased their textbook discount to 25 percent in exchange for a more limited return privilege. Given the current economics of the college textbook market, with publishers' costs on the rise and shrinking per title sales figures, it is doubtful that publishers will be prepared to make substantial concessions on discount. The often suggested solution—that publishers should simply raise prices—is hardly realistic at a time when many students are already refusing to purchase adopted titles.

The return privilege itself has been another area of controversy between store and publisher. Many publishers limit the portion of the store's purchase that may be returned, whereupon bookstores complain that this places the full burden on them when professors guess wrong and students fail to buy adopted materials. Publishers reply that they do not want to carry the full burden either, that accepting already large portions of unsold goods is punishment enough. Certainly neither store nor publisher can afford to continue absorbing the kind of punishment that has been meted out to them in recent years. There really should be ways that require the responsible institution or its faculty to absorb at least the excess burden that results from their actions and decisions.

One problem seems to be that many faculty members feel almost as hostile as some students do about bookstores and publishers. An example of this attitude is found in the demands certain faculty make on publishers for free books. Traditionally publishers have supplied free copies to professors for their examination in order to facilitate their decision making. When a book is adopted the publisher is prepared to furnish a free "desk copy," i.e., a copy to the teacher of the course (unless he has already received a free examination copy), or even several such copies if the course is large enough and is taught in several sections. Publishers usually stipulate that an adoption must result in an order for at least ten copies before they can justify supplying a desk copy. Unfortunately some college instructors apparently feel that the publisher should accommodate them with an almost unlimited number of free books, and they are decidedly unsympathetic when the publisher maintains that free books are a promotional expenditure that must be kept within bounds.

Another area where the publisher appears to be regarded as fair game by some faculty is unauthorized copying. Although the copyright law is clear and publishers have gone on record often that they regard the indiscriminate photocopying of their materials to be illegal, many college instructors continue to duplicate whole chapters and sections from books, distributing copies to students, sometimes even selling them through bookstores or in the classroom. So flagrant has this practice apparently become that Professor Robin Higham of Kansas State University felt compelled to write to *Publishers Weekly* (January 24, 1972) suggesting that publishers should sue some of his offending colleagues since only making examples of them was likely to stop the practice. Needless to say, publishers anxious to maintain good relations with the people who adopt their books have hesitated to follow this recommendation.

Sometimes, however, faculty compete with publishers quite legally by issuing proprietary textbooks, i.e., volumes specially prepared for use in their own classrooms. This interesting and growing phenomenon permits the teacher to construct his course materials entirely to his liking without having to depend on the approach of another man's textbook. A number of firms now exist who will publish such textbooks for instructors cheaply enough so that the price remains within the reach of students yet allows a modest income to the author. Such tailor-made texts are usually sold through the local bookstore. They add another challenge to the many problems currently facing college publishers.

Yet all participants in the process—the faculty, bookstore, publisher, and student—share enough common interests so that one hopes that marketing conditions in the field will soon improve. Most professors and students realize even now that bookstores and publishers basically want to serve them well and, granting a few unscrupulous exceptions, honorably. Bookstores and publishers themselves have engaged in fruitful dialogue and cooperative efforts thereby learning better to appreciate each other's needs and problems.

## REVIEWS AND PUBLICITY

One way to define the term "publicity" as commonly used in book publishing is as free advertising. Of course it is not entirely free. To obtain review coverage one must distribute review copies to the media, and to expose an author on television may involve a good deal of expensive time and effort on the part of a staff or a free-lance public relations expert. But the exposure in newspapers, magazines, or on the air is not itself paid for.

Although publishers of all descriptions seek to obtain review coverage of their titles, the more glamorous public relations efforts that send an author on tour or get him on a "Today" or "Tonight" show are undertaken by consumer-oriented trade and mass market paperback houses. In such houses there is usually a publicity manager who assumes responsibility for the whole free advertising area, sends out press releases, visits reviewers, arranges for the distribution of review copies, and attempts to gain public exposure for personable, photogenic, and newsworthy authors.

It's an uphill fight. Once again the sheer volume of titles and authors and the limited available news, review, and air space make for a fiercely competitive situation, one that is a source of constant frustration to publishers and authors. To begin with, there is only a very small number of regular consumer book review media. The *New York Times Book Review*, the *New York Review of Books*, and to some extent *Saturday Review World*, are now the only significant national publications in the field. While some magazines like *Time, Newsweek, Harpers*, and the *Atlantic Monthly* as well as the so-called journals of opinion (such as the *Nation, New Republic, Commentary, Commonweal*, and *National Review*) carry book reviews, all such media in combination cannot begin to treat even a fraction of newly published titles. The Sunday supplement *New York Times Book Review*, without question the leading medium in the field, can give prime attention to, perhaps, thirty titles a week and brief reviews to, possibly, another twenty. With fifty-two issues a year this means that at the very most some 2,600 titles can be noticed. This is not an unimpressive record but it appears slight considering that more than ten times that many original new titles are published each year. Although these releases include text and technical titles inappropriate for review in such a medium, it is probably fair to state that at best some 20 percent of all genuinely eligible items find their way into the *Book Review*'s pages.

There is, of course, some daily review coverage of books in the *New York Times*, just as there is in a number of other important newspapers. (A list of these media appears in *Literary Market Place*.) The *Times* has sometimes carried two reviews a day, so that in a year's time perhaps 500 titles or so are covered. For the most part these duplicate the attention given to these titles elsewhere, in the Sunday *Review* section and in other media, so they fail to increase the number of books that receive attention.

What is most discouraging about this situation is that it is growing worse rather than better. Until late in 1973 another weekly book review medium, *Book World*, existed as a separate supplement to the Sunday *Washington Post*. It was finally abandoned after floating in red ink for years. (Surprisingly, publishers failed to support it sufficiently with advertising.) And although there is every indication that American consumers read and buy more books each year, the news media have shown little awareness of this growing interest by their readers. Mourning the demise of *Book World* in a column in the *New York Times Book Review* of November 18, 1973, Richard Kluger, who at one time had edited its predecessor, *Book Week*, wrote:

One wonders, finally, why the press persists in regarding books as the limpest of watercress on its daily menu. Books are news, often decidedly more so than the toxic gruel dished out by flacks and advance men. Books are bearers of ideas, sometimes profound ones, if anybody would take the time and trouble to digest them, and the space to report them. Thus the ideas in John Kenneth Galbraith's latest book on the future imperatives of our economy were almost nowhere treated as the mainstream news they were. Perhaps a dozen such books a month are published, moreover, that scrutinize a major social problem with far more care and insight than the press itself, forever jostled by the deadline, can manage. When will newsmen recognize that books are not only good copy but also, at their best, the ultimate embodiment of their own craft?

The situation is slightly better in the many specialized media which review books in specific consumer and professional interest fields. Here at least there is more extensive, though far from complete, coverage. Unfortunately another, serious difficulty afflicts reviews in many professional and scholarly journals: delays of sometimes a year or more. Again one suspects that the sheer volume of new material is one cause of such delays: journals naturally attempt to choose the best people in their fields to write reviews, people usually spoken for for months on end because of the flood of reviewable titles—totally aside from the many other commitments such prominent authorities usually have. Other factors creating delays result from the specialized publications' budget limitations and the fact that their editors are usually volunteers who take on such chores in addition to too many other duties.

Most review media, until recently at least, displayed a reluctance to review paperbound books. Considering the importance of many titles published exclusively in paperbound form and the fact that the buying public is taking increasingly to the paperback format, this large-scale indifference to the merits of paperbacks has been, to say the least, astounding. It is apparently diminishing, as the *New York Times Book Review* has begun to give coverage to at least some outstanding paperback reprints and a few originals. This is progress—but it is still a long way from the ideal when each book would be selected for review on the merits of its content rather than on the incidental features of its manufacture.

Even when books are reviewed, however, publishers and authors are often frustrated by the nature of the reviews themselves. Criticism is an extremely difficult and challenging art—and in an age in which mediocrity is often widespread one has every sympathy for the reviewer who, while meaning to be constructive, finds himself put off by the inadequacies of the work itself. But as my father, the art critic Wilhelm Dessauer was wont to point out, the ultimate objective of criticism must be to enhance appreciation. This means that the critic should be motivated by a desire to serve the interests of both the work and its audience. He will therefore shy away from exploiting the occasion for narrow personal advantage: to demonstrate, for example, how he would have written the book or to air his own views of the subject which the author has treated. In its extreme form the egocentric review becomes a long essay in which the reviewer does his "own thing," using the author's work at best as a jumping off point, at worst as a foil. This certainly does little to enhance appreciation or to serve the cause of books.

Some of the large consumer review media use academic critics on an extensive scale. Academic critics, of course, vary greatly one to the next; some are extremely lively, dedicated to doing justice to the work under review, fair, generous, and determined to keep self-interest out of their assessment. Too often, however, academic reviewers become entangled in scholarly controversies and personal disagreements, and some seem unable to resist the temptation to grind their own axes. Too often, therefore, the book suffers and the cause of books generally is let down. In professional and scholarly media some controversy, one supposes, is essential to the critical process; after all, such reviews attempt not only to enhance appreciation but also to evaluate books as contributions to their scholarly or professional disciplines. Even here, however, emphasis should be on the book and on what its author has to say rather than on the critic and his viewpoint.

When it comes to literary criticism—the reviewing of new fiction—one prays for the day when authors will be discussed not by comparing them with every other writer since Dostoevsky but in the light of their own individuality, unique talent, and ability. There is a recognizable mannerism in much of the reviewing of fiction: an eager search for symbolism, much psychoanalytic interpretation of characters, and the discovery of a thousand similarities to other books and writers. The critic's language appears to make up in exotic coinage and tortured construction what it lacks in clarity and depth. So the reader does not receive what the price of admission entitles him to: a straightforward, to-the-point evaluation of the novel. Instead what he often gets is a display of verbal and intellectual pyrotechnics, a sort of doctoral dissertation exhibition of critical technique quite derivative and lacking substance. Will not such low quality reviewing encourage low quality writing?

Some of the best general criticism today, it seems to me, comes from professional critics: from the people who conduct the daily book pages in the *New York Times, Chicago Tribune, Los Angeles Times, Providence Journal, Boston Globe, St. Louis Post-Dispatch, Kansas City Star,* and *Milwaukee Journal,* among others. Reader-oriented and committed to the cause of books, these reviews, though often and deservedly very critical, make a genuine contribution to our evolving literary culture. If the media fail to review all eligible titles this is certainly not entirely their fault. Much of the responsibility must fall on overproducing publishers who have clogged the review channels as much as they have the channels of distribution.

## ADVERTISING AND PROMOTION

When authors of trade books air their grievances against publishers they usually complain about insufficient advertising. That trade publishers often fail to support a publication with sufficient promotion cannot be denied. But in most cases the lack of promotion is a symptom rather than a cause among complex factors that result in a title's failure in the market.

Trade publishers almost invariably engage in certain standard efforts on behalf of a book: they include it in their seasonal catalogs and in their "trade list" (i.e., a complete catalog of their publications in print which is distributed separately as well as bound into a massive compendium of such catalogs, the *Publishers Trade List Annual*, published by Bowker); they distribute some 200 to 500 review copies to general and specialized media; and they include the title in their announcement ads to libraries and booksellers appearing in special seasonal issues of *Publishers Weekly*, *Library Journal*, and other trade publications.

Books with major potential receive, in addition, advertising exposure in the national review media (notably the *New York Times Book Review* and the *New York Review of Books*) and in some major newspapers, magazines, and journals of opinion. These advertising efforts are intended to support the retail market, to alert the public to the existence and merits of a book, and to send interested customers to their bookstores inquiring for it. This approach works well if the book is available in the stores. If it is not, the effort is largely wasted. In rare cases the customer inquiries will result in enough special orders from bookstores to offset the cost of advertising, and in even rarer cases the demand may become sufficiently great to convince some stores that they should stock the book in question. In general, however, national advertising is productive only in the case of those few hundred titles each year which are bought in substantial quantities and featured and promoted by retailers.

Somewhat the same situation pertains with regard to the cooperative advertising publishers arrange with booksellers. Here the publisher contributes a major portion of the advertising cost (usually 75 percent) in return for which his title is promoted in local newspapers (taking advantage of the contract rate the bookseller usually enjoys because of his volume of advertising in the local paper). To justify such an insertion, however, both publisher and bookseller must be able to anticipate fairly wide sales of the title in question; in other words such advertising is again likely to be limited to major books which the bookseller has stocked in quantity.

Even then advertising cannot guarantee that a book will sell. Nor can a book's success be ensured by a favorable review or a personal appearance by the author on a national TV show. The book must have that mysterious appeal, that intrinsic fascination which makes readers respond; all the enthusiasm of publishers, booksellers, reviewers, and talk-show hosts will not necessarily make it go. There are many cases on record where such enthusiasm turned out to be largely fruitless. Of course enthusiastic reviews, TV appearances, and promotion by publishers and booksellers will help sell a title if it has the ingredients to which the public is ready to respond. As advertising men have been saying for decades: advertising will make a good product sell better; it cannot turn an unsalable product into a success.

Given the fact that most books are not adequately represented in bookstores and cannot be expected to sell in sufficient quantity to warrant the expense of national or cooperative advertising, it is hardly surprising that most books are simply not advertised to any great extent. This is less a sign of the publisher's unwillingness to support his book or of his lack of responsibility toward his author than it is an indication of the failures of the entire book distribution system to which we have repeatedly referred. Advertising is to total distribution what grease and oil are to an engine: necessary lubricants which will make the engine function more smoothly and successfully. If the engine lacks power, is antiquated, and in bad need of overhauling, pumping more oil into it or greasing it more will do little to improve its performance.

Of course advertising is a key tool of publishers who resort to direct selling; direct mail or coupon ads in popular or specialized media are ways of obtaining a consumer's order without relying on retailers. Sometimes such advertising can benefit even retailers, however, by sending them customers who prefer to obtain the book locally rather than order it from the publisher. At times publishers even imprint circulars for retailers who have good mailing lists or who specialize in mail order, thereby enlisting their partnership in the direct marketing effort. And, of course, there are many consumers who are far removed from any book outlet or whose local bookstore is a best-seller and cookbook haven where most books are simply unavailable. Direct marketing by the publisher or by an enterprising book club or mail order house may then be the only means of bringing books to that consumer.

Direct advertising to specialized audiences is particularly easy to justify, and specialized consumer books and professional and scholarly titles are usually promoted by mail or through ads in disciplinary publications. Costs of such efforts are proportionately lower and response higher, thereby creating a more favorable environment for the effort than exists in the general consumer field. Also, the retail exposure of specialized books is so limited that direct marketing by the publisher becomes almost a necessity.

In addition to space advertising and direct mail, publishers' promotional efforts include furnishing posters, display materials, and special racks (favored especially by trade and mass market paperback publishers); exhibits at meetings of booksellers, librarians, and professional and scholarly associations; and consumer book fairs (usually managed by booksellers with help from publishers). The industry as a whole, through such organizations as the National Book Committee which annually sponsors Library Book Week and the National Book Awards, engages in some promotional efforts on behalf of books and reading, as do the various trade associations, the AAP, ABA, and NACS, individually. Perhaps such general efforts, particularly those directed to the young, will be the most productive of all.

## INTERNATIONAL MARKETS

There are a number of ways in which American publishers place their books on foreign markets: they export copies of American editions to booksellers and libraries abroad; they arrange for the sale of entire editions to foreign publishers; they distribute their books in foreign countries through their own subsidiary companies; and they sell translation and/or publication rights of their titles to publishers in other lands. Since the marketing of rights, including those placed abroad, is discussed in the next section, we shall confine ourselves here to reviewing the sale of American *books* in foreign countries.

By far the most common arrangement involves the export of copies of American titles to foreign customers, be they individuals, booksellers, or libraries. Most publishers employ foreign sales representatives, usually American firms such as Feffer & Simons, a subsidiary of Doubleday, or Henry M. Snyder & Co. These firms engage sales travelers who call on bookstores, wholesalers, and libraries abroad, soliciting orders for the most salable titles. They also act as clearinghouses for special orders placed by dealers and institutions. Among the services export agents provide are credit checks on foreign customers, or even the assumption of all credit risks for an extra commission, a most important consideration since debts from foreign sources are very difficult to collect. They also keep their publisher clients advised on currency problems, another important consideration since certain Asian and African countries are periodically short of dollars, and export to them must at times be severely restricted or credit extended for unusually long periods.

For the most part the orders thus obtained are shipped by the American publisher from his domestic warehouse. However, the foreign representative usually has warehousing facilities in key locations abroad, and some publishers will stock some of their titles for immediate delivery at the foreign locations.

There are some striking differences in the level of export sales for different types of books. According to my estimates for 1972, only 3.5 percent of adult trade hardbound and 5.1 percent of adult trade paperbound total sales were exported, while 20.0 percent of professional and 14.1 percent of university press sales were shipped abroad. College text exports represented 9.8 percent of total sales, elhi text exports 9.0 percent, and mass market paperback exports 9.8 percent. It is not surprising therefore that among publishers operating their own facilities abroad are principally textbook, professional, and scholarly imprints. These facilities are usually incorporated in the foreign countries, staffed by indigenous personnel, and they operate as local publishers. While some import copies from the parent company in the United States, others manufacture editions locally, often translated into languages of that country, or with text adaptations that make them more marketable in their own area.

American publishers are well advised to institute such subsidiaries abroad—although, as Kenneth T. Hurst, Vice President and General Manager of Prentice-Hall International, points out, only substantial sales and a sizable program can justify such a move—for the nature of overseas interest in American text and professional publications is changing. Until recently according to Hurst and to Leo Albert, Prentice-Hall International's President, the unique quality of such books originating in America made them superior to most others emanating from other countries and therefore gave American publishers a significant dominance in the field. However, of late Japanese, Scandinavian, and other European publishers have begun to develop publishing programs in the sciences, technology, and business which not only rival U.S. books successfully, but which are more appealing to local audiences because of their indigenous orientation and focus. By developing similar publishing programs locally, American publishers can maintain positions, if not of leadership at least of competitiveness, in the world market. (Furthermore, to improve U.S. balance of payments, the government is encouraging American publishers in their foreign ventures.)

Even publishers who do not operate their own foreign companies, however, often find that titles they originate will have a sufficiently strong appeal abroad to justify indigenous publication. They may then make arrangements with a foreign publisher for the exportation of an entire edition, either in sheets to be bound abroad or of fully bound and jacketed copies. Not infrequently, in particular where expensive art books are involved, publishers from several countries will collaborate, each planning an edition for his own market with a text in his own language. Joint editions will then be manufactured, in whole or in part, in an area of the world where quality and price prove to be most advantageous for the entire venture.

International publishing is not without its hazards. In addition to credit risks and currency problems, publishers have had to deal with piracy, and with demands by underdeveloped countries for total freedom in reproducing copyrighted books. As the United States is a signatory to the Universal Copyright Convention (administered by UNESCO), and as American books with foreign sales potential are usually copyrighted simultaneously in Canada or another signatory to the Berne convention (which offers somewhat greater protection than does the Universal Copyright Convention but to which the United States has never been a signatory), American books are protected by international agreement in most countries of the world including, since 1973, the Soviet Union. Furthermore, an agreement concluded in Paris in 1971 is designed to offer maximum opportunity to developing countries for acquiring rights to books published in developed nations without, however, destroying the protection of international copyright.

Developed nations, including the United States, are aware that in the long run any contribution to the educational development of underdeveloped countries is bound to create new readers and therefore benefit publishers wherever they may be. In consequence the Paris agreement has warm support from U.S. publishers. What is more difficult to deal with is outright piracy: the unlicensed reproduction of American books by foreign publishers. Generally, the governments of the countries where such piracy has occurred have cooperated with the U.S. State Department, acting on behalf of American publishers, in bringing such offenders into line. Even Taiwan, which for a time harbored some of the worst culprits publishing and circulating pirated editions nearly unhindered in Asian markets, has now almost entirely suppressed this practice on its shores.

In addition to publishers, there are a number of wholesalers engaged in significant book export from the United States. Richard Abel & Co., with warehousing facilities in England and Holland, as well as Baker & Taylor, are among the most active in this area, as are a number of smaller firms which are shipping books to military installations, government operated schools, and Information Libraries abroad, under government contracts.

## MARKETING RIGHTS

Trade publishers in particular have such a great stake in the sale of subsidiary rights that the responsibility for handling such sales is usually placed in the hands of a skilled and experienced person or staff. Book clubs, reprint publishers, magazines, and other media that might use an entire work or part of it are approached, usually at very early stages of a book's production, to explore the extent of their interest. Galley proofs are a common means of exposing a project to a prospect.

Where book clubs are concerned, arrangements on major titles are usually made with the larger clubs on an exclusive basis: only one club may distribute the book to its members. Where smaller clubs and books of lesser drawing power are involved, the title may well be sold to more than one club. This is particularly true of titles that clubs acquire for use in introductory offers or as premium or bonus books to reward faithful members. Clubs have been known to use classics and reference works for such purposes which have been in print for years and where exclusivity would be meaningless.

When negotiating with reprint publishers, of both quality and mass market paperbacks, discussions are often initiated when a manuscript is first accepted or when a project is placed under contract. Like authors' agents, publishers may hold auctions on major titles inviting several paperback houses to submit simultaneous bids. Or joint publication might be arranged, under which originating and reprint publisher assume part of the responsibility for author's advance, promotional, printing, and other publishing expenses and also share income in proportion.

Foreign and translation rights are sometimes handled by special agents retained by the publisher to represent him in a foreign country (assuming, of course, that such rights have not been reserved to the author, as TV and film rights now usually are, and will therefore be disposed of by the author or his agent). There is also a great deal of visiting going on, with foreign publishers coming to this country and American publishers going abroad to discuss and conclude arrangements. Here, too, advance copies of manuscripts or proofs may serve as vehicles for examination, with foreign publishers requesting exclusive option for a limited time. Top items may well be subject to auction just as they are for domestic reprint. There is also a great international publishing meeting, the Frankfurt Book Fair, held each October in Frankfurt am Main, West Germany, where publishers do a great deal of buying and selling of international rights.

Serialization and excerpts by newspapers and magazines may involve use of the material before publication (first serialization) or after publication (second serialization). Both are encouraged not only because of the income they may yield but because of the valuable publicity for the book such use by mass media usually represents.

Finally, publishers derive a small but steady income on their own behalf and that of their authors through the granting of permission for the use of incidental passages or sections from their books, usually in other books. Collections of readings for college and secondary text use, anthologies for popular consumption, works of scholarship or literature utilizing extensive quotations, are typical of the projects to which such permissions are granted for a fee. Short quotations, exempted from copyright protection under the doctrine of fair use, are not usually charged for.

## SPECIAL SALES AND REMAINDERS

The term "special sales" covers transactions outside the publisher's usual channels, such as premium sales to industry. Enterprising publishers have found that handsome income awaits the house that has the imagination to promote its books off the beaten path. One need think only of road atlases imprinted for motel chains, for example, or various books on sports which are offered as giveaways on TV, to recognize the popularity and volume of distribution that is often enjoyed by such arrangements.

Remainders are overstock that has ceased to sell at full price and is therefore disposed of far below its usual cost. Some publishers run their own remainder sales by making special offers to dealers, or to consumers by mail. There are also wholesalers of remainders who buy overstock in bulk, disposing of it in a variety of ways, such as through one-priced assortments marketed by department and discount stores, through mail order catalogs imprinted for dealers, and through promotional sale ads run by department stores and bookstores. Some books do so well as remainders that the wholesaler will reprint them after the remainder stock is exhausted, and entire hard-cover reprint series have been developed to take advantage of this phenomenon. What makes such books especially attractive is the comparative price ("published at $25.00—now only $4.95"), while the sales volume created by the special promotion makes it economically possible and profitable to reprint the books at the lower price. The original publisher normally furnishes plates and dies for the reprint and earns a small royalty per copy on the deal.

What contributes to the success of remainders—and the reprints they spawn—is the fact that the titles thus promoted are often coming to the attention of a broad public for the first time. They are titles which on their original publication became lost in the shuffle, inundated and submerged by too many other books which were getting the lion's share of attention. Often, too, they were overpriced for their market and became successful only after they were sacrificed at the remainder or reprint price. Some dealers specializing in remainders, such as Marboro Books which operates a chain of retail stores and a large mail order business, even bring in such items from abroad as they have discovered that a reduced-price market will make an item popular and profitable which would have died on the vine had it been imported under normal circumstances.

The experience of remainders, and reprinted remainders, offers one more proof that consumer interest in books—serious and important books—is widespread and that often all that is required to exploit it is an aggressive and attractive way to market such books.

# Chapter VI.

# How Books
# Are Stored
# And Delivered

The "fulfillment" function discussed in this brief chapter embraces two principal areas: the processing of customers' orders, including billing, maintenance of accounts receivable, and related preparation of sales and inventory reports; and the warehousing and shipping of books. These appear at first glance to be humble and relatively insignificant tasks—housekeeping chores which have little or no bearing on the creative aspects of the publishing process. How fatal a conclusion that would be! Many a battle in publishing has been lost for want of a horseshoe nail—in fact, the inefficacies of the present system of book delivery are among the principal reasons why the industry is failing to fulfill its promise and potential.

## ORDER PROCESSING

Under AAP Survey definitions, "order processing" includes the following activities: "order editing, invoicing, preparation of credit memoranda, inventory control, maintenance of accounts receivable, credit control, and production of periodic sales and inventory reports. Also included is the so-called 'customer service' function—an activity devoted to handling order inquiries and complaints."

Since these tasks, as well as those of shipping and warehousing, are closely related to the other business and financial concerns, such as accounting, to which a publisher must attend, they are usually performed under the supervision of the business or financial manager of a house. And since they are today commonly performed with the help of automated equipment (usually referred to as "electronic data processing" or "EDP"), large portions of the work may be farmed out to service organizations, particularly by smaller houses which cannot afford to acquire or lease costly equipment of their own. Invariably, however, the publisher must exercise strict watch over the process whether it is conducted under his own auspices or delegated to an outside firm. So complex are the tasks of fulfillment, so easily disrupted, and so costly to restore once they have malfunctioned, that a publisher can simply not afford, financially or because of customer dissatisfaction, to neglect this vital area.

### Order Editing

It would be easy to assume that an order received from a bookseller, library, wholesaler, school, or individual would need simply to be invoiced and shipped—and there would be an end of it. Unfortunately it's not that simple. To begin with, many orders are incorrectly or incompletely prepared. Many fail to identify author or title properly; names are misspelled, words confused, or badly remembered (too many orders are obviously prepared from memory, without consulting catalogs), prices are wrong or outdated, International Standard Book Numbers (ISBN)—when used—are often misstated. Many orders fail to identify the edition wanted

*148*

when more than one is available, such as in cases of hardback and paperback versions. Many orders include requests for books that have been out of print for years or for books published by other publishers.

The publisher's first task, therefore, on receiving an order is to clean it up so that it can be billed and shipped. Authors and titles must be properly identified, and since most publishers now maintain their title file by the ISBN the correct number must be noted. Where such identification is not possible, where the customer must supply additional data or be advised that his order cannot be filled as placed, he must be notified either separately or on the invoice which covers his shipment.

To simplify the chore of notification, most publishers use a common code of abbreviations to cover the most frequently encountered problems. Notable among these are: OP (out-of-print), for books whose stock is permanently exhausted; TOP (temporarily out-of-print), where plans for reprinting the book are somewhat indefinite; OS (out of stock), where a title is temporarily unavailable but expected in the near future, with the estimated arrival date usually noted; NYP (not yet published), in cases where books are ordered in advance of the publication date; and NO (not ours), for titles not published by the house.

There are other reasons why an order must be examined before it can be billed. Since discounts in many cases are contingent not only on the type of book or the quantity ordered but also on the type of account placing the order (wholesalers and agency accounts are examples of customers who would be entitled to preferential discounts), instructions are often needed so that billing clerks will extend appropriate discounts in each case. Such discounts can vary considerably from title to title, even on the same order. To take an example, a retailer ordering books from a publisher of both trade and professional books may be entitled to the regular quantity-related discount on trade titles ordered, to an agency discount on certain of the professional titles, and to a standard short discount on other professional books not covered by the publisher's agency plan.

Many customers, notably those affiliated with governments and municipalities have highly complicated procedures for purchasing materials which necessitate a good deal of extra paperwork on the publisher's part. Some require the submission of advance quotations or competitive bids— even for a single copy of a book—before they can award a purchase contract. Others must be invoiced in sextuplicate or septuplicate, with notarized affidavits of compliance with numerous regulations attached. Similar demands accompany many shipments to foreign destinations. All such orders require careful inspection and instructions in advance to make certain that requirements are conscientiously followed.

Needless to say, the task of order editing is a demanding one and can only be assigned to a highly competent individual thoroughly familiar with the publisher's list, prices, policies, and customers. The developments which have automated—and necessarily so—much of the routine of order processing have placed even greater weight on the importance of the initial review, because orders can be handled effectively and correctly by automation only if they have first been subjected to the most rigorous and intelligent editing. Machines don't think—they only carry out orders, hopefully issued by people who think!

## Credit Control

Any business can make a great many shipments and issue a great many invoices, yet little is accomplished unless customers pay their bills. Since in the field of bookselling as in many other mercantile fields, some customers pay slowly or not at all, publishers cannot indiscriminately process every order received without ascertaining that the account in question has a good credit standing.

In the case of existing accounts this requires an examination of their indebtedness and past payment history. A customer who owes for excessively long periods and whose indebtedness has built up to a dangerously high level, may have to be told that shipment cannot be made until payment is received. The terms publishers normally extend to their customers are 30 days net, requiring payment within a month. When payment is not received within the specified period, statements are forwarded to the delinquent account and, after 90 days or so, the customer may well be "cut off," i.e., be refused further shipments on open account.

Exceptions are of course made for institutions whose cumbersome payment procedures often makes it impossible for them to pay even within 90 days. Also certain accounts—like college stores during the summer months—may be given "advance dating" on their invoices, i.e., payment does not become due until a later specified date, normally to give the customer an opportunity to sell some of the merchandise before having to pay for it. Similarly, longer terms are extended to foreign accounts to allow for the additional time consumed in transporting goods to overseas destinations.

Should a customer fail to pay even after repeated warnings, he is usually turned over to a collection agency, i.e., a commercial service that collects past due accounts for a percentage (usually 50 percent) of the overdue amount. Only in the case of a very sizable debt would the publisher find it worthwhile to go to court after the collection agent has failed; instead he would simply "write off" the uncollectable amount (i.e., treat it as an expense of doing business).

Accounts that establish a reputation for nonpayment of bills are simply refused credit and are asked to pay for their books in advance of shipment. Since the known offenders are usually impartial in owing all publishers with whom they deal, a regular warning system, exchanging information among publishers, helps to identify them and prevent too many publishers from running into difficulty. Among the sources of such information are the collection agencies, such as Stanley K. Oldden Inc., who issue confidential bulletins about bad accounts to their clients.

When a new trade account requests credit, he is usually asked for references, notably from other publishers with whom he deals or for evidence at any rate that he has the resources and the integrity to honor his debts. Sometimes the publisher will extend credit only up to a certain limit because the data provided by the customer indicate that his resources are too limited to argue for unrestricted credit. Institutions and governments are not subject to such controls, of course. Nor are individual consumers in most cases. The publisher who deals with individuals as a matter of policy recognizes that the cost of checking the credit of each one would exceed the collective bad debt that would result from extending ready credit to all applicants.

In theory, then, a customer who fails to pay his bills with reasonable promptness will not be shipped on open account and the business management of a publisher is usually ready to stick by this sound policy. Unfortunately, such a policy has a tendency to keep down sales, and so the sales management of the same publishing house will often argue for more liberal terms. Not infrequently this leads to rather unfriendly discussions between sales and business managers, and top management must step in to arbitrate. Characteristically it arbitrates on the side of sales harkening to such arguments as "books in the warehouse do no one any good," or "how can we increase sales when you tie our hands this way?" In vain will banks that lend money to publishers hold seminars urging them to be less liberal in extending credit to doubtful accounts. In vain will collection agents warn that such liberality may only have the result of encouraging a bookseller or wholesaler to overextend himself and hasten his bankruptcy, a bankruptcy that might have been prevented had he been treated with sound business restraint. "Good" sales figures—whether they turn out ultimately to be really sales or not—are apparently too much of an enticement to keep some publishers from taking the long view.

### Invoicing, Payments, Credit Memoranda, and Reports

Most invoicing is done through automated systems, and EDP can even perform some functions involved in credit control, such as checking an account's indebtedness and automatically rejecting an order if the account has exceeded its limits. Most systems, too, are able to assign appropriate discounts automatically—particularly if exceptions have been noted in editing.

In the course of billing, important information is gathered or updated: inventories of titles on hand, advance orders for unpublished titles, and sales information, usually broken down by title, type of customer, and customer's geographic location. The inventory data include warning of titles running low so that reprint orders can be placed early enough to keep most active titles in stock, at least most of the time.

The system is designed, further, to post payments and to prepare periodic statements (i.e., summaries of accounts) for customers who owe money. When books are returned or errors are made in billing, credit memoranda are issued, in effect reversing the billing, with resulting additions to inventory and deductions from sales records.

Very often systems fail and chaos sets in. This has been particularly true when a system has first been installed by a publisher; customers have learned to expect malfunctions and disruptions in service whenever a publisher announces conversion to a new system. Both publishers and booksellers are then tempted to blame computers for their troubles—as though computers had minds of their own or were faultily constructed. The truth is, of course, that computers follow human instructions and commands. Many if not most of the installations made in the publishing field are programmed by people who are not familiar with the book industry, who assume that because the book world bears a superficial resemblance to other mercantile industries, the same procedures as would work in processing hardware or canned goods might safely apply to books. Screws and bolts don't have authors or titles, however; they are not sold under significantly different circumstances to a variety of markets and different types of customers; they don't come in different editions on which different discount schedules might apply. Nor is their inventory control and stock replenishment as frought with complexities, nor must cumbersome records be kept so that royalties can be paid correctly in accordance with intricate contractual arrangements.

Most, if not all, of the difficulties computer installations have caused in the book field have been due to a profound lack of communication between the people who furnished the computers, did the programming, and made the installations, and the staff of the publishing houses who were subsequently asked to work with the new systems. Unbelievable though it may sound, case after case is on record involving computer installations where the installers did not acquaint themselves with the business they were about to serve, where the first conversation they held with the publisher's fulfillment crew occurred *after* the computer was on the premises and all the programs were already written. Subsequent failures were then often blamed on the hapless staff that had not been prepared for their new assignments; they were accused of hostility toward the new system, uncooperativeness, or even lack of intelligence.

Because so much grief has come to publishers and their customers as a result of such ill-conceived and badly executed systems installations, an almost mystical distrust of computers has been bred into the souls of many publishers and booksellers. They see automation as the wicked world of technology taking over and destroying the vital, humane, and urbane world of literature. That their vital and urbane world is riddled with near fatal inefficiencies that could be effectively resolved by the computer when properly programmed and that, in fact, nothing may save that world but such effective application of the new technology does not apparently persuade them. Yet their antipathy represents a formidable obstacle to attempts to put the industry's fulfillment house in order.

## WAREHOUSING AND SHIPPING

Just as there is a variety of order processing arrangements, involving internal installations as well as the use of outside services, so there is a variety of warehousing and shipping arrangements in use within the industry. Large publishers usually operate several warehouses located in different parts of the country; others utilize only one warehouse. Some middle-sized and smaller houses share joint facilities; still others make use of commercial shipping services. Nearly all publishers stock inventories at binderies and may occasionally make very large shipments of single titles directly from binderies.

The major problem is that for the most part they "go it alone." Every day a vast tonnage of books is shipped from eastern locations to other parts of the country, for example, without any attempt to consolidate these shipments. Conceivably several trailer trucks or railway freight cars could be filled daily with books traveling from New York to San Francisco, yet no one bothers to organize such an operation. Still—nothing would seem to be more logical. The book industry, though sizable and complex, is concentrated to a significant extent in larger metropolitan areas. Considerable time and money could be saved just by consolidating a vast number of small shipments many of which now travel by book post (at increasing rates), and most of which are directed to a relatively small number of wholesalers, booksellers, libraries, and institutions in a few urban centers.

In past decades the idea of regional warehouses operated by the industry has often been mentioned. This was a sound concept when fewer books were published and before many of the larger publishers invested large sums in constructing warehouses of their own. But while regional warehouses might no longer be practical, regional processing centers might be. Such processing centers need not stock inventories but could consolidate orders from wholesalers, booksellers, and institutions, receiving consolidated shipments in return, which they could then distribute, in reconsolidated form, to customers. The processing centers, located perhaps in some twelve key locations throughout the country, could function with the use of a central computer, and could use standard order forms, standard book and customer numbers, standard billing and reporting procedures (though still, of course, implementing faithfully each publisher's specific discount schedule and operating policies). The centers could also employ consolidated shipping services, operating, conceivably, their own fleet of trucks. They would be industry-owned and operated not-for-profit.

It is possible, of course, that the increasing role played by wholesalers might sooner or later lead them to assume a greater part in the process and help make the industry's delivery system more efficient. Yet there are serious questions whether wholesalers will ever find it sufficiently profitable to process the many special orders at short discount that now constitute a significant portion of the shipping volume that requires consolidation—especially as the number of such special orders is likely to increase impressively in future.

Assuming that wholesalers, although likely to perform increasingly valuable services—by making books that sell well more promptly available to bookstores, for example—may indeed find it impractical to take on the bulk of the industry's delivery burden, a system of nonprofit, regional processing centers may well prove to be the solution to the industry's very critical fulfillment impasse.

# Chapter VIII.

# How Publishers Finance, Plan, And Manage

The organization, structure, and business and financial management of publishing houses are the final subjects in this survey of the industry. Like other aspects of the field, business and financial characteristics vary from house to house and depend on the type of publishing in which it is engaged. These aspects are also heavily dependent on corporate size, type of ownership, and management philosophy.

## STRUCTURE AND ORGANIZATION

In Figure 8, the organization of a publishing house is shown. What is envisioned here is a medium-sized enterprise engaged in, basically, only one kind of publishing (such as trade or college). In a smaller house, some of the management positions charted would probably be combined and managers would be involved substantially in the everyday activities of their departments. Thus an editor-in-chief would probably do a great deal of procurement and be his own managing editor (i.e., control the flow of work in the department and supervise the copy-editing staff directly). The head of the house may function as an editor, or be his own marketing manager, and the roles of sales, promotion, and advertising manager may be combined. Small houses, furthermore, rely more on outside or free-lance assistance; they might farm out all copy editing, possibly all production work and, very likely, all fulfillment.

In larger houses, on the other hand, specific functions additional to those shown in Figure 8 would probably have to be charted. The editorial department, for example, would probably include manuscript readers. The marketing department may well have a separate international sales manager, a direct mail manager, a market research director and staff, and regional sales managers. Reporting to the business manager may be a legal counsel, a financial planning and/or corporate research department, and a manager of Electronic Data Processing (EDP) with a staff of programmers.

A subsidiary rights manager is shown on the chart, a position that would probably function on such a high level only in a trade house. The organization of an elhi publisher, on the other hand, would have to include consultants in the marketing area. Furthermore, the terms used to designate certain responsibilities vary greatly from house to house as does the distribution of these responsibilities themselves. As in other contexts, we have employed the concepts and definitions utilized in AAP Surveys, thus representing what is at least majority practice in the industry.

Relatively few major publishing houses are today engaged in only one type of publishing and their organization charts would therefore show several divisions (such as professional, elhi, and college). Such divisions may operate almost autonomously so that their individual charts may well look much like the one we have illustrated. More commonly, however, each

156

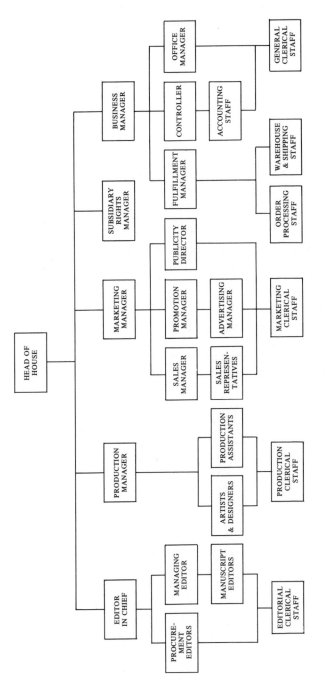

**Figure 8.** Organization chart of a publishing house.

division will control only its own editorial and marketing departments and will share joint production and business services with the other divisions.

Behind the method by which a multidivisional publisher is organized lie important concepts of management philosophy. Some managements believe in strong centralization, arguing that the more services that can be performed under a single supervisor, the more efficient and economical the entire operation will become. Others are convinced that the more autonomy is granted to a division and the more of its services it can render under its own auspices, the more productive and excellent its performance is likely to become. There are strong and persuasive arguments for either point of view and there are many examples of good and efficient management under either alternative, just as there are examples of failure under both. In the end what seems to make the difference between such success or failure is not so much the theoretical structure employed or the philosophy espoused as the ability and commitment of the people, both in top management and on the operating level, who must carry out their responsibilities within the structure. A well-managed, productive organization appears to be one in which senior management is able to inspire its staff to do their best, and where operating executives and personnel are both capable of and committed to performing their tasks well.

It matters a good deal who the people performing the various functions are and under what conditions they will perform them best. If like Judith M. Kennedy, business manager of the medical division of Little, Brown, one is enthusiastic about a decentralized structure, one should also be as fortunate as that division has been in recruiting excellent people for their production department, for example. Good people are not always available for every opening, however, and sometimes a particular post is extremely difficult to fill. Even though, in theory, decentralization may be the more desirable arrangement, it will not always be possible to realize it in practice unless the resources of the house and favorable circumstances permit it to attract the first-rate talent it seeks. To a large extent intelligent organization will be less inspired by theory than by the pragmatic consideration: what type of structure will work best for the people on our staff?

Multidivisional houses are today faced with an additional organizational challenge: overlapping markets. At one time, notably before World War II, a house that organized itself by product or editorial divisions found that its marketing structure naturally followed suit: trade books were marketed to trade outlets, college books to college outlets, elhi books to schools, etc. Today, of course, this identity of product and market sphere no longer holds, as many trade books are marketed to schools and colleges, college books to secondary schools, and so on.

Most multidivisional publishing houses are still organized according to product-editorial criteria even today, however, with the result that a division's marketing department is usually unable to dispose of all of its own products in its own market, and is engaged in selling a good deal of another division's materials in addition to its own. Since divisions are conceived to be profit centers (i.e., their profit and loss performance is carefully analyzed by management and division heads are held responsible for that performance), financial adjustments must be made within multidivisional companies to allow for the interdivisional selling of products. A variety of methods is used to achieve these adjustments, such as one division actually selling its books to the other, or paying its sister division sales commissions for marketing services performed.

## OWNERSHIP AND SIZE

Closely related to questions of structure are, of course, those of corporate size and ownership. According to popular mythology, "big" publishing is destroying the spirit of the industry, is curtailing its venturesomeness, is making it too commercial. Authors published by "big" publishers supposedly receive less attention than they would at small houses; the "big" company is far too impersonal, far less conscientious, far less humane than its small counterpart. What is usually referred to as "big" publishing in this context are the large, multidivisional houses, in particular those which have in recent years been acquired by conglomerates or giant parent companies.

There can be no question that large size in any organization tends to make that organization excessively bureaucratic and impersonal, tends to diffuse responsibility and therefore to lessen commitment by its executives and staff. I say "tends" because these traits are far from inevitable, particularly if management takes steps to counteract the tendency. Among publishing organizations that would qualify for the "big" label there are now those whose policies, practices, and performance are as effective and reputable as any to be found in the industry, as well as others who display all the unfortunate traits one associates with bigness. Again one suspects that people make the difference. Where management takes the needed steps to ensure integrity, courage, and excellence, such traits are likely to be found in the largest as well as the smallest house; where management or ownership are not so motivated the imprint, large or small, will display far less stature.

Few situations are black or white. More often than not publishers are as guilty as the rest of mankind of mediocrity, of a complex mélange of virtue, vice, and indifference that is far closer to daily human experience than either sainthood or corruption—all the more reason to reject the popular oversimplification that smaller publishing houses are more virtuous or effective than the large ones. The evidence simply does not support such a myth. A small publisher may be as consumed by greed, or by worries about money, as any corporate giant. A small publisher may be as arbitrary as any big house in accepting or rejecting a manuscript; in fact in small houses the publisher's own personal taste and opinions often carry far too much weight. If it is true that in large houses books can get lost in the shuffle, it is also true that a small house may not have the strength in the marketplace to gain for a book the attention it deserves. The entrepreneur who heads a small house may be a genius whose attentions greatly benefit an author— but the larger house may have the means to attract some of the industry's best editors, designers, and marketing people to its staff and may therefore have as much access to talent or more than the small house does. Generalizations rarely work. The one about the horrors of "big" publishing and the sterling qualities of small houses is no exception.

## PERSONNEL POLICIES AND MANAGEMENT

### Management Attitudes

The key to good publishing, we have suggested, is primarily good people: good people at the top who will in turn attract good people to the middle and to the bottom and create such an environment and atmosphere for their work as to enable them to do their best. No doubt it is possible to violate these rules for a time, to enjoy brief periods of success even while ignoring every good and responsible personnel practice, but it is very doubtful that a publisher can hope to survive and prosper for a long while disregarding the essential fact that the quality and effectiveness of his program must ultimately depend on the quality and effectiveness of his staff.

Publishing is a people business. From the editor who must gain an author's confidence and nurture him along to turn out the best manuscript of which he is capable, to the shipping clerk in the warehouse who must care enough so that an order is picked and packed correctly, the entire industry rises and falls with the capability and commitment of its people.

It is astonishing that some publishers seem to disregard, or pay inadequate attention to, this vital fact. Although for years—in books published by publishers—industrial psychologists have attempted to encourage sound personnel policies, certain publishing executives appear to be unaware of them. Apparently they don't read their own books!

The insights industrial psychologists have emphasized are that people look upon work as a source of self-fulfillment, that they want to be able to believe in and take pride in what they do, that they want to feel that they are making a contribution, and that they are motivated as much or more by these considerations as by the money they are paid or by the fear of losing their jobs. If this is true of people in general, how much more so of the creative people who are likely to be attracted to and be engaged in most publishing jobs! More sensitive, more highly motivated, more committed to their self-development than the average, creative people are likely to respond more readily to good personnel management and far more adversely to poor personnel practices than most.

How does some publishing management, however, hope to gain the commitment of its people when it shows slight regard for their efforts, firing editors and marketing people because a product does not live up to expectations? Publishing is after all a business of risks; even people with excellent judgment are bound to make mistakes sometimes, particularly since overproduction has glutted distribution channels and even worthy titles often suffocate for sheer lack of breathing space.

Or will certain publishing management motivate its staff when it fails to utilize their talent and judgment, refusing to delegate authority to people well able to handle it? Why hire an editor, production man, designer, or salesman—ostensibly because of his creative capability and sound judgment—then make him toe a narrow line, allow him no creative leeway, and ask him to be no more than a rubber stamp for his superiors?

Will some publishing management inspire its employees when it appears unclear in defining its policies and objectives, changes them suddenly without warning, and acts indecisively, capriciously, and arbitrarily? Or will some management enlist the warm commitment of its staff if it is devious and dishonest and asks the staff to act dishonestly toward authors, suppliers, and customers?

Should not management in a communications industry communicate with its employees, or in a cultural industry show respect for their dignity as persons and for their sensitivity as human beings? Publishers who treat their staff as partners in their creative enterprise, who fully utilize the talents of their employees and extend to them the simple courtesy to which they should be entitled reap great benefits from such seemingly obvious and basic attitudes. Their people work with enthusiasm and concern. They make the publisher's objective their own and identify readily with his interests.

Let me not be misunderstood. Not all employees, particularly the talented, are reasonable or capable of responding to courteous, responsible management. We live in emotional times in which personalities often tend to extremes, the creative unfortunately more than the average. Hostility to all authority, to all business enterprise, even a culturally oriented one, afflicts some, particularly among the young. Nothing that management can do is likely to enable such people to come to terms with a world with which they are fundamentally at odds, or with a social structure they despise. Unfortunate though it may be, such people cannot be humored; if they cannot adjust to the necessary routine of a publishing house, no alternative is available but to dismiss them. Such instances are tragic because, were it not for their personality difficulties, such people could be highly useful to the industry and happy in their work.

But a manager who decides that he is dealing with a hopelessly rebellious personality should ask himself first whether the hostility he is encountering is really incurable or whether it is simply a response to his own ineptness and heavy-handedness as a manager. From what I have observed in the industry, far more discontent is engendered by poor management than by cultural disorientation or personal alienation.

### Education and Training

One factor that aggravates the entire personnel picture is the dearth of available training in book publishing which handicaps most applicants for first jobs in the industry. Astonishingly, despite the growth of academic programs in the so-called communications fields in recent years, there are very few courses available offering a comprehensive, detailed view of the book publishing process. New York University has been offering a program for some years—attended, in fact, more by people already working in New York publishing houses than by students seeking advance information—and a few courses are available at other academic institutions in the New York area, again attended mostly by working staff at publishing houses. A brief survey course is given each summer at Radcliffe College of Harvard University, and here or there a university or school of library science makes a summary course available to students of journalism, literature, or librarianship. To my knowledge there is not now any significant program available anywhere which gives primary emphasis to training students for a career in book publishing.

Nor is even general information available to students in colleges or universities that might enable them to plan for such a career and to seek adequate academic preparation for it. For several years some individuals in the book field have advocated that such information be made available in simple form to interested students. To date nothing has come of the idea.

As a result, most of the education and training given to employees in the industry is imparted on the job. While much may be said in favor of on-the-job training—it is often more realistic in its approach than academic career training—when it becomes the only method of preparing people for a career it turns out to be very costly for both employer and employee. The employer must invest a staggering amount of supervisory time in the training process, and the employee often does not discover until long after he has started on a job that he is in the wrong spot or even in the wrong industry. High dropout rates and excessive turnover result which are inherently costly for all concerned. Furthermore, some people do not learn well under the kind of pressure characteristic of on-the-job training, and some supervisors are poor teachers.

On-the-job training inclines, furthermore, to be rather narrow in its approach, concentrating on the job at hand and on little more. It is amazing how many capable editors, production people, marketing people, and accountants in the industry know little more than the editing, production, sales, or financial tasks they must perform daily; they are literally insulated from other people in the field, even from others within the same house. Few individuals in this "knowledge" industry appear to acquire a broad, comprehensive knowledge of the field in which they earn their livelihood, to place their own role into industry context, or to place the industry itself within the context of the world at large.

Some publishing houses have begun to offer formal and broadly oriented training courses within their own walls—and these have been of genuine help to their staffs, providing exactly the sort of background and breadth of understanding needed to perform with full effectiveness in almost any job in this highly complex field. But such "cram" courses—and they can afford to be little else—still cannot solve the problem of the person who entered book publishing because he dreamed of working closely with authors and of influencing the course of American literature, only to discover that trade editorial positions are very few and far between and are usually not awarded to people until after they have spent many years learning their craft. Just a little advance information about the industry, how it works and what opportunities are available in it, might have saved such an individual a good deal of frustration and disappointment.

**Recruiting Talent**

As it turns out, many a person with noble editorial ambitions now accepts what he considers to be second best—such as a production, sales, or clerical job—just to be in the publishing world, or in the hope of eventually realizing his first dream. Others drift into professional or educational publishing as a second choice when they discover that the trade publishing job they sought is just not available. Since man's accidents are often God's purposes, such people sometimes become sublimely happy in the positions in which they eventually find themselves. Very frequently, however, this happens only after much painful trial and error, and all too often things don't work out at all.

Although the industry has no formal recruiting program, and few general publishing houses engage in recruiting on their own, in professional and educational publishing, conditions are somewhat better because these publishers are in closer contact with their readership and draw much of their talent from it. Many a professor, school teacher, or professional person with literary flair and an interest in publishing has gone to work in a publishing house as an editor, sales representative, or consultant. College publishers actually engage in intensive recruiting of students about to graduate from college, who usually begin their careers as field representatives, many eventually rising to editors and managers. As McGraw-Hill Vice President James Bowman, himself the product of such a career, points out, statistically many more publishing executives began as college travelers than in any other capacity.

Like other industries in recent years, book publishing has struggled with the problems of minority employment—with little notable success. It is probably fair to say that the atmosphere for ethnic minorities is more hospitable in cultural industries than in other segments of the economy; the artistic and intellectual strata of society—whatever their other failings—have always been less riddled with raw prejudice than most. At the same time, members of minority groups have been quite diffident about seeking employment in cultural industries, an understandable attitude in view of the cultural and educational deprivation to which they have been subjected. Outreach programs, such as one sponsored by AAP, in which active recruitment of minority employees is coupled with intensive efforts to make up for educational and cultural disadvantage, have met with only marginal response from both publishers and minority candidates. One fears that in this area, as in so many others involving civil rights, what has been lacking has not been enthusiasm and good will so much as time and patience. The notion of patience is very unpopular at the moment, particularly with respect to minority development; nevertheless it has been an indispensable ingredient in any progress mankind has ever made. Patience need not imply relaxation of one's good efforts—merely the lack of illusions about how quickly things can change for the better.

The position of women in the industry is actually fairly good—compared to most other industries. Women have headed publishing houses in the past and they do so now—Helen Meyer of Dell and Joan Manley of Time-Life Books come readily to mind—and women often hold chief editorial, production, business, and sales positions. There has certainly been more opportunity for women in this and other cultural industries than in the general manufacturing and mercantile fields that constitute the bulk of American commerce. This does not rule out the fact, however, that women are often paid less than men for identical responsibilities; in fact some of the advanced positions women have earned in the field have at least in part been awarded to them because publishers know that they could pay them less than men. And undoubtedly in some of the larger houses, particularly some educational and professional imprints owned by conglomerates, formidable obstacles exist for women who hope to rise to the top. One surmises, however, that the innately more hospitable attitudes prevailing in the field will continue to result in more rapid gains for qualified women here than perhaps in other industries.

## Promotion, Advancement, and Compensation

The matter of promotion and advancement in the industry is itself a delicate issue because here as in so many other fields where special skills earn the recognition of management, people are often promoted to managerial positions even though they may lack the qualifications for holding them. It is simply not true that a superb editor, excellent designer, highly effective salesman, or first-rate financial planner will necessarily make a good editor-in-chief, production manager, or sales or business manager. On the contrary—the very fact that his talents are concentrated in a special field may make him less qualified than others to be a manager.

To be a good manager in a people industry calls primarily for the ability to work well with people and to inspire them. It is not likely that an individual will succeed as a manager unless he fundamentally likes people, can relate to them easily, empathize with them, take a genuine interest in them, and develop honest regard for them. Obviously people with hang-ups, with strong neurotic tendencies, make very poor managers; their excessive preoccupation with self and their insecurity will constantly get in the way of their developing constructive relationships with others. Similarly professionals whose first love and major interest lies in the pursuit of their craft, may simply not be able to muster the psychic energy a manager must be able to invest in his relationships with employees.

Promotion to managerial responsibility should never be regarded as a reward for good professional performance. Professional excellence deserves professional rewards, both financial and in public recognition; however, as in the academic and other professional fields, honors can surely be bestowed on people without inflicting them on others as managers. The true facts regarding qualifications for management call for a major reorientation on the part of some ownership and top-level administrators in publishing who must begin to appoint people to such vital roles only on the basis of the belief that they will really make capable managers.

One suspects that once the quality of management improves, some of the disastrous and debilitating interdivisional and interdepartmental conflicts one witnesses so often in publishing houses will also begin to subside. Now frequently tugs of war between editors and production people, between editors and sales people, between business people and all the rest, disrupt the orderly and productive process of work and victimize authors and customers. Good managers could keep professional jealousies in check and put dampers on unruly egos, at least sufficiently to prevent the publisher's work from suffering.

As for financial compensation, the book field reached a general level of parity with most other enterprises during the prosperous sixties, thus eliminating inequities that had soured the lives of many publishing people for decades. Today most of the salaries, commissions, and fringe benefits paid in the field are commensurate with those which individuals of comparable ability and training would be likely to earn elsewhere. If there is still room for improvement, therefore, it is of the sort applicable to the economy as a whole.

It is important to note, finally, that in addition to full-time staffs a major labor resource in the industry consists of the many free-lance editors, production people, and commission salesmen, as well as a variety of fulfillment and other service organizations. These are utilized particularly by smaller publishers, although even larger houses often call on them for special projects or to supplement their own staffs. Because the free-lancers make highly skilled and experienced labor available on an ad-hoc basis they give even the smallest house an opportunity to avail itself of competent professional services and enable larger organizations to overcome problems caused by seasonal or temporary fluctuations in their work load. (A list of such individuals and service organizations, though not entirely complete, appears in *Literary Market Place*.)

## FINANCIAL MANAGEMENT

### Accounting and Its Role

A convenient way of approaching the economics and financial dynamics of book publishing is to examine some characteristic financial statements. For accounting is really nothing more than an attempt to portray the circumstances of a business in quantitative, i.e., numerical terms, and financial statements are the means accountants use to illustrate their findings. I have therefore developed two fictitious sets of operating statements and balance sheets, one for a small trade publishing house, the other for a medium-sized elhi imprint. While these statements are wholly imaginary—and any resemblance to actual operation would be entirely accidental—they do incorporate the experiences a publishing house might encounter in today's economy and could therefore be termed fairly typical.

I hasten to add that "typical" allows for a wide range of circumstances. Because publishers deal in products of highly individualized nature, each with its unique character and performance in the marketplace, and because publishers themselves act and think very individualistically, there are no two publishing houses wholly alike or even very nearly alike in their income, cost, cash flow, and other fiscal experiences. Thus while the data we shall discuss may be instructive in revealing the type of economic activity or performance factors one is likely to encounter in analyzing the finances of a publisher, there will be wide departures from the specific amounts and ratios cited in the actual experiences of houses.

The very methods of accounting and preparing financial statements reflect diversity. Contrary to popular notion—and contrary to the impression accountants sometimes manage to create—accounting is not an exact science. While any capable and conscientious member of the profession will adhere to "generally accepted" standards of practice, he has a great deal of leeway in selecting alternatives from a wealth of approaches and treatments in portraying the financial operations of an enterprise. What may be proper or not in his exercise of judgment is governed by rules and opinions handed down by the profession's governing body, the American Institute of Certified Public Accountants (AICPA), as well as by law, and by various regulatory agencies, such as the Internal Revenue Service and the Securities and Exchange Commission.

The basic motivation behind any sound accounting decision and the supreme standard that governs all practice, is the honest and accurate portrayal of what is actually transpiring within the enterprise. While unscrupulous managements and their accountants may occasionally attempt to falsify records or to hide rather than to disclose facts which owners and stockholders should know, normal practice dictates that the fullest possible information be provided by whatever statements are prepared. The need for disclosure, then, dictates much of the style, format, and methods used in accounting; the desire to leave an accurate impression with the reader of a statement will influence many decisions regarding treatment and fiscal policy.

So fundamental is this concept, and so ready are all parties to honor it, that the government even allows a business to keep two sets of books: one to inform management and ownership of goings-on, the other for tax purposes. Then if under the tax law a business chooses to adopt practices which give it certain advantages but which would result in a distorted or inaccurate portrayal of the business' condition, it will not be forced to confuse the issue by having to share with management the reports designed to take advantage of tax loopholes rather than to disclose facts.

One of the basic concepts in accounting, designed to provide an accurate picture of the health and vitality of a business is that, insofar as logical and possible, the income a business enjoys should be related to the expenses incurred in generating that income. In other words, an expense should be shown on a statement covering the time period during which the income toward which it contributed is shown. For many businesses, including most publishing, this means that very often an expense is not shown when the cash was actually spent, or income when it was actually received, but at the time when the relationship between income and cost can be most meaningfully established. The accounting approach that matches income with expense irrespective of the time of cash flow is known as "accrual" accounting; it is distinguished from the method which records transactions at the time money actually flows and which is therefore known as the "cash" method.

Accrual accounting makes sense. If a large advance is paid to an author this year, yet the book he is writing will not be published until two years from now, it would not provide a realistic picture of the loss or gain on that book if the advance were reported on this year's statement. It would be more revealing to report the royalties covered by the advance as they are earned by sales, two and three years hence. Similarly if the printing of a book were to arrive late in the year it would be more instructive to report the cost of that printing as the books are sold during the coming year rather than burden this year's sales with expenses unrelated to them.

Time, generally, is a very important factor in accounting. A year is the basis on which major assessments and analyses of businesses are normally undertaken, not only by examining the experiences of the year itself but by comparing it with the previous and even earlier years. During the course of the year, monthly or quarterly statements are usually prepared so that the progress of the enterprise can be carefully watched. Even though short periods, influenced as they often are by incidental factors, are less reliable than longer time spans for revealing trends and patterns, intelligent watch over performance indicators, particularly as they relate to budgets and forecasts prepared in advance, and the ability to make enlightened decisions because of the information provided, are essential to sound management. Incidentally, a "year" or "quarter" may not always mean a calendar year or quarter; many businesses, including some publishing houses, operate on "fiscal" years which may end with any month and which are usually chosen because the seasonal character of the enterprise—or the history of its incorporation—provided some advantages for so doing.

Another very important consideration in accounting is consistency. Once a practice is established it should not be departed from or changed without very strong reason since such changes make comparison with previous periods very difficult if not impossible. If a change becomes inevitable, the statement which incorporates it must be adequately footnoted to call attention to the change and to warn the reader to take it into account.

### Small Trade Publisher's Operating Statement

The Small Trade Publisher's Operating Statement shown in Figure 9 covers the calendar year 1972, and data are furnished for 1971, for comparison purposes. This operating statement (or income statement or profit-and-loss statement, as it may also be called) has been prepared on an accrual basis, showing income and expense in the closest advisable relationship. By its nature an operating statement is a history—so what we are observing is a quantitative description of what happened during 1972 (and 1971) to make the house come to the state it is in on December 31.

**Small Trade Publisher's Operating Statement**
*December 31, 1972*

| | 1972 | | 1971 | |
|---|---|---|---|---|
| | Dollars | Percent of Net Sales | Dollars | Percent of Net Sales |
| Gross sales | 4,746,101 | 114.7 | 4,650,381 | 112.2 |
| Less: returns and allowances | 608,262 | 14.7 | 505,656 | 12.2 |
| Net sales | 4,137,839 | 100.0 | 4,144,725 | 100.0 |
| Cost of sales | | | | |
| Plant costs | 339,303 | 8.2 | 352,302 | 8.5 |
| Paper, printing, and binding | | | | |
| Beginning inventory | 1,497,898 | 36.2 | 1,487,956 | 35.9 |
| Purchases | 1,419,279 | 34.3 | 1,492,101 | 36.0 |
| Total available | 2,917,177 | 70.5 | 2,980,057 | 71.9 |
| Less: ending inventory-net of | 1,547,552 | 37.4 | 1,497,898 | 36.1 |
| write-downs: 1972–$144,824 (3.5%) | | | | |
| 1971–$132,631 (3.2%) | | | | |
| Less: cost of free copies | 45,516 | 1.1 | 41,447 | 1.0 |
| Net paper, printing, and binding | 1,324,109 | 32.0 | 1,440,712 | 34.8 |
| Royalties | 504,816 | 12.2 | 472,499 | 11.4 |
| Total cost of sales | 2,168,228 | 52.4 | 2,265,513 | 54.7 |
| Gross margin on sales | 1,969,611 | 47.6 | 1,879,212 | 45.3 |
| Other publishing income | 277,235 | 6.7 | 256,973 | 6.2 |
| Total operating income | 2,246,846 | 54.3 | 2,136,185 | 51.5 |
| Operating expenses | | | | |
| Editorial | 264,822 | 6.4 | 240,394 | 5.8 |
| Production | 70,343 | 1.7 | 78,750 | 1.9 |
| Marketing | | | | |
| Salesmen's salaries and commissions | 182,065 | 4.4 | 194,802 | 4.7 |
| Space advertising | 128,273 | 3.1 | 120,197 | 2.9 |
| Free copies (including postage) | 57,930 | 1.4 | 45,592 | 1.1 |
| Departmental salaries | 111,722 | 2.7 | 111,908 | 2.7 |
| Travel and entertainment | 53,792 | 1.3 | 58,026 | 1.4 |
| Other marketing expense | 219,305 | 5.3 | 203,092 | 4.9 |
| Total marketing expense | 753,087 | 18.2 | 733,617 | 17.7 |
| Fulfillment | | | | |
| Order processing | 173,689 | 4.2 | 174,078 | 4.2 |
| Shipping and warehousing | 256,545 | 6.2 | 248,683 | 6.0 |
| Total fulfillment expense | 430,243 | 10.4 | 422,761 | 10.2 |
| General and administrative | | | | |
| Management salaries | 86,895 | 2.1 | 74,605 | 1.8 |
| Other salaries | 115,859 | 2.8 | 120,197 | 2.9 |
| Occupancy | 74,481 | 1.8 | 66,156 | 1.6 |
| Employee benefits | 57,930 | 1.4 | 53,881 | 1.3 |
| Other general and administrative | 198,616 | 4.8 | 232,105 | 5.6 |
| Total general and administrative | 533,781 | 12.9 | 546,944 | 13.2 |
| Total operating expenses | 2,052,276 | 49.6 | 2,022,466 | 48.8 |
| Other (nonpublishing) income (or expense) | ( 24,827) | ( 0.6) | ( 33,158) | ( 0.8) |
| Net income (or loss) before taxes | 169,743 | 4.1 | 80,561 | 1.9 |
| Federal, state, and local income taxes | 82,757 | 2.0 | 37,420 | 0.9 |
| Net income (or loss) after taxes | 86,986 | 2.1 | 43,141 | 1.0 |

Figure 9.

That state itself is portrayed in the balance sheet (Figure 10) and the two documents will be examined in conjunction in order to provide a meaningful analysis of this fictitious enterprise.

The following is an explanation of each of the line items in the operating statement.

*Gross sales* include all regular sales to bookstores, wholesalers, individuals, etc., after the deduction of all discounts from the list price of books. (Transportation charges are not included here. If they are paid by the customer, they do not appear in the statement at all; if they are paid by the publisher they are shown as an expense under "Fulfillment.") Also included here are sheet sales and remainder sales, not, however, sales of rights which appear under "Other publishing income."

*Returns and allowances* include credits extended to customers for books returned, or special allowances (such as a credit permitting a bookseller to mark down books rather than return them). Credits to adjust billing errors are excluded, since billing errors should be eliminated by adjusting gross sales.

*Net sales* represent gross sales less returns and allowances. Net sales provide the basis—or yardstick—for establishing ratios for income and expense entries, thus making comparison between specific items easier and facilitating analysis of differences between the current and previous years. (In the statement ratios appear in the columns to the right of dollar amounts, for both 1972 and 1971.) Some publishers, such as mass market paperback houses which experience very sizable returns, find it more meaningful to show their ratios on the basis of gross sales.

*Cost of sales* is a broad category which includes manufacturing costs, both plant and running, and authors' royalties. Also sometimes referred to as "cost of goods sold," it seeks to identify and separate those expenses which vary directly with the number and volume of books sold from those shown under "operating expenses" which are not affected—at least not as directly—by the sale of specific books.

*Plant costs* include nonrecurring manufacturing costs (such as typesetting, negatives, and reusable plates) plus artwork supplied by the publisher. The way in which nonrecurring development costs are treated varies considerably from publisher to publisher, and some even regard certain editorial expenses as "plant costs" (thus departing from the AAP definitions which we are using in this book). In the present statement, we are "writing off" plant costs at the time of publication—i.e., we do not show them until the month (or year) in which the book is released.

Our rationale for "writing off" plant costs, even though some of the books on behalf of which they were incurred may not be sold for some months, is that the life expectancy of most trade books is short, that very often inventories (in this case including paper, printing, and binding values of the books only) must be written down to reflect their loss in sales potential, and that therefore to stretch out the application of plant costs in some way—such as by including them in inventory values—would only result in larger write-offs a few months from now. Since our objective is to portray the condition of the enterprise as realistically as possible, it seems more appropriate to bring the entire plant expense into cost of goods sold at the time of publication rather than to defer it.

Publishers who disagree with this position may include plant costs in inventories—some even incorporating certain editorial expenses there as we have noted—or they may amortize them (i.e., apportion the expense in accordance with a predetermined pattern over a period of months or years). In trade book publishing, amortization over several years would be justifiable only if the life expectancy of the title were to be considerably above average, such as in the case of dictionaries and other reference works. In other words, the criterion for deciding how plant costs or other development expenses should be treated should be the life expectancy of the product: how long is it anticipated to be in print in its present form (i.e., before extensive revision would require new plant expenses, for example). Since different treatment for individual titles would be cumbersome and confusing, policy is usually established for whole categories or lines of books. Some trade publishers have different policies for their hard-cover and paperback books, for example, or for adult and juvenile titles.

*Paper, printing, and binding.* As just explained, these costs are carried into inventory in our case, and, true to the concept that we want to include only values of books actually sold—not the entire cash investment in inventory—we must take steps to isolate the value of the books sold from the rest. One way to do this would be to record the value of each book as it is sold, and houses using computers are able to do so and to prepare a cumulative entry for statement purposes. To verify the accuracy of such an accumulation and to reconcile it with physical inventories at the beginning and end of the statement periods, or to calculate inventory consumption in cases where computerized summaries are not available, the method shown in our statement is employed. (This also has the advantage of showing the values of the inventories at the beginning and end, as well as of the cash investment in "purchases" during the year, i.e., new printings completed in whole or in part, and additions to paper and cloth on hand.)

When we add "purchases" to "beginning inventory" (note that beginning inventory for 1972 and ending inventory in 1971 are identical) we obtain a "total available." By deducting "ending inventory" from that total, and by deducting, further, the books we have given away for promotional and other purposes (free books are not books sold) we arrive at a net "paper, printing, and binding" cost figure of inventory consumed or of books sold. Note that in the stub of the statement we also show the amount of inventory "write-downs" in 1972 and 1971, i.e., decreases in assigned values we have had to apply to the inventory during the year because parts of it had become unusable or only nominal income could be realized on some books through remaindering or pulping (i.e., destroying) them.

*Royalties.* Included here would be royalties paid to authors, other publishers, *et al.*, throughout the year; also fees in lieu of royalties (e.g., flat fees to illustrators of juveniles). Furthermore, any royalties that had been guaranteed in advance and proved to be unearnable during the year would have to be written off here. Thus had a given book, on which a guarantee of $20,000 had been paid, stopped selling after earning only $18,000, a sum of $2,000 would have to be included in the royalty entry in addition to amounts actually earned during the period. (In our case, however, a reserve for unearned royalty advances has been set up on the balance sheet, and therefore only additions to the reserve made during the period would be added to earned royalties in our entry; cf. the balance sheet discussion of royalty advances.)

*Gross margin on sales* represents net sales less cost of sales.

*Other publishing income.* This statement includes two categories of "other" income, i.e., revenues other than those resulting from the sale of books. The entry on this part of the statement is called other "publishing" income because it contains other revenues, such as income from rights, directly connected with and resulting from the book publishing program. The second, or other "nonpublishing" income is incorporated on the line designated "other (nonpublishing) income (or expense)" just before the pretax income (or loss) entry at the end of the statement. The income included there represents earnings from outside investments and enterprises, or income from good money management, and is therefore only indirectly related to book publishing activities.

Included in the "Other Publishing Income" category are revenues from subsidiary rights (reprint, book club, permissions, foreign and translation, serial, etc.) as well as such items as income from the renting out of mailing lists.

*Total operating income* represents gross margin on sales plus other publishing income.

*Operating expenses.* By their nature most operating expenses involve the publisher's cost of doing business and are "expensed," i.e., shown in their entirety and not deferred or amortized in any way. There are exceptions, however, involving real estate, equipment, and vehicles, for example, whose acquisition is usually amortized or depreciated over a period of time (and which would be shown under "fulfillment" or "general and administrative" expense). As one would expect in a people business, salaries and salary-related costs make up a significant portion of total operating expense.

In assigning costs to departments, such as editorial, production, and marketing, compensation to staff and free-lance employees (salaries, bonuses, and commission) is included, as is travel and entertainment, and such supplies as stationery, reference materials for editors, and art supplies for designers. Employee benefits (pensions, retirement plans, deferred profit sharing, insurance programs, etc.) are not included on the departmental level but are considered a general and administrative expense. So are mandatory insurance programs (workmen's compensation), payroll taxes, telephone and telegraph charges, occupancy costs, heat, light, and power, and maintenance (except for warehouse occupancy, utility, and mainte- nance expense which would be shown under "fulfillment"). While some publishers accumulate certain of these overhead charges on a departmental basis, the majority do not, and AAP definitions accordingly provide that they be classified under "general and administrative" costs.

AAP definitions also require that in cases where members of top management are engaged in departmental tasks, such as editing and sales management, appropriate portions of their compensation, based on their departmental time involvements, be charged to the departments. In such cases the entry for management salaries under general and administrative (G & A) expense is proportionately reduced.

*Editorial and production.* Our statement entries for editorial and production conform to the principles just outlined.

*Marketing.* Under marketing expense some details are isolated because of the importance of and interest in these items. The entry for "free copies" differs from the deduction made under cost of sales in that postage spent in mailing the books has been included. Departmental salaries include those of the sales manager, promotion manager, advertising manager, publicity manager, copywriters, and other promotional staff. "Other" marketing expense would include the cost of catalogs, circulars, direct mail, posters, displays, and exhibits.

*Fulfillment* costs can be incurred completely inside the house, or entirely outside (as envisioned in this example) by engaging commercial services, or the operation can be conducted partly inside and partly outside. If the publisher operates his own warehouse, all occupancy costs related to it (rent or mortgage expense and maintenance of the premises) are included here rather than under G & A where all other occupancy expense is normally reported.

*General and administrative expense.* The entry for general and administra- tive expense again provides some of the more significant details separately. Management salaries are confined to those of top-level executives, with any portion of their time devoted to departmental activity extracted and added to department charges. "Other" salaries are those of the accounting, general office staff, and clerical staff (e.g., telephone operators, secretaries to top management, etc.). "Other general and administrative" expenses would include payroll taxes and other nonincome taxes (except real estate taxes which are classified as an occupancy expense); general travel and entertainment; EDP expense (other than that of fulfillment, or otherwise of a departmental nature such as the maintenance of production records which should be charged to production expense); telephone and telegraph; general stationery and supplies not charged to departments; bad debts (i.e., uncollectable bills) written off (or additions to balance-sheet provisions for doubtful accounts); professional fees to accountants, lawyers, and consultants; insurance (except as classified under employee benefits or occupancy); and depreciation on general office equipment.

*Other (nonpublishing) income (or expense).* Interest paid on borrowings, or interest earned on investments, and cash discounts given or earned (i.e., incentive discounts for prompt payment of bills) are examples of the items that would be incorporated in this figure. The brackets around the number in our statement indicate that the net total of all income and expense is a negative figure (i.e., aggregate expenses exceeded aggregate income) and that this amount will have to be *deducted* in calculating our net income (or loss) before taxes figure.

*Net income (or loss) before taxes.* Total operating income less total operating expense, with other (nonpublishing) income (or expense) added or deducted depending on whether the figure is positive or negative. Should the result indicate a loss (negative figure) it would be shown in brackets.

The final entries in the statement show the income taxes paid (to federal, state, and local governments—all nonincome taxes have been shown under "occupancy" or "other G & A expense"), and the net profit or loss earned by the house after paying its taxes. A loss would be shown in brackets, of course.

### Small Trade Publisher's Balance Sheet

We shall return to an analysis of this operating statement after we have acquainted ourselves with the Small Trade Publisher's Balance Sheet (Figure 10) since the two documents are closely related and are intended to be reviewed together.

The balance sheet is basically a state of condition report as of December 31, 1972 (and 1971, again for comparison purposes). It is divided into two sections, the first headed "Assets," the second "Liabilities and Shareholders' Equity," and each section totals to the same amount. This explains the document's name—the statement shows the "balance" between assets on the one hand and the liabilities and net worth of the business on the other. Assets are tangible values, either actually in the possession of the company (such as cash, securities, inventories, and fixtures) or due in future, such as accounts receivable (i.e., invoices covering goods shipped but not yet paid

**Small Trade Publisher's Balance Sheet**

*December 31, 1972*

|  | 1972 | 1971 |
|---|---|---|
| **Assets** | | |
| Current assets | | |
| Cash | $ 16,415 | $ 14,680 |
| Marketable securities–at cost | | |
| (Market value: 1972–$8,570; 1971–$12,300) | 8,570 | 11,800 |
| Accounts receivable (net of allowances for | | |
| doubtful accounts: 1972–$44,120; 1971–$41,810) | 1,360,865 | 1,340,740 |
| Inventories | | |
| Finished goods | 1,112,680 | 1,057,920 |
| Work-in-process | 347,860 | 375,658 |
| Paper and other raw materials | 87,012 | 64,320 |
| Total current assets | 2,933,402 | 2,865,118 |
| Fixtures and equipment–at cost | 18,450 | 17,970 |
| Less: accumulated depreciation and amortization | 7,318 | 7,115 |
|  | 11,132 | 10,855 |
| Royalty advances | 620,600 | 580,200 |
| Less: reserve for write-off of unearned guarantees | 53,400 | 48,600 |
|  | 567,200 | 531,600 |
| Prepaid and deferred expenses | 9,846 | 11,394 |
|  | 3,521,580 | 3,418,967 |
| **Liabilities and shareholders' equity** | | |
| Current liabilities | | |
| Accounts payable | $ 744,809 | $ 725,356 |
| Royalties payable | 226,830 | 231,616 |
| Notes payable | 22,700 | 30,670 |
| Accrued income taxes | 19,680 | 8,473 |
| Other accrued liabilities | 2,485 | — |
| Total current liabilities | 1,016,504 | 996,115 |
| Long-term debt | 782,730 | 747,862 |
| Shareholders' equity | | |
| Capital stock–$1 par value | 100,000 | 100,000 |
| Additional paid-in capital | 860,000 | 860,000 |
| Retained earnings | 762,346 | 714,990 |
| Total shareholders' equity | 1,722,346 | 1,674,990 |
|  | 3,521,580 | 3,418,967 |

**Figure 10.**

for). In accrual accounting a prepaid expense must also be considered an asset until such time as related income is realized and the expense can be reported in the operating statement. Liabilities are monies owed, payable in the near or distant future. The net worth of a business, or the equity its stockholders have in it, represents the value of their investment (to the extent that a balance sheet can reflect it).

Again, let us review each line item in turn.

*Current assets.* Current assets are those likely to be consumed or to be subjected to change in the near future: cash, securities (short-term investments), receivables, and inventories, as opposed to equipment which is likely to remain in use for a few years, or author's royalty advances, a prepaid expense that may not be earned or written off for some time to come.

*Cash.* This would include cash on hand and in banks.

*Marketable securities.* Any business wants to have a small money reserve to meet seasonal or unexpected demands without having to borrow too much or under unfavorable conditions. However, to leave money lying around without putting it to work is foolhardy. For this reason businesses make short-term investments, usually in stocks, bonds, debentures, and other securities that are likely to show favorable earnings while held and can easily be disposed of when the need arises. On balance sheets they are usually listed at cost because market values are subject to too much change, but market values are shown to inform the reader of the amount at which the securities could be sold should it be deemed necessary.

*Accounts receivable.* Under this heading fall payments from customers that are outstanding at the time of the statement. It may be noted that an "allowance for doubtful accounts" has been deducted from actual billings prior to listing the receivables. The amount of such an allowance—reflecting a realistic expectation of what portion of the amount due cannot be collected—is based on the publisher's past experience in collecting receivables, modified by changing conditions in the marketplace. (In bad times collections slow down noticeably and more people default or go bankrupt.) Any addition to the provision made during the year must be shown as an expense on the operating statement under "other general and administrative expense." (Certain publishers such as those of mass market paperbacks whose returns are very high, may also carry a reserve for anticipated returns against their accounts receivable.)

*Inventories.* Separate entries have been made for finished (bound) books, work-in-process (which could be books at any stage of completion: flat sheets, folded and gathered sheets, or partially bound sheets) and paper and raw materials, notably cloth. The value of the inventory will have been subject to any write-down necessitated by declining sales potential of the stock. Some books may actually be in inventory without value (usually in anticipation of their being remaindered) or with some of the stock wholly or partially depreciated. There are a variety of methods used in writing down inventory; some people employ mathematical formulas, others simply evaluate the potential of each title periodically and then adjust inventories accordingly. What is critical is that inventories not be overvalued, particularly in the trade-book field where depreciation of books is so rapid.

*Fixtures and equipment.* These items are shown at their original acquisition cost, with accumulated depreciation deducted to arrive at the actual value at which they are now carried on the books. The portion of depreciation and amortization applicable to the past year will have been included as an expense under "other general and administrative" costs on the operating statement.

*Royalty advances.* This entry includes a provision for unearned guarantees since in our judgment a portion of the contractually committed advances will not be earned. Additions to the provision during the past year will have been included in the royalty expense shown in the operating statement.

*Prepaid and deferred expenses.* These expenses would include such items as prepaid service contracts, retainers for professional work not yet completed, advance tax deposits, and the like.

*Current liabilities.* In this category are liabilities which will be settled in the near future, as opposed to long-term debts which will not be retired for some years.

*Accounts payable.* Unpaid bills from vendors, manufacturers, suppliers, service agencies, etc., are included here.

*Royalties payable.* Most trade contracts provide that royalties be computed for the periods January 1 to June 30, and July 1 to December 31 of each year. A December 31 balance sheet will therefore reflect a sizable accumulation of royalties earned during the second half of the year but not yet paid to authors.

*Notes payable.* Despite the fact that they may command nominal cash reserves and hold portfolios of marketable securities, most businesses will find it opportune to take out short-term loans during periods of the year when their payables and receivables are both high, in effect when they must pay some big bills before receiving large payments due from their customers. Unless a business is thought to be a very poor credit risk, or interest rates are abnormally high, a short-term loan (say 90 to 120 days) may be more advantageous than to sell portions of a good investment portfolio which may yet rise in value or continue to show solid earnings. Since many publishers regularly experience periods of tight cash flow (i.e., when payables substantially exceed current receipts), short-term loans regularly make their appearance on their balance sheets.

*Accrued income taxes.* These are taxes payable on business already transacted.

*Other accrued liabilities.* This item includes, for example, contractual arrangements providing for payments of specific fees by certain dates.

*Long-term debt.* Such debt could involve real estate mortgages, bonds or debentures issued by the company, or notes held by banks, other corporations, or private individuals.

*Shareholders' equity.* "Equity" represents the value of the owners' holdings. The term "shareholders" is used because our venture is a corporation and has issued shares to obtain capital. A sole proprietorship (i.e., a business owned by one individual) or a partnership (which is owned by several individuals, yet with a different legal structure from that of a corporation) might speak of a "proprietor's equity" or "partners' equity." Most publishing houses find the legal character of the corporation most advantageous for their circumstances; however, there are also advantages in proprietorship and partnership arrangements. When a business is founded, the various legal and fiscal alternatives for establishing it are investigated and the course most advantageous to the founders is adopted.

*Capital stock.* Stocks are certificates of ownership issued by a corporation to raise capital. There are several types of stock. Common stock, the variety most widely in use, entitles its owner to vote for corporate officers, but earnings (known as dividends) must be authorized by the company's directors before they can be distributed. Holders of preferred stock do not always enjoy a vote but are usually guaranteed some specific earnings from the company's profits. Some companies issue several classes of common or preferred stock, with the higher classes enjoying priority call on dividends. To complicate matters further, nonvoting stocks are often sold on a "convertible" basis, i.e., they may be exchanged for common stock under certain conditions. Corporations sometimes also sell so-called "warrants" (i.e., certificates entitling the owner to receive or acquire shares when they become available).

Corporations may also issue securities which are not shares of ownership but rather interest-bearing loan certificates, debentures, and bonds, for example. Often these securities are made more attractive by being convertible for common stock, however, because they are not shares, they would not be listed under "shareholders' equity" on our balance sheet, but under "long-term debt" (with necessary details fully disclosed).

Most corporations and most publishing houses—including the fictitious company we are analyzing—are "privately held," i.e., their shares are not offered for sale publicly but are in the hands of founders, their families, heirs, close associates, friends, employees, etc. The public sale of securities, the method by which they are offered, the information that must be disclosed to prospective purchasers, and the circumstances surrounding the relationship of a publicly held company with its stockholders, are all strictly governed by law and regulated by the Securities and Exchange Commission. Not every public company is listed on stock exchanges, however; that listing is reserved only to the largest, whose securities are most actively traded. (Very few publishing houses or even corporations with publishing subsidiaries are so listed.) The securities of unlisted public companies are "traded over the counter," i.e., they are made available through brokers, and quotations on their value are usually published through standard financial sources. (Publishing stock reports also appear periodically in *Publishers Weekly* and in newsletters published by Knowledge Industry Publications.)

In our case, as we note from the balance sheet, only one class of stock was issued: 100,000 common shares at par value of $1.00. Par value is a nominal worth placed on a stock at the time of its issuance—some stocks may be issued without par value, in fact—and in many cases even the original paid-in capital exceeds par value. As this is true also in the present case, we note an *"additional paid-in capital"* entry, which represents that amount of cash which the stockholders have invested in the company above and beyond the par value of the stock.

*Retained earnings.* When a corporation shows a profit it is usually required to distribute it to its stockholders. However, a business often needs increases in "working capital" (i.e., cash necessary to keep the business functioning), and the best source (in many ways) of additional working capital is from the profits generated by the company itself. The company may, therefore, keep back (retain) some of its earnings for operational use. Such disposition of profits must be judicious, however; excessive retention is subject to heavy tax penalties.

It must be noted that what the balance sheet describes as "total shareholders' equity," or the net worth of a company, is not necessarily the price such a company would bring on the market if it were sold by its owners. Rather it represents only what accountants call "book value" (i.e., the worth carried on the company's books). Were the house actually sold it might be for substantially more or possibly less than book value. There are a number of reasons for this not the least of which is that the balance sheet fails to list a publisher's "intangible" assets which may be as important or more important to his health and success than the tangible items listed: the people on his staff, his reputation, the authors on his list, his relationship with customers and suppliers. One can conceive, for example, of two publishing imprints with almost identical tangible assets, liabilities, and operating experience, but with very different future prospects: one rather unimaginative and routine in its product and management approach, the other vital, aggressive, keenly attuned to what the market demands and shooting effectively ahead of its target. Would the purchaser considering the acquisition of these two companies be willing to pay the same price for both? Hardly. For he would be convinced that the ultimate effectiveness of the aggressive house, and therefore its future earnings, would be considerably greater than those of the quietly unimaginative one.

What may be said of purchasing an entire company can be said with equal validity about purchasing its stock. Obviously if I have my choice between investing my money in the shares of a house with an exciting and promising future and one whose outlook is rather lukewarm, I shall choose the bright prospect. What buyers of companies or of shares of companies consider primarily, then, is the likely future course of the enterprise in which they are asked to invest. And since, in purely financial terms, the measurement of success is earnings (i.e., profits), the basis for appraising whole companies or the value of their shares is usually some multiple of the earnings of that company. For example, the price for a publishing house may be formulated as follows: average earnings over the past five years, multiplied by fifteen. The multiple chosen would reflect the confidence of the purchaser in the future of the enterprise. Stocks, similarly, tend to reach their market value (represented by a multiple of current or recent dividends paid) based on analyses of where the business may be heading. Trading factors, such as the supply and demand of the stock as well as general market trends and moods, will of course modify the value pattern.

Appraisals of a company may therefore exceed or be smaller than the book values shown on balance sheets (although financial statements are, of course, vital components in the analysis that arrives at that appraisal). Similarly the market value of a share of stock may be greater or less than the book value of that share (the latter calculated by dividing stockholders' equity by the number of shares issued, making due allowances for different types and classes of stock).

In recognition of the various factors, tangible and intangible, contributing to the correct analysis of a business, the law requires corporations to issue periodic reports to their stockholders. Here financial experience is disclosed as well as such facts involving the management, productivity, and plans of the enterprise as will enable owners and shareholders to form an accurate picture of its progress and likely future course. To assist in making operating and balance sheet reports more meaningful and easier to dissect, the following information is usually provided: footnotes to the statements, explaining the accounting methods and treatments employed as well as providing additional detail or background whenever required for adequate disclosure of the facts; reports on shares outstanding, dividends paid, and earnings per share; and changes in the level of retained earnings and in the amount of working capital, together with other related so-called "changes in financial position."

Since we are attempting to keep this discussion as simple as possible we have avoided including complicating features in our fictitious statements, such as "extraordinary items" (usually substantial losses or expenses not likely to recur that deserve separate listing and explanation because they might otherwise distort the company's position); or "contingent liabilities" (obligations the company will apparently have to meet, or losses it will have to sustain, even though circumstances have not evolved to the point where the liability has become actual). We have also kept share distribution simple, listing only one class of common stock, and assuming no further sale of stock during the reporting period, nor the payment of stock dividends (where additional shares, rather than cash, are distributed to shareholders), nor the existence of "treasury stock," i.e., undistributed shares held by the company.

As we have explained the various line items, we can dispense with footnotes to the statements. As for dividends paid on our 100,000 shares issued, they amounted to $39,630 or 39.6 cents per share, for 1972. We shall be referring to changes in retained earnings and working capital during the analysis which follows.

### Analysis of Trade Publisher's Statements

Beginning with the operating statement, we notice that gross dollar sales were up slightly (2 percent) in 1972 over 1971. (In view of general price increases that may actually denote a drop in unit sales over the previous year.) But the gross sales increase was quickly wiped out by an increase in the level of returns, so that net sales in 1972 were actually marginally lower than in 1971.

Yet when we look at the bottom line, net profit after taxes, we see that it more than doubled in 1972. Why?

For one thing, cost of sales was down compared to the previous year. Other publishing income was up. And while operating expense rose, other nonpublishing expense fell. The net difference of all these factors (2.2 percent of net sales) was sufficient to more than double pretax profit, from 1.9 percent of net sales in 1971 to 4.1 percent in 1972. Although our taxes rose somewhat more than in proportion, our bottom-line profit still showed a handsome increase of 101.6 percent!

Let us compare the differences between the two years more closely. Note, for example, that plant costs dropped in 1972. Although inventory levels were up at both beginning and end (and inventory write-downs increased by 9.2 percent), purchases were down. This, together with the drop in plant costs, suggests a modest curtailment in new title production, possibly in actual number of titles, or size of first printings, or both. In any case, manufacturing costs dropped sufficiently to offset an increase in royalties. Total operating income improved by 2.8 percent of net sales.

Some operating expenses increased—notably some salaries—others declined. Editorial expense was up, as were management salaries, suggesting that staff of many years' service received increases in compensation. Other salary costs, as in production, marketing, and in the general clerical area remained stable or declined marginally, implying some turnover of staff or even some cutbacks in lower level positions. Although this publisher farms out his fulfillment he was able to keep order processing costs at level, suggesting systems improvements and greater efficiency. His warehousing costs did rise by 3.5 percent.

So far it is not a bad picture. What does the balance sheet tell us? Our publisher's cash resources are up, but the value of his investments declined. His accounts receivable are up 1.5 percent, but his allowance for doubtful accounts had to be increased by 5.5 percent, no doubt due to greater difficulties in making collections. As inventories have also increased by 3.3 percent, his current assets have been augmented by 2.4 percent.

The publisher apparently acquired some equipment during the year, probably to replace outworn items, but the increase after depreciation was only 2.7 percent. What is more serious is that royalty advances have climbed by almost 7 percent and that the allowance for unearned guarantees has had to be increased by 10 percent! That accounts for the royalty increase shown on the operating statement, and it warns us that a pattern is developing that may consistently cut into the publisher's profits in future years. In all, the publisher's 1972 assets increased by 3 percent over 1971.

The liabilities shown on the balance sheet reveal that the house has been experiencing cash problems, which is not too surprising when we consider that the level of royalty advances increased by almost $40,000 during the year, that a dividend of nearly the same amount was declared, and that inventories and accounts receivable together increased by nearly $70,000. The cash flow difficulties are apparent from the fact that the level of payables increased (i.e., the publisher has been paying his bills more slowly); but even more significantly, long-term debt went up by nearly $35,000, or 4.7 percent. Otherwise liabilities reveal no startling or unexpected changes. It is logical that royalties payable should decline slightly with the decline in sales and the apparent change in the character of the sales mix (more backlist, somewhat less new materials). Short-term borrowing was apparently down, mainly because the cash needs the publisher experienced were of a long-term nature and he could see no way of solving them with a short-term loan. Accrued income taxes would naturally rise with increases in profits.

Retained earnings increased by $47,356. Why, you may ask, didn't the publisher distribute all his profits; why did he retain such a substantial amount? The cash flow problem referred to and the apparent trend of increasing royalty advances provide the answer. In order to pay the current dividend and the necessary royalty guarantees, the publisher was forced to increase his long-term indebtedness, even despite the retention of some profits. To borrow even more, at high interest rates, would have been unwise and impractical.

Working capital is calculated by deducting current liabilities from current assets (resulting, in our case, in $1,916,898). To establish what has happened to working capital and reveal related "changes in financial position" we must analyze how additional working capital was generated, how it was used, and what factors account for its increase or decrease. In other words, how was the cash employed in operating the business raised, how was it spent, and what changes in assets and liabilities were responsible for the fact that the amount of cash now tied up in the enterprise has increased or decreased. In this analysis, we must adjust some of our records in order to remove the effects of accrual accounting; as we are now determining solely cash experience, we must concern ourselves only with transactions that would affect cash income or disbursement.

We begin by establishing the sources of working capital. Our first source is, of course, income from operations. In accounting for that income (on the operating statement) we have shown a net residue after all expenses of $86,986. However, some of the expenses we have included have not involved cash outlays but have instead represented accounting entries designed to spread out cash expenses incurred in the past, such as depreciation and amortization of equipment. These entries, totaling $4,455 in our case, must be added to profits so that the actual cash yield from operations may be determined.

We look to the balance sheet for discovering other sources of working capital: $34,868 increase in long-term debt, and a decrease of $1,548 in deferred and prepaid expenses (which freed that much additional cash for use). We find, then, that all our sources yielded us working capital totaling $127,857.

Some of this cash was disbursed: $39,852 in additional royalty advances, $480 in the acquisition of equipment, $39,630 to pay cash dividends. Some of the cash remains tied up in the business, however, as we discover when we compare each 1972 entry with the comparable 1971 amount under current assets and current liabilities. The net difference of all these entries in our case is plus $47,895, which therefore represents our increase in working capital for the year.

Wise and knowledgeable financial managers observe statements and related performance analyses with an eagle eye. They are quick to detect changes which alert them to favorable or unfavorable developments and send them into action if need be to take advantage of or try to prevent the trends from developing further. Financial publishing executive George A. Hall, for example, puts much store by what is revealed by various performance ratios, particularly balance sheet ratios. Indeed these ratios when carefully watched are excellent indicators of positive and negative trends. "Return on investment," "return on assets," "inventory turnover," and the relationship between various balance sheet items and operating entries (accounts receivable and net sales, for example) are particularly worthy of attention. "Return on investment" (ROI) relates net profit to shareholder's equity or net worth (in our case it is 5.05 percent). "Return on assets" relates net profits to total assets (in the present instance it amounts to 2.47 percent). Inventory turnover, designed to measure the efficiency of inventory management, is calculated by dividing total inventory cost (paper, printing, and binding) by the average of beginning and ending inventories after write-down. (In our example 1972 inventory turnover was 0.87.)

According to these performance measures and earlier analyses, our trade publisher is not doing too badly, but he is also experiencing some problems. His inventory turnover, for example, is slow; his ROI is, however, rather good—as trade houses go—and his return on assets is passable. Like many trade publishers he often finds his profits fluctuating wildly and his control over his market is shaky, as witness the high percentage of returns. But he has apparently exercised good judgment in controlling his product mix in 1972—and probably should go further in that direction in the future. He has improved the relationship of his cost of sales to sales, and he has managed to keep operating expenses generally in check.

One of the most interesting aspects of his experience is his ability to improve profits without increasing sales, an indication that growth isn't everything. But he is experiencing potentially serious cash problems and will have to try to improve his cash flow. He should concentrate on collections and try to reduce his accounts receivable, as well as improve his credit control in order to reduce bad debt risks.

There is little he will be able to do about rising royalty advances and the need to write off increasing unearned portions of guarantees so long as much of the industry is caught up in the current inflationary trend. This represents, possibly, the most serious of his problems because it will continue to make heavy cash demands on him and cut into his profits. After all, he can go only so far in reducing his new book program and relying on backlist sales before his list begins to show signs of stagnation and lack of vitality.

But assuming his ability to stay on his present course while improving his cash position—a combination of good publishing judgment, good management, and good luck, in other words—he should continue to show a modest profit and maintain his position in the field.

### Elhi Publisher's Statements

Turning now to the Medium-Sized Elhi Publisher's statements, we will first look at the operating statement (Figure 11). Some slight differences are apparent between the line entries found here and those in the trade publisher's statement. Plant costs, for example, are listed after gross margin, separately from cost of sales, and the entry for paper, printing, and binding costs does not detail beginning and ending inventories, purchases, or write-downs. The reason for the plant cost arrangement is that for an elhi publisher, whose development expenses including plant costs are sizable,

**Medium-Sized Elhi Publisher's Operating Statement**

*December 31, 1972*

| | 1972 Dollars | 1972 Percent of Net Sales | 1971 Dollars | 1971 Percent of Net Sales |
|---|---|---|---|---|
| Gross sales | 14,787,482 | 103.2 | 12,812,966 | 103.4 |
| Less: returns and allowances | 458,527 | 3.2 | 421,317 | 3.4 |
| Net sales | 14,328,955 | 100.0 | 12,391,649 | 100.0 |
| **Cost of sales** | | | | |
| Papers, printing, and binding | 4,169,726 | 29.1 | 3,593,578 | 29.0 |
| Royalties | 874,066 | 6.1 | 755,891 | 6.1 |
| Total cost of sales | 5,043,792 | 35.2 | 4,349,469 | 35.1 |
| **Gross margin on sales** | 9,285,163 | 64.8 | 8,042,180 | 64.9 |
| **Plant costs** | 1,146,316 | 8.0 | 978,940 | 7.9 |
| **Other publishing income** | 272,250 | 1.9 | 247,833 | 2.0 |
| Total operating income | 8,411,097 | 58.7 | 7,311,073 | 59.0 |
| **Operating expenses** | | | | |
| Editorial | 745,106 | 5.2 | 656,757 | 5.3 |
| Production | 186,276 | 1.3 | 161,091 | 1.3 |
| Marketing | | | | |
| Compensation to salesmen and consultants | 1,074,672 | 7.5 | 916,982 | 7.4 |
| Departmental salaries | 444,198 | 3.1 | 384,141 | 3.1 |
| Travel and entertainment | 315,237 | 2.2 | 247,833 | 2.0 |
| Depository expense | 343,895 | 2.4 | 285,008 | 2.3 |
| Free copies | 544,500 | 3.8 | 446,099 | 3.6 |
| Other marketing expense | 874,066 | 6.1 | 805,457 | 6.5 |
| Total marketing expense | 3,596,568 | 25.1 | 3,085,520 | 24.9 |
| Fulfillment | | | | |
| Order processing | 315,237 | 2.2 | 297,400 | 2.4 |
| Warehousing and shipping | 630,474 | 4.4 | 557,624 | 4.5 |
| Total fulfillment | 945,711 | 6.6 | 855,024 | 6.9 |
| General and administrative | | | | |
| Management salaries | 200,605 | 1.4 | 185,748 | 1.5 |
| Other salaries | 272,250 | 1.9 | 247,833 | 2.0 |
| Occupancy | 257,921 | 1.8 | 235,441 | 1.9 |
| Employee benefits | 229,263 | 1.6 | 210,658 | 1.7 |
| Other general and administrative | 730,777 | 5.1 | 619,582 | 5.0 |
| Total general and administrative | 1,690,816 | 11.8 | 1,499,262 | 12.1 |
| Total operating expenses | 7,164,477 | 50.0 | 6,257,654 | 50.5 |
| **Other (nonpublishing) income (or expense)** | 28,658 | 0.2 | 37,175 | 0.3 |
| **Net income (or loss) before taxes** | 1,275,278 | 8.9 | 1,090,594 | 8.8 |
| **Federal, state, and local income taxes** | 616,145 | 4.3 | 520,450 | 4.2 |
| **Net income (or loss) after taxes** | 659,133 | 4.6 | 570,144 | 4.6 |

Figure 11.

and the life expectancy of whose products is considerably greater than that of most trade books, it is appropriate to amortize such plant expense over the number of years for which he expects his product to be active. While the practice of amortization is not universal among school publishers, it is more common than that of write-off and it is therefore practiced by our fictitious publisher. He amortizes his plant expense over a five-year period, and to emphasize the fact that these costs are deferred separately and therefore not directly related to the books sold during the year, the entry is made separately rather than as part of cost of sales.

The character of the paper, printing, and binding entry is determined in this case by the fact that the publisher accumulates his cost of goods sold data through EDP and is therefore relieved of the necessity of making an inventory/purchase calculation, in the traditional manner. The balance sheet does, of course, show beginning and ending inventories for the year (ending inventory in 1971 is identical to beginning 1972 inventory), and write-down information can be footnoted.

Under "marketing expense" we find some novel entries, such as "compensation to salesmen and consultants" and "depository expense" which are characteristic of the school publishing business. It is also worth noting that the proportions to net sales of certain items vary substantially from those in the trade publisher's operating account; in particular, returns, royalties, and other publishing income, all of which are substantially lower in elhi experience.

There are comparable differences in the balance sheet also. No provision for writing off unearned royalty guarantees needs to be made in the elhi publisher's long-term assets, for such write-offs are usually moderate and infrequent. But there is an entry for "unamortized plant costs" representing that portion of plant costs incurred which is to be written into operations in future years.

In analyzing the elhi publisher's experience, his operating statement shows that his sales increased substantially (15.6 percent) in 1972. Yet the relationship to sales of his bottom-line profit remained the same. This would seem to indicate that the sales increase was due to an expansion of his program and the development of new products, a fact confirmed by the respectable level of plant amortization and the unamortized plant costs listed on the balance sheet. In general the publisher seems to have exercised remarkable cost control: nearly every item on the operating statement has fluctuated only one or two tenths of a percentage point in relation to sales, and total operating expense is down one half of one percent.

As for the balance sheet (Figure 12), it reflects the consequences of expansion. While the current assets total changed only slightly from that of the previous year, there is a significant shift from liquid assets (cash and securities) to receivables and inventories, indicating that the liquid assets are now substantially tied up. There are increases in equipment investment,

**Medium-Sized Elhi Publisher's Balance Sheet**

*December 31, 1972*

|  | 1972 | 1971 |
|---|---|---|
| **Assets** | | |
| Current assets | | |
| Cash | $ 278,420 | $ 413,536 |
| Short-term investments–at cost | 495,081 | 1,340,512 |
| (approximates market value) | | |
| Accounts receivable (net of allowance for | | |
| doubtful accounts: 1972–$25,700; 1971–$22,300) | 2,865,691 | 2,478,329 |
| Inventories | 5,153,447 | 4,485,777 |
| Total current assets | 8,792,639 | 8,718,154 |
| Fixtures and equipment–at cost | 227,109 | 214,440 |
| Less: accumulated depreciation and amortization | 58,200 | 54,600 |
|  | 168,909 | 159,840 |
| Royalty advances | 859,737 | 743,499 |
| Unamortized plant cost | 5,513,273 | 5,026,144 |
| Other deferred charges and prepaid expenses | 22,550 | 21,970 |
|  | 15,357,108 | 14,669,607 |
| **Liabilities and shareholders' equity** | | |
| Current liabilities | | |
| Accounts payable | 1,500,371 | 1,497,062 |
| Royalties payable | 462,322 | 379,520 |
| Notes payable | 1,744,752 | 1,214,824 |
| Accrued income taxes | 303,777 | 261,003 |
| Other accrued liabilities | 14,375 | 17,820 |
| Total current liabilities | 4,025,597 | 3,370,229 |
| Shareholders' equity | | |
| Capital stock–$1 par value | 850,000 | 850,000 |
| Additional paid-in capital | 5,900,300 | 5,900,300 |
| Retained earnings | 4,581,211 | 4,549,078 |
| Total shareholders' equity | 11,331,511 | 11,299,378 |
|  | 15,357,108 | 14,669,607 |

**Figure 12.**

in plant costs being capitalized (i.e., amortized), and in royalty advances. Liabilities have risen, particularly short-term loans. However, it is noteworthy that this publisher does not carry any long-term debt.

The publisher paid almost his entire earnings to stockholders, $627,000 (or 73.7 cents per share), retaining only $32,133. (In view of his shrinking cash resources, should he have retained more?) Working capital stood at $4,767,042 and decreased $580,883 for the year. Return on investment (ROI) was 5.82 percent, return on assets 4.30 percent. Inventory turnover was 0.86 (which would be slow for a trade publisher but is about par for the course of a middle-sized schoolbook imprint).

I think we can conclude that we are looking at a fairly successful enterprise. Being a middle-sized publisher, being a middle-sized business for that matter, has peculiar problems. The economics of scale are frequently against you. In a very small enterprise, the owner often contributes most of the capital as well as much of the management and professional expertise, pays himself a fair salary, and cares not too much whether or not he earns dividends. To capitalize the growing small or middle-sized business usually requires investments by outsiders who had better be paid dividends to be kept happy. Furthermore, the nature and volume of the work load of a middle-sized business requires that it employ professionals at good salaries, with the result that it usually carries a relatively high payroll. A large business, on the other hand, again enjoys advantages: it can more easily attract capital by selling shares to the public, and the proportionate cost of retaining managers and professional people is less prohibitive because their contributions are utilized on a wider scale and with greater productivity. Furthermore, large businesses can purchase raw materials and manufacturing at lower cost because of the purchase volume they command.

Given these factors, our publisher has done well. He has realized a fair profit, he has utilized his resources wisely, he is free of long-term debt, and indications are that he will continue along this path. Maybe he should have retained a larger portion of his 1972 earnings to give him a bit more liquidity, but then his stockholders may be a restless lot who require soothing with cold cash.

### Statements of Multidivisional Publishers

We have looked at the statements of two fictitious, independent houses, each engaged in a different kind of publishing. The statements of a multidivisional house would require certain modifications in the formats we have discussed. To begin with, the house would probably "consolidate" its statement to stockholders, i.e., it would combine the various divisional data under rather broad headings that would minimize their differences. However, management would still want to be able to assess the performance of each division, and would want the divisional manager to be fully apprised of that performance. Consequently at least simple operating statements would be prepared regularly for each publishing unit.

This would raise certain problems. Most divisions share the services of some departments: production, fulfillment, and accounting, for example; they often occupy the same building, use some of the same equipment, and are directed by the same top management. How is the use of these shared talents and facilities to be accounted for? There are two basic approaches, each with fervent advocates and opponents. The more common method produces a complete statement down to the bottom line of profit. It measures all expenses incurred solely by the division directly: manufacturing, royalty, editorial, and marketing expense, and/or any other over which the division has exclusive control, are simply recorded and detailed. Shared expenses are "allocated," i.e., estimated portions of the expense are assigned to each division on the basis of some formula, such as a relationship to net dollar sales, or number of units sold, or a combination of both, or time consumed by managers in working with divisions, or time-based utilization of EDP and other equipment, etc.

The alternative method reports only the direct expense over which the division has substantial control. The resulting profit margin is regarded as the division's "contribution" to a common pool of revenues from which shared expenses are met and profits derived. Because of its character, this method is said to employ the "contribution concept" of cost accounting.

Advocates of the contribution concept point out that all allocations are essentially arbitrary. Short of undertaking extremely detailed and expensive time-and-motion studies and space utilization surveys, there is no way of doing full justice to a division when charging it with estimated costs. Are dollar net sales to be the basis for allocation? Then high-priced books are likely to receive an excessive share of the expense and cheaper books are likely to escape much of the burden. Are units to be the basis? Then cheaper books will suffer while costly titles will be favored. Even dollar-weighted unit figures cannot achieve just attributions of fulfillment costs where the size of a transaction (i.e., the number of books billed and shipped at one time) has a considerable bearing on actual expense incurred. Nor do most allocation formulas take into account the substantial costs of processing returns incurred by some books and not by others, or the expense created by books that are not selling at all.

Defenders of the allocation approach retort that these problems may be real enough, but contribution-based reporting is not the answer. While it is true that a divisional manager does not have sole control over shared services or facilities, his decisions, the volume of his output, and the nature of his product still have a great deal to do with the costs incurred on his behalf. Therefore he should share some responsibility for those costs. Furthermore, bottom-line profit is profoundly affected by the performance of the divisions and should be related specifically to their performance. Under the contribution method, net profit is not so related, thus failing to disclose the full effect of divisional activities on the earnings of the company.

My own inclination is to favor allocation, to devise the best possible and most equitable formulations for attributing costs, while fully recognizing their limitations. (Constructing allocation formulas is becoming easier after all with the help of computers now utilized by most multidivisional houses.) Not only do I find the argument relating bottom-line profit to divisional performance persuasive, but I think the initiative of a divisional manager will be stimulated more by the more complete disclosure resulting from a full report. Contribution may be a "purer" method in the sense of including a greater proportion of "hard" figures, but purity is not our prime objective here. Producing information designed to facilitate planning and decision making is our objective. If in the process of accomplishing this goal we have to work with estimates that are a little "softer" than actual cost data would be, so be it, so long as the estimates are intelligently and conscientiously prepared.

There is another reason why allocations are essential, in my judgment. The basic decision in publishing is made when an individual title is selected for publication and therefore the most important profit or loss analysis is that which involves the individual book. Such analyses are impossible to construct without making use of some allocations, and in multidivisional companies they cannot be made at all unless divisional allocations have been devised first.

### Analyses of Individual Title Performances

To illustrate the importance and value, as well as some possible methods of analyzing the profit performance of specific books, I have devised three fictitious statements which examine alternative approaches to the same title. The title in question we imagine to be a work of history, written by a professor at a prominent university. Some 450 pages in length, illustrated with a few plates and maps, well-written and well-conceived, it appeals solidly to historians and students as well as to laymen interested in the subject. It is being published by a trade house (perhaps the one whose statement we examined earlier).

The publisher has guaranteed the author a $15,000 advance against royalties (10 percent of list price) and subsidiary rights income. The contract grants only domestic rights to the publisher; foreign publication will be negotiated by the author directly. A small book club has selected the title, and the royalty income from the book club sale, representing 10 percent of the club's price to members, is to be shared equally by author and publisher. Reprint rights have also been sold to a quality paperback house which will release its edition, intended principally for use in college courses, 18 months after hard-cover publication. The paperback publisher has advanced $5,000, which the contract provides will be shared—60 percent by the author, 40 percent by the original publisher.

The first alternative is illustrated in Figure 13. Here the publisher has decided to price the book at $15.00, extend the customary trade discount (averaging 41 percent) to retailers and wholesalers, and to print initially 10,000 copies; 300 copies are being distributed free, mostly to reviewers, and $5,000 is being appropriated for advertising in general and specialized media. To offer an attractive saving compared with the publisher's list price,

**Profit/Loss Analysis**

*History Title: Alternative One (List price $15.00—Trade discount)*

|  | Dollars | Percent of Net Sales |
|---|---|---|
| Gross sales: 8,100 copies at full price | 71,685 | 110.6 |
| 2,450 remaindered at 80¢ | 1,960 | 3.0 |
| Total gross sales | 73,645 | 113.6 |
| Less: returns and allowances | 8,850 | 13.6 |
| Net sales | 64,795 | 100.0 |
| Cost of sales |  |  |
| Plant costs | 7,200 | 11.1 |
| Paper, printing, and binding | 20,952 | 32.3 |
| Royalties | 10,650 | 16.4 |
| Total cost of sales | 38,802 | 59.8 |
| Gross margin on sales | 25,993 | 40.2 |
| Other publishing income | 7,970 | 12.3 |
| Total operating income | 33,963 | 52.5 |
| Operating expenses |  |  |
| Editorial | 5,300 | 8.2 |
| Production | 1,600 | 2.5 |
| Marketing |  |  |
| Advertising | 5,000 | 7.7 |
| Free books | 648 | 1.0 |
| Other | 8,400 | 13.0 |
| Total marketing expense | 14,048 | 21.7 |
| Fulfillment | 6,900 | 10.7 |
| General and administrative | 6,100 | 9.4 |
| Total operating expense | 33,948 | 52.5 |
| Net income (or loss) | 15 | 0.0 |

**Figure 13.**

the book club plans to sell its edition for $9.95 and is advancing $11,940 on its anticipated distribution of 12,000 copies.

As so often happens in publishing, not everything goes according to plan. During the first eight months of the book's existence, 5,100 copies are sold, but 1,000 are returned at the end of that period. In the succeeding ten months 3,000 more copies are sold, but by that time the sale has slowed to a trickle and the paperback edition is due to be released. The publisher reviews his inventory, remainders 2,450 copies for 80 cents per book, and writes off 150 copies which have disappeared, been stolen or damaged, as a total loss. He then examines the record and discovers that he has just about broken even.

Let's look at the statement. Gross sales cover the 8,100 copies shipped, at full price, as well as the yield from the remaindered copies; returns represent the 1,000 copies that came back. Cost of sales show plant costs separately, then the paper, printing, and binding expense of 10,000 copies at $2.16 per copy, less the cost of the 300 copies given away. Royalties represent earnings of $1.50 per copy on 7,100 copies sold at full price, (remainder sales are, as is customary, exempted contractually from royalties). Other publishing income shows only the publisher's share, of course. It includes $5,970 from the book club and $2,000 from the paperback house.

Operating expense was computed as follows. Editorial, production, and most marketing expenses were established directly by surveying the time involvements of the editors and of the production and marketing staff, determining sales commissions, advertising expenditures, and the value of free books distributed. Fulfillment expense was allocated in accordance with the number and size of the transactions involved in invoicing, shipping, and processing returns of the title, as well as its warehouse occupancy during the period of its life. General and administrative expenses were variously treated. Management and general salaries, occupancy, and other largely indirect expenses were apportioned in accordance with the book's list price and the number of units sold (the formula employed in effect assigns lower proportionate costs to titles with higher list prices). Salary-related costs (such as fringe benefits and payroll taxes) followed directly whatever salaries were directly attributed, but were subject to the list price/unit formula insofar as they were attached to indirectly allocated salary expenses. (Since "other nonpublishing income or expense" or income taxes have no direct bearing on the profitability of a title, our analysis is carried no further than to net operating profit).

Now let's look at alternative approach number two, illustrated in Figure 14. Here the publisher decides to be more aggressive. He has experienced the sort of disappointment demonstrated in the first alternative with this type of title before and hopes to overcome it with a slightly harder sell. He decides to price the book at only $12.50, trusting that this will expedite sales and improve his earnings. He also decided to give away more copies, 350, and to spend more money on advertising, $6,500. It works—up to a point. The first printing (10,000 copies) sells out in six months (too early to have received any sizable returns), and the publisher rushes into a reprint of 3,000 copies (at a cost of $2.47 per copy). Of the second printing 1,650 are also sold, but returns cancel out these additional sales, resulting, after 18 months, in a total net sale of 10,000 copies. In other words, the publisher did accelerate and increase the sale of the book through the lower price and greater sales effort, but he was left with as large an inventory, 2,450 copies, in the end. He is forced to remainder these books at 80 cents each, writing off losses and damages on 200 copies.

**Profit/Loss Analysis**

*History Title: Alternative Two (List price $12.50—Trade discount)*

| | Dollars | Percent of Net Sales |
|---|---|---|
| **Gross sales:** 11,650 copies at full price | 85,919 | 113.5 |
| 2,450 remaindered at 80¢ | 1,960 | 2.6 |
| Total gross sales | 87,879 | 116.1 |
| Less: returns and allowances | 12,169 | 16.1 |
| **Net Sales** | 75,710 | 100.0 |
| **Cost of sales** | | |
| Plant costs | 7,200 | 9.5 |
| Paper, printing, and binding | 28,254 | 37.3 |
| Royalties | 12,500 | 16.5 |
| Total cost of sales | 47,954 | 63.3 |
| **Gross margin on sales** | 27,756 | 36.7 |
| **Other publishing income** | 7,817 | 10.3 |
| Total operating income | 35,573 | 47.0 |
| **Operating expenses** | | |
| Editorial | 5,300 | 7.0 |
| Production | 1,800 | 2.4 |
| Marketing | | |
| Advertising | 6,500 | 8.6 |
| Free books | 756 | 1.0 |
| Other | 9,500 | 12.6 |
| Total marketing expense | 16,756 | 22.2 |
| Fulfillment | 9,800 | 12.9 |
| General and administrative | 6,700 | 8.8 |
| Total operating expense | 40,356 | 53.3 |
| **Net income (or loss)** | ( 4,783) | ( 6.3) |

Figure 14.

Was it worth the extra effort? Apparently not. Our analysis shows that while net sales were higher than in alternative one, the lower price, higher inventory costs, and increased marketing and fulfillment expense combined to create a sizable loss for the publisher. To aggravate his problem, the publisher had to pay more royalties to the author ($1.25 on each of 10,000 copies), and the book club, basing its price on the title's list price, lowered it to $8.95. While this resulted in a somewhat larger book club sale (13,000 copies), the net effect was to lower the club's royalty payments to $11,635, of which the publisher's share was $5,817.

Now suppose that our publisher were to conclude that traditional hard-cover publishing methods were no longer adequate for a book of this sort and that he should try a new approach entirely. He might then arrive at the scheme illustrated in our third alternative shown in Figure 15. Here the

**Profit/Loss Analysis**

*History Title: Alternative Three (List price $17.50—Short discount)*

| | Dollars | Percent of Net Sales |
|---|---|---|
| Gross sales: 4,800 copies at full price | 67,200 | 105.7 |
| Less: returns and allowances | 3,640 | 5.7 |
| Net sales | 63,560 | 100.0 |
| Cost of sales | | |
| Plant costs | 7,200 | 11.3 |
| Paper, printing, and binding | 11,136 | 17.5 |
| Royalties | 7,945 | 12.5 |
| Total cost of sales | 26,281 | 41.3 |
| Gross margin on sales | 37,279 | 58.7 |
| Other publishing income | 8,417 | 13.2 |
| Total operating income | 45,696 | 71.9 |
| Operating expenses | | |
| Editorial | 5,300 | 8.3 |
| Production | 1,600 | 2.5 |
| Marketing | | |
| Advertising | 3,000 | 4.7 |
| Free books | 464 | 0.7 |
| Other | 7,300 | 11.5 |
| Total marketing expense | 10,764 | 16.9 |
| Fulfillment | 6,200 | 9.8 |
| General and administrative | 6,000 | 9.4 |
| Total operating expenses | 29,864 | 46.9 |
| Net income (or loss) | 15,832 | 25.0 |

**Figure 15.**

publisher decides to narrow rather than to broaden his focus, to pinpoint his efforts at the core market for the book: historians, libraries, and intensively interested laymen. Since individuals in this market can be reached with greater effectiveness by direct methods rather than through current bookstore channels, the publisher decides to sell the book at a higher price, $17.50, and at a short discount (averaging 20 percent). He realizes, of course, that the number of units sold will therefore be substantially fewer than under the other alternatives, so he decides on a printing of only 5,000 copies (at a cost of $2.32 per copy). He also reduces the number of free copies to 200, limiting them to media that are really likely to review the title and do it some good. Space advertising is also curtailed, to $3,000, to be spent predominantly in specialized media. Marketing efforts will be heavily weighted in favor of direct mail.

The results are spectacular. Gross sales are only 4,800 copies, but of these only 260 are returned as bookstore involvement is limited largely to special orders. (The returns, including damaged copies, are too few to warrant remaindering at this time, so the stock is simply written off.) Substantial savings in inventory expense, royalties, advertising, and fulfillment work together to produce a substantial profit. Even the book club lends a hand, deciding that it will maintain the higher membership price of $9.95 and that, because of the publisher's more restricted marketing approach, its sales will benefit to the tune of 13,000 copies. The club's guarantee therefore becomes $12,935, of which the publisher's share is $6,417.

Fine, you say. But what about the publisher's responsibility to the book and its author? Is the publisher really exercising his "best effort" for the book, as the contract requires him to do, with the third approach? I think he is. I think he has come to recognize that crowded distribution channels make it unwise for him to attempt marketing a specialized title in the traditional fashion, that he is likely only to bark his shins if he does so, and that his resources must sooner or later give out if he continues on that path. He is certainly not evading his responsibilities; he is not only making the book available in his own edition but he has also sold rights to a book club which will reach additional readers through sales of a hard-cover edition, and to a paperback house which will keep the work in print, for the benefit of students and consumers, probably for years to come. I don't believe that a publisher has a responsibility to lose money or to tread water in developing his program.

On the contrary, I would argue that a publisher has a responsibility at this point to publish fewer books and to print them in smaller quantities. Paper is already short, other raw materials are growing short. The waste resulting from overproduction in the industry is appalling. It also endangers the economic health of bookstores and wholesalers. If a publisher succeeds in reducing this waste and in improving his own economic position in the process, I think he is actually performing a public service.

It is true, of course, that the author will earn less on the third alternative than on the others. (Interestingly enough, the author will receive the largest income—$21,317—from the second alternative, which is the most ruinous one for the publisher. Alternative one will yield the author $19,620; alternative three, $17,362). This is not to suggest that the long-term interests of authors and publishers are not the same, they obviously are. But it does illustrate the fact that their short-term interests sometimes diverge. The author would obviously like nothing better than to amass as many sales through bookstores, as many reviews in all sorts of media, and as many promptly earned royalties as possible. He may not give a second thought to the publisher's profitability in this connection. But can he really afford not to? If the publisher is unable sooner or later to find alternatives to obviously self-defeating publishing methods, will he not conclude that he simply cannot afford to publish hard-cover books appealing to specialized interests?

Suppose enough publishers were to reach that conclusion—some have already—so that a book like our history title would in future be available in paperback only. Would the author really prefer to forgo the benefits and income of a hard-cover edition including the possibility of a book club sale? Would he not rather accept the reduced earnings of alternative three and enjoy publication in a format which, in many ways, is the one closest to his heart?

There are other lessons to be learned from the alternative analyses we have made: for example, that conventional ideas about generating profit may not always work. More sales and larger printings are obviously not always the answer, nor are lower prices and more aggressive marketing. More important than such conventional techniques may be the accurate definition of a market and the choice of optimal means to reach it. Prudence, restraint, and good judgment may be more effective business tools than blind enthusiasm, vigor, and high pressure.

### Budgeting and Planning

All the gathering and analysis of financial data will be of little use unless the lessons learned are applied in making decisions on future titles and programs. The time to ask basic questions about the income, cost, and profit of a publishing venture is before, not after, a commitment is made. Accordingly the various revenue and expense factors we have identified in our statements should be estimated and projected for a product in advance of the decision to publish and how to publish. Alternative approaches should be weighed whenever options exist so that the most enlightened decisions regarding format, price, size of printing, promotional efforts, and subsidiary rights arrangements can be made.

A number of publishers have devised sophisticated methods for forecasting profit or loss of titles under consideration, many of them making imaginative use of computer capability. One of the most interesting of these has been developed at John Wiley & Sons under the direction of William S. Diefenbach. Mr. Diefenbach believes that editors, production managers, sales managers, and others involved in making publishing decisions should have the opportunity to view the impact of their plans for the production, pricing, and promotion of forthcoming books before they are required to make a final recommendation. Accordingly these managers prepare forms in which they list basic production specifications and marketing plans. The computer digests these, adds allowances for overhead costs, and produces a financial forecast which indicates whether or not the given specifications will result in a profit that meets Wiley's standard for return on investment. A notable feature of the program is that cash flow is "discounted," i.e., the value of various revenues and expenditures is adjusted upward or downward depending on when they are received or spent, taking into account the changing value of money over periods of time. Should a projection fall short of standard, editors and managers have the opportunity to modify specifications until an acceptable plan results. (Wiley markets a version of the program to interested publishers.)

No projection is better, of course, than the estimates that go into it, and every forecasting program is therefore dependent on the quality of judgment managers bring to it. But while no forecast is foolproof, it is vastly better to undertake such estimates than to rely on the uncorroborated divinations or inspirations on which so many publishers seem to depend when they make serious publishing decisions. Inspiration has its place, of course. It leads a publisher to discover a potentially important book in the first place, or to recognize the quality of a manuscript on initial reading. But in today's demanding publishing world, given the sizable risks involved, more than strokes of genius are required to justify a final determination. The muse needs hard facts and figures to demonstrate she is really a muse —not just a dreamer.

If projections are needed to publish individual titles effectively, they are equally necessary to operate a whole program for a season or a year. Most sound businesses make forecasts for each line item on their statements and, as the year progresses, compare actual performance with projections, thus alerting themselves to gains or shortfalls, and giving themselves the opportunity to deal effectively with either. In preparing their comprehensive forecasts, publishers will, of course, base them on the projections they have made for individual titles.

Plans involve more than figures or finances, of course. They involve people and working space, warehouses and trucks, computers, furniture, and equipment. Personnel plans must be formulated as carefully as financial forecasts in order to deal efficiently and humanely with any expansion or cutbacks that may be contemplated. It takes time to train new people or to help established personnel adjust to new circumstances. The installation of new facilities, machinery, and systems, may involve months, even years of preparation. A good manager, furthermore, must always be conscious of the greater world outside, the economy as a whole, the social and physical environment. A good publisher must be responsive to the world of ideas, the cultural climate, the literary atmosphere. No businessman, and certainly no publisher, is an island.

But there is a limit to planning, especially in a cultural industry. To develop the necessary resources, human as well as financial, one must indeed make long-range forecasts covering periods five or even ten years hence. But such projections will have to be very broad, based more on the experience and imagination of the forecaster than on factual details which are at this point simply unavailable. In book publishing the unknown remains a large factor; one never really knows what will happen in the world of knowledge, education, entertainment, and consumer taste even a year or two years from now. A forecast for next year, based on titles already scheduled or planned for publication, can and should be amply detailed. But a long-range forecast can never be more than a sophisticated, wide-sweeping guess.

Many clever and capable people in other businesses, notably the executives of corporations that own publishing subsidiaries, cannot quite understand this fact. They are accustomed to "scientific" long-term planning and product development, undertaken after years of sophisticated research. Their markets are often more predictable, less dependent on taste and whim or on fashion and mood than the markets for books. These executives cannot believe that the bright young economists who so confidently predict the fate and future of their giant corporations should not be able to do so as readily for publishers.

As a result such corporate owners often demand that some unnecessarily complicated and frequently futile forecasting be done by the managers of their publishing subsidiaries. What is even worse, the owners often take such forecasts quite literally despite the honest disclaimers made by the people who prepare them regarding the impossibility of predicting specific sales and performance details five and ten years into the future.

Like the managers of their publishing companies, these owners should realize that publishing is really much like a poker game: a fascinating exercise combining skill and chance. Like the card player, the publisher will be quickly forced out of the game if he does not react capably to what fortune deals him. But if he is successful he would be presumptuous to attribute his prosperity entirely to his own skill. For he never really knows what card will be dealt to him next when he places a bet.

## Capital and Its Sources

For the publisher planning his future, raising capital has always been one of the principal problems. Book publishing is reputed to be a field which one can enter with very little capital (which supposedly explains why there are so many small publishing houses in the United States). To a considerable extent this is true, of course. To enter publishing one does not need to build a large plant, purchase expensive machinery, or spend huge sums developing patents. But to establish a significant publishing imprint has always taken a good deal of money, and it takes more today than ever. In school publishing for example, a major new series may require an investment of several million dollars. In professional and college publishing, building an imprint to competitive size and eminence usually takes years and large sums. And in trade publishing intense competition for good authors and big books is making increasingly heavy cash demands on struggling houses.

The need for capital was one of the principal reasons why so many publishers passed into the hands of larger corporate owners during the last decade. Some of these owners, who acquired publishing houses in the belief that they would fulfill the glowing predictions for growth and prosperity that had been made for them, have since been disappointed. Had some owners known at the time what they know now, they would probably not have acquired their publishing subsidiaries. In fact, some of these corporations have already divested themselves of their publishing holdings and others have indicated strong interest in doing so.

The performance records illustrated in this chapter explain why. While there are some outstanding educational and professional publishing houses, in both public and private hands, that yearly compile superb earnings records and are a source of great satisfaction to their stockholders, much of the industry, particularly many of the smaller and middle-sized imprints, are not in such enviable positions.

To raise capital when it is needed is therefore a weighty problem for many publishing executives. There are just too many other opportunities available to the investor who is looking for a quick, easy profit, to make many publishing stocks seem a prize. And in times when the stock market is despondent and the vision of investors is jaundiced, even the shares of highly successful publishers with outstanding earnings records have been known to decline alarmingly in value. Of course other cultural industries, and even other mercantile and manufacturing enterprises, are in the same boat. That is small comfort for the publisher who is looking vainly for operating capital.

Yet—there are still investors, corporations as well as individuals, willing to invest in even the less glamorous and the less profitable publishing houses and publishing stocks. Interested in more than money, they are looking for cultural as well as cash dividends. Like patrons in other ages, they are prepared to risk capital in the pursuit of intangible profits.

The problem has always been to find such people. There never seem to be enough to go around. But although the task of the publisher seeking venture money remains an arduous one, we should not be too surprised to discover that even in this respect publishing experience extends beyond the purely monetary or material. For in the last analysis, the very existence of books, and of the enterprises that publish them, is concrete testimony to the fact that man does not live by bread alone.

# Epilogue:

# What Does
# The Future Hold?

People who make carefully calculated and specific predictions about the future have always filled me with admiration—not because of the accuracy of their prophecies, but because of their cool courage. I lack the fortitude to join their ranks.

But we must think of the future and so we look to events in the present for some clues. We know, for example, that enrollments in schools and colleges will reflect the declines in birth rates of recent years; elementary schools are already finding it so, high schools will soon follow suit, and colleges will begin to feel the full impact by 1980. Colleges are already suffering some undergraduate declines over the peak years of the sixties because some of the principal motivations for attending college—to avoid fighting the Vietnam war and the notion that college is the only gateway to success—are no longer felt. On the other hand, vocational and adult education have been growing rapidly and many colleges and universities are redesigning curricula and facilities to adjust to new trends. The whole structure of education, from kindergarten to graduate school is under close scrutiny. Some shibboleths and fads may well be overturned by the very practical and honest questions communities and educators are asking about the entire process.

Publishers have always known that education is an adventure that does not stop at the schoolhouse door. The same curiosity and practical need that gave birth to schools gave birth to books in our ancient past. Now that more leisure and affluence allow more people to indulge their curiosity, both education and books will be the beneficiaries.

Educational publishing may in the future place more emphasis on vocational subjects, on continuing and adult education, on the informal acquisition of knowledge, or semiformal means such as classes on TV. Consumer reading has been steadily on the increase and there is no reason to assume that the trend will stop. Paperbacks are growing daily in popularity even while more people are buying expensive, handsomely illustrated tomes by mail. Bookstores have been multiplying in number and many, I believe, are growing in quality. Bookselling is rediscovering its professionalism, a vital factor in making bookstores more responsive to the needs of their patrons.

What exciting opportunities, then, await publishers! The big question is how will they respond? Will they show the judgment and wisdom necessary to take full advantage of these opportunities?

Much will depend, I think, on how effectively the industry solves its three main problems: the need to curtail overproduction, the need for greater standardization in manufacturing, and the need for an effective distribution system. I say "industry" advisedly. To satisfy these needs is beyond the capability of any single publisher, even the largest and most successful. These are challenges that only the publishing community acting in consort and in consciousness of its common interests can hope to tackle. And to do so will first of all require that publishers muster an awareness of their common purpose which has so far eluded them.

The chances for this happening are better than ever. New owners, new minds, new courage, new imagination, new sophistication have been infused into the field. In many publishing houses today there are young people much aware of the industry's problems and anxious to see them resolved. The new forces acting together may well introduce this ancient profession to a new and exciting era made possible by cultural and technological progress.

Accomplishment, however, is the reward of resolution. One hopes that the publishing community will develop the enlightened self-interest, and muster the determination to remove self-made obstacles and to forge common tools, so that the promising future can be realized.

# Glossary

*AA*—author's alteration: text change in proof made by author

*AAP*—Association of American Publishers

*AAUP*—Association of American University Presses

*ABA*—American Booksellers Association

*accountability*—demand for demonstrable results from educational programs and materials

*accounts receivable*—monies due from customers

*accrual*—accounting method that reports expense not necessarily when incurred but in coordination with related income

*adoption*—choice of educational materials for classroom use

*advance* 1. monies paid to author prior to publication, to be earned subsequently from royalties on sales. 2. books ordered by customers prior to publication

*advance dating*—use of future date on invoice delaying requirement for payment

*agency plan*—marketing arrangement enabling bookseller to earn preferential discount on short-discount titles in return for his commitment to stock a minimal title selection

*agent*—author's representative

*AIGA*—American Institute of Graphic Arts

*ALA*—American Library Association

*allocation*—attribution of indirect expense

*alternate*—secondary book club offering

*amortize*—to spread out accounting of an expense over a period of time

*antique finish*—velvety surface texture of paper

*auction*—simultaneous submission of manuscript to several publishers, awarding contract to highest bidder

*audiovisual materials*—educational and professional products utilizing pictorial or sound media to communicate: films, cassettes, records, slides, etc.

*autographing party*—author's visit to bookstore to inscribe copies and meet admirers

*AUPS*—American University Press Services, a subsidiary of the Association of American University Presses

*backbone* (also *spine*)—back of bound book

*backlist*—titles selling steadily year after year

*balance sheet*—financial report, balancing the assets of a business against its liabilities and net worth

*binding*—the folding, gathering, and sometimes sewing, of press sheets, and the attaching of covers

*binding die*—form used to stamp binding case

*bleed*—extending printing image to the very edge of the page

*blind stamping*—blank stamping, without ink or foil

*BMI*—Book Manufacturers Institute

*body*—base on which type character is mounted

*body type*—type employed in setting main text, exclusive of headings and footnotes

*boldface*—heavy-weight type

*book club*—marketing organization that distributes special editions of books to its members on preferential terms, in return for their minimal purchasing commitment

*book post*—parcel post at special book rates

*broken price*—merchandising technique which prices books slightly below amounts customarily employed (e.g., 99 cents, $2.49, $4.95)

*building-in machine*—case-binding machine

*bulk*—thickness of book paper or book

*burning a plate*—etching of an offset printing plate

*calendered paper*—paper processed for smooth finish

*Cameron Belt Press*—printing press in which plates for individual pages are hung on a movable belt and which prints and perfect-binds books in one operation

*cap*—capital letter

*capitalize*—1. to invest capital in. 2. (also *amortize*) to spread out accounting of an expense over a period of time

*carload price*—cost of book paper in rail freight car lots

*case binding*—hard-cover binding

*cash discount*—discount given for prompt payment of bills

*casting off*—1. breaking type into pages. 2. estimating number of pages in advance.

*character*—single type letter or symbol

*character count*—determining exact length of manuscript prior to design

*coated paper*—paper surfaced with clay, enamel, or plastic, particularly suited for printing illustrations

*cold type*—typesetting process, by typewriter or computer, which dispenses with the hot metal castings of traditional techniques *collating* (also *gathering*)— assembling folded press sheets in sequence

*college store*—retailer, institutionally or privately owned, catering predominantly to college faculty and students

*colophon* (also *logo*)—publisher's trademark

*color separation*—method of preparing images, by hand or photographically, from which color printing plates are made

*commission man*—free-lance salesman representing several publishers

*comp*—complimentary copy

*comparative price*—quotation of original and reduced price in promoting markdowns or remainders

*composition*—typesetting

*compositor*—typesetter

*computer composition*—methods of typesetting utilizing computers instead of traditional systems

*computer program*—instructions to computer for performing a routine

*condensed type*—type compressed in width

*consignment*—merchandise shipped to customer which does not become payable until sold

*consultant*—teacher retained by elhi publisher to demonstrate products

*consumable book*—educational book designed to be marked up, cut up, or otherwise used up, during its employment

*continuity program*—mail order marketing arrangement in which the customer agrees to accept periodic shipments of books in series, with option to cancel at any time

*cooperative advertising*—ad run by bookseller, the cost of which is shared by publisher

*copy*—single book unit

*copy editing*—meticulous working over of manuscript prior to typesetting

*copyright*—legal protection enjoyed by literary property. Unpublished works are protected under common law; published materials must follow statutory regulations in order to enjoy protection

*copyright page*—verso of title page listing copyright notice

*CPDA*—Council for Periodical Distributors Associations: trade association for wholesalers of magazines and mass market paperbacks

*crash*—sturdy gauze glued to backs of pages, and to boards under endpapers, in case-bound books

*creative editor*—editor who conceives of a book project, and subsequently finds an author to execute it

*credit control*—screening out unfavorable credit risks from customer list, and denying further credit to past due accounts

*crop*—to trim an illustration

*customer service*—handling of order inquiries and complaints

*cut*—letterpress engraving

*deep-etched plate*—offset printing plate that can be used repeatedly

*defer*—to delay the accounting of an expense, usually in order to achieve better coordination with related income

*depository*—state-designated warehouse where adopted titles must be stored

*depth*—vertical measurement of type on page

*desk copy*—copy furnished free to college teacher upon adoption of a text

*development expense*—cost incurred in developing a new product

*display type*—decorative type used for headings or title pages

*dummy*—mock-up of pages or book

*dump-bin*—combination shipping carton and display unit favored by mass market paperback publishers

*dust cover*—jacket or plain wrapper placed over binding

*editing*—1. selecting, creating, or soliciting materials for publication. 2. close working over of manuscript to prepare it for typesetting

*edition*—specific version of a book, which may differ from other versions because of content, format, or market (e.g., revised edition, paperbound edition, text edition)

*elhi*—embraces elementary (grades K–8) and high school (grades 9–12)

*em*—space consumed by lower case letter m; basic measurement for length and cost of typesetting

*EMPC*—Educational Media Producers Council: division of National Audio-Visual Association (NAVA), enrolling producers of educational software

*endpapers*—heavy, sometimes decorated pages at beginning and end of case-bound books

*engraving*—letterpress printing plate

*even forms*—full utilization of press sheets; no blank pages at end of book

*examination copy*—complimentary or on-approval copy furnished to college teacher for possible adoption

*exhibit*—book display at professional, scholarly, or book trade meetings

*extended type*—type that is cursive and/or widely spaced

*fair use*—limited quotation of copyrighted matter which, according to legal precedent, does not constitute violation of copyright

*F&G's*—folded and gathered sheets

*first reading*—initial review of manuscript to determine whether it should be considered further or rejected

*first serialization*—see *serialization*

*flatbed press* (also *sheet-fed press*)—prints on flat sheets of paper

*flat sheets*—unfolded, printed sheets

*folio*—page number

*font*—the characters which are available for a given typeface in a specific size, slant, or weight

*foreign rights*—right to translate and/or to publish a work abroad

*form*—section of pages printed on one side of press sheet

*Frankfurt Book Fair*—major international publishing meeting; held each October in Frankfurt am Main, West Germany

*free sheet*—book paper free of low-grade pulp, therefore of longer lasting quality

*front matter*—material preceding the main body of a book: title, copyright, and dedication pages, preface or foreword, acknowledgments, and table of contents

*fulfillment*—activities embracing order processing, invoicing, handling of accounts receivable, payments and collections, credit control, shipping and warehousing, and the maintenance of sales and inventory records

*G&A*—general and administrative costs; incurred on a company-wide, as opposed to a departmental, basis

*galleys*—long type trays from which galley proofs are pulled

*gathering* (also *collating*)—assembling folded press sheets in sequence

*grain*—direction in which paper fibers flow

*gravure* (also *intaglio*)—printing process in which impression is made from plates into which image has been grooved

*guarantee*—minimum royalty agreed upon, usually paid in advance of publication

*gutter*—margin adjoining inside vertical (unbound) edge of page

*half title*—the recto, preceding the title page or a section of a book, on which the title or the name of the section is shown, normally in display type

*half-tone illustration*—black-and-white reproduction of a shaded image, such as a photograph or painting

*hardware*—see *software*

*head- and footbands*—woven, often brightly colored ribands decorating the back edges of the sheets in case-bound books

*home field*—market of homes and offices covered directly by field representatives of subscription reference book publishers

*ID*—independent distribution: dissemination of mass market paperbacks through independent wholesalers

*imposition*—arrangement of pages on the press sheet which results in correct sequence after folding

*imprint*—name of publisher or series, identified on title pages and bindings

*income statement*—see *operating statement*

*independent wholesaler*—local wholesaler of magazines and mass market paperbound books

*integrated book manufacturer*—enterprise capable of manufacturing complete books, from composition to bound copy

*initial galleys*—copies of new titles shipped automatically to wholesalers by mass market paperback publisher *instant book*—work of great current interest written, produced, and marketed on a crash schedule

*ISBN*—International Standard Book Numbering System; assigns identifying numbers to books, publishers, retailers, and institutional purchasers

*italics*—slanted version of type (*abc*)

*jacket*—decorative dust cover placed over binding for protection and promotional purposes

*jobber*—wholesaler to bookstores or libraries

*justify*—setting type in lines of equal width, resulting in even right-hand margin

*juvenile*—children's book

*lamination*—plastic coating applied to covers

*leading*—spacing between lines of type

*letterpress*—printing process in which impression on paper is made by raised surfaces

*library reprint* (also *scholarly reprint*)—short-run, hard-cover reprint of out-of-print title

*lightface*—regular weight type

*line illustration*—black-and-white illustration without tones or shadings, e.g., a geometric diagram, or a pen-and-ink drawing

*linofilm*—derivation of linotype in which lines of film are output rather than metal castings

*linotype*—metal typesetting process, casting text by the line

*list*—publisher's entire output of titles, in-print and forthcoming

*list cleaner*—service provided by post office informing mailing list owner of address changes

*literary agent*—author's representative

*lithography*—see *offset printing*

*live returns*—new books in unopened cartons returned by wholesaler to mass market paperback publisher

*LMP*—*Literary Market Place*: annual directory of book publishing industry

*logo* (also *colophon*)—publisher's trademark

*lower case*—small letter

*mail order publication*—title produced primarily for distribution by mail directly to the general consumer

*makeready*—setting up of press in preparation of print run

*manipulative materials*—educational materials that are touched and handled rather than read or viewed: rocks, sea shells, toys, games, craft kits, etc.

*manufacturing*—process of making the physical book, principally typesetting, printing, and binding.

*manuscript editing*—see *copy editing*

*mass market*—book market that extends beyond traditional trade outlets (such as book, department, and stationery stores) to include newsstands, drugstores, chain stores, and supermarkets *mass market paperback*—see *paperback*

*measure*—width over which a line of type is set

*module*—unit or section of multi-unit educational product

*monofilm*—derivation of monotype in which film rather than a metal casting is output

*monograph*—narrowly specialized, scholarly study

*monotype*—metal typesetting process, casting each letter individually

*ms.*—manuscript

*multimedia product*—educational materials package containing components in two or more media: books and cassettes, filmstrips and records, booklets, cards, slides, and tapes, etc.

*multiple contract*—agreement binding author and publisher for the publication of two or more books

*multiple insertion*—use of several enclosures in direct mail

*NACS*—National Association of College Stores

*NAVA*—National Audio-Visual Association

*negative*—photographic transparency used in preparing offset printing plates

*negative option*—book club marketing technique whereby member receives selection automatically unless he notifies club to the contrary

*NO*—not our publication

*NYP*—not yet published

*objective test*—testing materials sold in conjunction with textbooks or materials to measure student's learning progress

*offset printing* (also *photo-offset, lithography*)—process in which impression on paper is made by rubber blanket on which print image has been "offset" from etched cylindrical plate

*on-approval copy*—book furnished to college teacher for possible adoption, which must be returned or paid for if not adopted

*on-demand publishing*—method of publication which manufactures books only in response to specific purchase orders

*OP*—out of print: stock exhausted; no longer available

*opacity*—density of paper which prevents image on reverse page from showing through

*operating statement*—financial report establishing the profit or loss of a business by showing its income and expenses

*option*—opportunity of first refusal granted by an author to a publisher on a future manuscript, or by one publisher to another in negotiating for reprint or foreign publication rights

*order editing*—review and annotation of customer's orders to ensure their accurate processing

*OS*—out of stock; temporarily unavailable

*over the transom*—unsolicited manuscript

*page proof*—final proof in typesetting process

*pallet*—see *skid*

*paper merchant*—wholesaler stocking book papers from several mills

*paperback*—softbound book. Quality or trade paperbacks are distributed largely through book and college stores; mass market paperbacks are distributed, in addition, through chain stores, drugstores, supermarkets, and newsstands

*PE*—printer's error: error made by typesetter

*perfect binding*—process in which the backs of folded press sheets are abrased and the cover is attached with a strong adhesive

*perfector press*—prints both sides of sheet simultaneously

*permission*—granting of the right to use a book excerpt

*photo-offset*—see *offset printing*

*pica*—type measurement, a little less than 1/16 inch (12 points)

*plant costs*—nonrecurring manufacturing costs (such as typesetting, negatives, and reusable plates) plus artwork (outside artwork only in the case of educational books). Some publishers may include certain editorial and other development expenses as well

*plate*—metal or other form from which printing image is impressed or offset onto paper

*point*—type measurement, a shade less than 1/72 of an inch

*printing*—1. process of impressing images on paper. 2. (also *impression*) a particular lot of copies printed at one time

*process color*—method of full-color reproduction, requiring separation of colors by a special photographic process

*production*—task of planning and supervising manufacturing process

*professional books*—books created predominantly as tools of work for the professions and the trades

*profit-or-loss statement*—see *operating statement*

*promotion*—marketing activity other than direct personal selling, such as space advertising, direct mail, exhibits, and publicity

*proportional spacing*—making allowances for the varying widths of letters in equalizing the spacing between them

*proprietary textbook*—college textbook published exclusively for an instructor's use in his own course

*publicity*—achieving news and review exposure for books and authors

*publishers' overstock*—see *remainders*

*pulping*—destruction of unsalable books

*PW*—*Publishers Weekly*, the industry journal

*quad open front and foot*—see *rough front and foot*

*quality paperback*—see *paperback*

*rack allowance*—contribution made by mass market paperback publisher to the cost of his customers' display racks

*ream*—500 sheets of paper

*recto*—right-hand page

*religious books*—Bibles, testaments, hymnals, prayer books, and other works of specifically religious content

*remainders* (also *publishers' overstock*)—unsold books disposed of by publisher, usually below cost, to wholesalers, retailers, and consumers

*reprint*—1. new printing in original format. 2. reissue in new format (e.g., paperback)

*reproduction proof*—proof of exceptional quality used in making negatives or plates

*resource center*—facility, similar to a library, serving one or several schools

*returns*—1. unsold books shipped back to publisher. 2. responses to direct mailing

*rivers*—unsightly blank streaks running through pages of inexpertly set type

*review copy*—free book furnished to newspaper or other medium for review purposes

*rotary press* (also *web-fed press*)—utilizes cylindrical plates and prints on rolls (webs) of paper

*royalties*—shares of sales income, paid to authors and others, usually based on the number and price of copies sold

*running heads*—captions at tops of pages identifying book, parts, or chapters

*saddle-wire stitch*—wire-stapling booklets through the backs

*sans serif*—typeface that lacks serifs (cross strokes at line endings)

*second serialization*—see *serialization*

*selection*—title chosen by book club as its prime offering

*scholarly books*—books in highly specialized areas of knowledge and advanced research

*self-mailer*—brochure mailable without envelope

*school books* (also *elhi books*)—textbooks for grades K–12

*SCOP*—Single Copy Order Plan: ABA-sponsored plan in which booksellers earn preferential discounts on prepaid orders for single books

*score*—indentations on sheets and covers facilitating folding

*screen*—transparency, marked with criss-cross lines or other pattern, used in preparing printing plates for half-tone illustrations

*serialization*—publication of a book in installments by a periodical, either before (first serialization) or after publication (second serialization)

*sheet-fed press*—see *flatbed press*

*sheets*—unbound printed pages

*short discount*—lower than the standard trade discount of 40 percent

*short run*—small printing

*side-sewing*—stitching signatures through the sides rather than through the backs

*signature*—folded press sheets, usually of 32 or 16 pages

*sizing*—1. coating paper preparatory to offset printing. 2. specifying the reduction, enlargement, or cropping of illustrations

*skid* (also *pallet*)—wooden platform used to store books, sheets, or paper

*smyth-sewing*—threading signatures together prior to attaching covers

*software*—1. audiovisual software: films, filmstrips, tapes, etc., as distinguished from audiovisual hardware: cameras, projectors, players etc. 2. computer software: programs, as distinguished from computer hardware: machinery and equipment

*space advertising*—advertisement in periodical or newspaper

*special library*—library limited to business, industrial, professional, music, art, historical, or other special collections

*special order*—order for title not carried in bookseller's regular stock

*special sales*—sales outside normal distribution channels

*spine*—back of bound book

*split test*—simultaneous sampling of several direct mail approaches

*spoilage*—sheets and raw materials damaged beyond repair during printing or binding

*square-backed*—bindings with backs which have not been rounded

*stamping*—imprinting or embossing of titles and other matter on binding case

*Standardized Test*—test measuring intelligence, ability, aptitude, achievement, and other personality traits

*state adoption*—approval of elhi materials by state selection board, permitting purchase by local school districts

*stripping*—preparation and assemblage of offset negatives prior to platemaking

*subscription reference books*—multivolume encyclopedias marketed predominantly to the consumer on a door-to-door basis

*subsidiary rights*—rights to use of a book in ways other than original publication: reprint, book club distribution, serialization, translation, film adaptation, etc.

*substance weight*—ream weight of paper in standard sheet size (25 inches × 38 inches for book papers)

*superior number*—small raised number ($^1$) used in references to footnotes

*test*—1. standardized test: measures intelligence, ability or personality traits, not related to specific books or materials. 2. objective test: accompanies specific textbooks and materials to measure student's learning progress. 3. direct mail test: measures appeal of title or promotional approach by means of small sample mailing.

*textbook*—book created predominantly for use in formal educational settings and equipped with educational apparatus, such as summaries and test questions

*title*—1. name of a book. 2. a specific book on publisher's list

*title page*—page at book's beginning, usually of special design, listing title, author, and publisher

*TOP*—temporarily out of print: plans for reprinting title are indefinite

*top-stain*—color applied to top edges of pages

*trade books*—titles created predominantly for the general consumer and marketed through bookstores and to libraries

*trade customs*—BMI-approved policy standards for printers and binders

*trade discount*—40 percent or better

*trade list*—publisher's complete catalog of books in print

*trim size*—page size, exclusive of binding

*typeface*—specific design in which various sizes and weights of type are available

*typography*—art of designing and setting type

*university press*—publishing arm of a university, museum, or research institution

*unjustified margin*—ragged right-hand margin, resulting from type set in lines of unequal width

*unsolicited manuscript* (also: manuscript received *over the transom*)—manuscript submitted to publisher directly by author (not through an agent) and which publisher has not requested for consideration

*upper case*—capital letter

*validation*—field-testing and verifying the effectiveness of educational materials

*vanity publishing*—publication entirely or substantially paid for by the author

*varnish*—light protective coating applied to some jackets and covers

*venture capital*—cash sought for funding a new enterprise

*verso*—left-hand page

*web*—roll of paper

*web-fed press*—press printing on rolls of paper

*widow*—dangling word or short line at end of paragraph, preferably eliminated during typesetting

*working capital*—cash tied up in enterprise; amount is determined by deducting current liabilities from current assets

*write down*—to reduce the value of inventory or other asset in financial reports

*write off*—to show an expense in full, or to fully eliminate the value of an asset, such as inventory, in financial reports

# Bibliographic Note

A listing of "Reference Books of the Trade," which includes materials and directories covering the book publishing and related industries, appears in *Literary Market Place*. The following titles, in addition, are noteworthy for their treatment of book publishing in general or of certain of its facets:

*The American Reading Public: What It Reads—Why It Reads*, ed. by Roger H. Smith (New York: R.R. Bowker Co., 1964). Although now somewhat dated, still a valuable collection of essays on the cultural environment in which the industry functions.

*The Art and Science of Book Publishing*, by Herbert S. Bailey, Jr. (New York: Harper & Row, 1970). A concise survey, with particularly interesting discussions on projecting printing requirements.

*Book Publishing in America*, by Charles A. Madison (New York: McGraw-Hill, 1966). Concise, detailed, if somewhat plodding, chronology.

*Bookmaking: The Illustrated Guide to Design and Production*, by Marshall Lee (New York: R.R. Bowker Co., 1965). A solid and detailed introduction.

*The Bookman's Glossary*, ed. by Jean Peters (New York: R.R. Bowker Co., 5th ed., 1975). Defines the terms used in publishing, bookselling, and book collecting.

*A Guide To Book Publishing*, by Datus C. Smith, Jr. (New York: R.R. Bowker Co., 1966). Prepared primarily as a handbook for establishing publishing programs in developing countries, this volume provides sound, basic information on the publishing process.

*Now, Barabbas*, by William Jovanovich (New York: Harper & Row, 1964). Wise and witty reflections by one of the industry's most articulate leaders.

*Publishers on Publishing*, compiled by Gerald Gross (New York: Grosset & Dunlap, 1961). Essays by leading practitioners in England and America.

*To Advance Knowledge*, by Gene R. Hawes (New York: American University Press Services, Inc., 1967). A handbook on American university press publishing.

*The Truth about Publishing*, by Sir Stanley Unwin (New York: R.R. Bowker Co., 7th ed., 1960). A lively and urbane classic by one of the great

*217*

British publishers. A companion volume by Sir Stanley, *The Truth about a Publisher* (New York: R.R. Bowker Co., 1960) is also worth the education and the fun of reading.

*What Happens in Book Publishing*, ed. by Chandler B. Grannis (New York: Columbia University Press, rev. ed., 1967). Practitioners representing various aspects of the publishing process offer practical insight into their areas of expertise.

As for periodicals, *Publishers Weekly*, published by Bowker, is the industry's trade journal. Educational publishing, in addition, is served by the *Knowledge Industry Newsletter* and the *Educational Marketer*, two newsletters published by Knowledge Industry Publications, White Plains, N.Y.

# Index